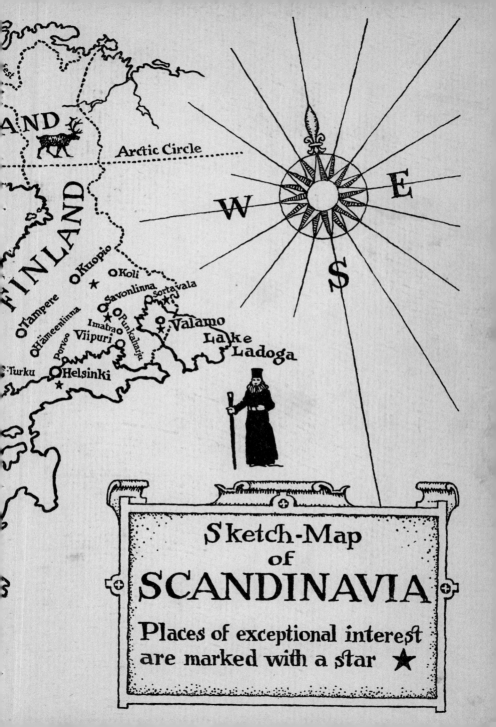

A Bride of the
Hardanger Fjord

SCANDINAVIA BECKONS

by
Mrs. (Ewing) AMY OAKLEY

Illustrations
by
THORNTON OAKLEY

♛ ♛ ♛

D. Appleton-Century Company
Incorporated
New York   1938   London

To
Håkon, Carl, Merete, and Yrjö

Viking

Table of Contents

CHAPTER VI

CHAPTER VII

CHAPTER VIII

CHAPTER IX

List of Illustrations

PAGE

LIST OF ILLUSTRATIONS   xix

Introduction

THE WORD Scandinavia has been used in the title of this book in its widest sense—that is, to include Finland. Although not racially, linguistically, or even geographically Scandinavian, Finland has, nowadays, political affiliations with the original group—Norway, Sweden, Denmark, and Iceland. "The Nordic Countries" was suggested to me as a more accurate expression, but the word "Nordic" has been used too vaingloriously by a dictator of late to be in good repute in English-speaking lands; nor is "Northern Countries" definite to one living on another continent, though full of meaning to a European.

Much has been written by experts on social legislation, education, and the coöperative movement in Scandinavia. These subjects are hardly within the sphere of this book, which, as I see it, is the personal impressions of travelers whose dominant interests are in nature, human contacts, and the arts. The stars upon the end-papers denote pic-

turesque regions or intellectual centers. During
two consecutive summers every place named upon
the map has been visited by the artist and by the
author.

Certain characteristics are outstanding in these
lands: the racial affinity of the peoples to each
other and to Anglo-Saxons; the ability of the
more cultured natives to speak English without
accent; the physical geography which varies dramatically. There is more sparkle in Finland and
in Norway—the brilliance of lake and fjord seems
to be reflected, too, in the personality of the people. Sweden and Denmark glow with the mellow
radiance of opaque gems—symbolic of the more
brooding temperament of Danes and, especially,
of Swedes; yet pearls are no less precious than
emeralds and diamonds.

Norway: land of midnight sun; of nomadic
Lapps; of wealth of culture—prehistoric, Viking,
modern; of sagas; of an astounding literary awak-
ening; of polar expeditions; of glacier and
fjord...

Sweden: land of an ancient nobility and of
ultra-modern legislation; of scientific research; of
conservation of folkways; of architectural renaissance; of iron and steel magnates; of industry
and of agriculture...

Denmark: land of paradox; of democratic king,
feudal nobility, and Socialist prime minister;
pioneer in adult education, old-age pensions, and

Scandinavian coöperatives; land of Viking stones, of storks and windmills...

Finland: country of lake and primeval forest; home of an educated and enlightened people—first in Europe to give suffrage to women, leaders toward new goals—a full-fledged republic; land of *Kalevala,* and of Sibelius...

Scandinavia! Your English-speaking brothers salute you as fellow-pioneers of world democracy.

AMY OAKLEY

There is no foreign land; it is the traveler only that is foreign.

R. L. S.

SCANDINAVIA BECKONS

Part One
NORWAY

Bergen ‡ The Fish-Market

SCANDINAVIA BECKONS
Chapter I
BERGEN, Gateway to Scandinavia

Harbors of the Northern Countries, any one of which might be our gateway to Scandinavia, compete with one another not only as to commerce but as to which should rightfully wear beauty's crown as queen of Scandinavian ports. Stockholm assumes that it is rightfully hers—but so does Copenhagen; Helsinki has a lucid freshness, Göteborg an innate robustness; Oslo is a subtle competitor, yet, when all is said, to my mind the laurels should crown inimitable Bergen.

Whether the charm of Bergen depends more upon hills or the sea should be a question easily answered in this haven where ships of all nations foregather; but Bergen could ill spare her seven hills which, in beauty, outshine those of Rome. It is Mount Ulriken that dominates with its two

3

thousand feet, but in popularity Flöien, the
Weather-Vane, is foremost with its restaurant
reached by funicular railway. On three sides is
Bergen sheltered by hills, while on the fourth the
Skjægård, a maze of islands, guards the peninsula
on which the city stands from the tempestuous
North Sea. Adequate protection in another respect has been in the past unfortunately lacking.
That Bergen is still so outstandingly picturesque
seems hardly short of miraculous, considering not
only the disastrous fire of 1855 but the conflagration in 1916. Tyskebryggen (the German Quay),
although having but one building that survives
from the time when the Hanseatic City controlled
all trade, still conserves a reminiscent style of
architecture; and the adjoining fish-market on
Torvet (the Market-Place) need fear no competition.

Bergen was founded by Olaf Kyrre (Olaf the
Quiet) in the year 1070, but prior to that date
the Vikings had known the harbor. Harald
Håfagre (Harold Fairhair) is acknowledged as
the founder of Norway in 872—two years before
the discovery of Iceland. It was Viking Leif Ericsson (son, that is, of Eric Raude, discoverer of
Greenland) who, returning to his father's settlement from a visit to Norway in 999, was blown
from his course and discovered the North
American continent—his encounter with the Indians of "Vinland" antedating that of Columbus

by nearly five hundred years. The founder of
Bergen was son to that Harold the Obstinate,
killed in 1066 while attempting the conquest of
England, who met his match in Harold the Saxon
less than a month before the latter succumbed to
William the Conqueror.

It is, however, with Håkon Håkonsson, later
known as Håkon the Old, that we are more concerned—him who in addition to being King of
Norway was "lord of the vassal lands of Iceland,
Greenland, the Faroe Islands, the Shetlands, and
the Orkneys." The coronation took place in
Bergen in 1223, in a mighty hall—lately restored,
with decorations by Gerhard Munthe—upon the
Fortress Quay. The feasting lasted three days
and three nights. It was in this Håkon's Hall that
the same king entertained Snorre Sturlasson of
Iceland, then at work upon his *Edda* or Norse
mythology, to whose *Heimskringla* or "Saga of
the Kings" (from Odin down to 1177) we owe
knowledge of Viking ways.

As descendants of the English, Irish, Scotch,
and French, we in America are apt to associate
the Vikings primarily with their overseas raiding.
Ruthless and unneighborly as were these on-
slaughts upon peoples of western Europe, they
bear witness to the vitality of the raiders. The
Vikings had, moreover, a strict code of honor—
the Haavamaal. Through the sagas of Iceland we
may trace the history of the Northmen from a

time prior to the settlement of that land in about
875 A.D.

"No," says du Chaillu, in *The Viking Age,* "the
people who were then spread over a great part
of the present Russia, who overran Germania,
who knew the art of writing, who led their conquering host to Spain, into the Mediterranean, to
Italy, Sicily, Greece, the Black Sea, Palestine,
Africa, and even crossed the broad Atlantic to
America, who were undisputed masters of the sea
for more than twelve centuries, were not bar-
barians."

Without shadow of doubt the seafaring English
race owes its adventurous spirit to Viking inheritance.

Nowadays it is the British who come on peaceful raids to Norway. Not a day passes during the
season but boatloads of invaders are discharged.
Minding the unwarranted advice of Cook's guidebook, they allow a day for Bergen—the morning
for sightseeing, noon luncheon at Flöien, the afternoon for the classic excursion to Fantoft Church
and to the house of Grieg. On the morrow these
modern rovers continue their cruise to the North
Cape or, like as not, take the early train for Oslo.
With a larger allotment of time at one's disposal
it is hard not to be peremptory in condemning
the scurry of those who have, as a matter of fact,
done well to come so far to spend a fortnight's
holiday.

Clerks at the Hotel Norge extend a courteous greeting to one and all, supplying the demand for the London *Times,* arriving daily by air mail. (How Britons pore over the list of new peers, proposed changes in the Marriage Bill, the item that "The Lord Chancellor took his seat on the Woolsack at three o'clock"!) A coal fire burned in the grate on the day of our entrance into the lobby. Parties sat at tables over coffee. Americans shivered in coats while the English and a group of Scots, wearing kilts, seemed impervious to drafts from the frequently opened door. To sit long enough here or at the Grand in Oslo is to court recognition almost as surely as at Morgan's in Paris.

The Hotel Norge is situated on the Ole Bulls Plass—so named from the monument to this famous son of Bergen whose statue stands with well-poised bow above a musical fountain. It was Ole Bull, the pupil of Paganini, who first recognized the genius of Grieg and arranged to have him study at Leipzig at the age of fifteen. Four years later Grieg gave a piano recital in Bergen, playing his own compositions. An ineffectual representation of the composer has been erected near the bandstand in the Town Garden.

The builders of the Norge and of the Grand Café opposite—across the way from the Ole Bull fountain—were incorrigible optimists or ignorant foreigners: no others would have risked the crea-

tion of sidewalk cafés in such a climate. Norwegians, however, are capable of eating an ice
while sitting in a cold damp wind that would discourage the sons of less hardy races. From the
windows of the hotel, Flöien, the weather-vane
mountain, could be seen, encouraging us to saun-
ter forth without umbrellas on days when clouds
had lifted, or disclosing the restaurant whose
lights winked a final good-night.

"Have you heard this one about Bergen?" we
had been asked as we entered the harbor. "A
certain captain started to put into Bergen and
it wasn't raining, so he thought he had made a
mistake and changed his course. They say the
dogs at Bergen bark at the man who doesn't carry
an umbrella."

It amused us as we ventured forth betimes on
our first morning—having observed sunshine on
Flöien—to see the stenographers and women
clerks scurrying to work in mackintoshes and
rubber knee boots. My Illustrator was armed with
sketch-books and kodak, and to the fish-market
we repaired. It was a Saturday. The mart was
at its height. Nowhere else may the amateur of
such events find so rewarding a juxtaposition of
hills and harbor, of jumbled Old World houses,
of gleaming fish and fishermen silhouetted against
a mass of weathered smacks. In Marseilles, one of
the world's most picturesque markets, we had
noted the burly fishwives—the mates of seamen;

but in no other city do I remember having seen
the fish sold by the men who made the catch,
within sight of the boats that would later bear
them home—in this case to the barren outer
reefs. Eels and mackerel and cod, tunny and
salmon and plaice vied to tempt the purchasers.
Much of the catch was swimming in tanks, for
Norwegians—like the Danes—stipulate that fish
must be cooked on the day of killing. (Gourmets
delight in the result, as the standard in sauces
is no less exacting.) Ragged clouds added to
the dramatic effect of the whole but did not arouse
our suspicions, ignorant as we were of Bergen
and its ways, until gusts set our hats aswirling.
A downpour followed the whirlwind. Housewives
scattered. Fishermen pulled on oilskins which
made them more than ever resemble Gloucester-
men off for the Banks. For ourselves it was a
rout.

We took refuge beneath an arcade, but when
a row of Scandinavian flags was blown with their
poles to the street, we retreated to a bakery and
purchased buns. Others were seized with the
same hunger and crowded into the warmth of the
little shop, whose vestibule was now flooded. Be-
draggled and drenched, anticipating at least a
week's stay in Bergen, I awaited my chance to
paddle, between showers, across the Torvalmenning to the shop where Bergen rubber boots
and woolen socks were to be had. Thereafter I,

 BERGEN ‡

Queen of Scandinavian Ports

too, could walk proudly, with head in air, like
Bergen's army of business women. It seems that
dwellers in the city take a pride in the vagaries
of their climate...I remembered the boast at
Singapore, "It rains every day in the year!" Umbrella brooches are sold as souvenirs. No one can
deny that Bergen downpours are spectacular.

The Torvalmenning offers temptations to tourists in arts and crafts (not to mention Ciro's
antiques at Store Markevei 2 A!) and especially
in furs. The establishment of Brandt, a specialist
in silver fox, is world-famous, and no one should
miss a visit to the basement to see the polar-
bear skins from Spitzbergen, where the supply
seems unlimited. It grieved us to learn that for
a mere eleven hundred kroner we might purchase
the skin of a creature so shaggy-haired and mammoth in stature as once to have been King of the
Bruins.

The German Quay adjoins the fish-market and
tempts with its steamers from all portions of the
globe, drawn up casually at unsheltered docks, its
quaint houses or *gårds* of the Angel, the Golden
Shoe, the Man, the Stag, the Unicorn—each with
appropriate statue enshrined. It is Finnegården,
owned by a Hamburg merchant at time of the
Hanseatic League (from 1350 to 1700), that has
been preserved as a visual testimonial of the
period in dusky low-ceilinged antiquity. A steep
stair leads to the musty office where, behind lat-

ticed panes, the German representative of those who monopolized the trade in Bergen for centuries received his customers. False measures are shown which enabled the merchants by the addition or elimination of a portion of a weight to trim the scales to their own advantage in transactions with the fishermen. Doubtless such double dealings led to their final overthrow. What a penance it would be thought nowadays to sleep in shuttered beds! Even the dog in his kennel fared better than foreman and apprentices. Hanseatic law forbade the entrance to the buildings of female servants, who were obliged to make the beds through apertures giving on the alley. There were at one time two thousand Germans, perforce bachelors throughout their stay, living in this congested quarter, the Hanseatic city. The entire trade with northern Norway was theirs—a trade in the export of dried fish assembled at Bergen. It is easy to recreate the picture, even to the wick lamps swinging overhead in which cod-liver oil was burned, providing as much smoke as light. Mariakirken, still Bergen's most distinguished house of worship, was erected in 1130 and in 1408 came into possession of the German merchants. This accounts for the tombstones with inscriptions in the Teutonic tongue still to be seen in the churchyard.

"That's the kind Lincoln rode in!" said an elderly fellow-countryman, indicating the four-wheelers drawn up at the foot of the funicular railway. Like ourselves he was about to mount to the Flöien Restaurant.

"Bergen's a lonesome place to be if you don't speak the language," he went on. "But do you know this?" He addressed my Illustrator. "Any man at hotel or restaurant may ask any girl to dance? You don't need an introduction, nothing shady about it. You just click your heels and say, '*Dans?*' and, at the end, '*Takke.*' "

As he spoke we had risen, as though in a balloon, until ships and wharves and many-funneled steamers lay spread as on a map below us, resembling toys. From Flöien the view extends not only over the branched By Fjord, on which Bergen crowds to the base of fir-clad hills, but over the skerries to the ocean.

The waitresses at the restaurant wear the costume most frequently seen in Norway, that of the Hardanger Fjord. The becoming red caps and snug bodices made the gentlemen say that, if dancing started, the waitresses would be their choice. Evenings at Flöien are glamorous, but despite the lights and music on the heights my preference is for the subtly illuminated restaurant of the Norge Hotell. Here the Janus Quintet plays Sibelius and Grieg to one's heart's content, interspersed with Stephen Foster melodies which appeal not only to touring Americans but to Norwegians who have acquired the taste while living

in the United States. There is indeed a similarity
in these plaintive airs to certain Norwegian folk-
songs.

It is to the violinist Ole Bull, discoverer of
Grieg, that posterity owes another debt as the
founder of the National Stage in Bergen. With
remarkable perception Bull employed (at about
a dollar a day!) an unknown and singularly
gauche youth as stage director. Without such preliminary experience this man might never have
flowered into the genius he was to become—Henrik Ibsen. The first production, with a prologue
by Ibsen, was given on January 2, 1850, in what
is now known as the Old Theater. This building
is still used for occasional performances, although
it has been replaced by a modern edifice and, with
the moving of the capital to Oslo, no longer holds
the unique position that it did at the time of its
foundation. No sojourner in Bergen should fail to
visit this quaint theater with its museum of
shabby things theatrical, its photographs with
names to us unknown (how local is the fame of
actors!), its wreaths in commemoration of Ludvig Holberg—born at Bergen during the time
of Denmark's supremacy and frequently compared to Molière. Acknowledged as the foremost
dramatist who has written in the Danish tongue,
Holberg and his satires are still popular in Copenhagen. His statue overlooks Bergen's market-
place.

We pored over cases containing the waistcoat of Ole Bull (his violin may be seen at the art museum on Christiegarten), letters and other souvenirs of Ibsen and Edvard Grieg. There is a copy of *Catilina,* Ibsen's first play, written at Grimstad and published in 1875 at Copenhagen. Perhaps most significant are the photographs of *Per Gynt,* on which the two collaborated...words or music alone have power to evoke the Norwegian scene. In the corridor may be found a print of Henrik Klausen, the rather full-blown first Per Gynt, and Froken Parelius as Åsa. Jacob Nilsen, *teaterchef* of the New Theater, now plays the rôle. The Old Theater connects by an overhead bridge with the house in which Ibsen lived from May, 1853, to July, 1857, and Björnstjerne Björnson from December, 1857, to August, 1859, each, in turn, as theater director.

On the day that we stood gazing at the tablets which record the above facts, the picturesque curator of the museum emerged from the historic dwelling. He evinced pleasure to hear that we had, within the year, seen in America productions of *Ghosts* and *An Enemy of the People.*

We asked him to enlighten us as to pronunciation: in Henrik Ibsen *Hen* is plain "hen," but *Per Gynt* is the more tricky "Père Günt."

No Bennett bus is necessary to explore Bergen's Corniche—Sandvikvei. We found a taxi adequate. A latest V8 swept us past the German

Henrik Ibsen

Quay, past Håkon's Hall, and up the road that skirts a semblance of the Mediterranean. So remote is the peninsula, with its high inland lake, its peasant carts hauling milk cans from Bergen, that in these wilds the urban is forgotten. Not

so rural did we find the more inland regions.
Here our first excursion combined a fleeting view
of Gamlehaugen, former country-place of the late
prime minister Christian Michelsen, bequeathed
as a residence for the King, and a visit to Herr
skibsreder Odfjeld at Minde.

Mr. Odfjeld's mansion is set among birches,
aspens, and evergreens upon the border of a lake.
A ship-owner, like his father before him, the gentleman would not feel at home except within sight
of water. Even within doors his walls showed
prints of merchant ships at sea. Our host, standing before a Munthe tapestry of the prince turned
into a black bear, seemed not to regret that the
weather had ruined the salmon fishing—otherwise he would not have been at Minde. Calling
hours, in Norway, are between twelve and three.
It being twelve thirty, we accepted Sola (fruit-
juice) and Hansa (soda-water) with cakes, but,
to our host's evident perplexity, declined more
convivial drinks. Families, Mr. Odfjeld explained,
meet at the midday meal, returning later to school
or business; only at Oslo, with its cosmopolitan
ways, do offices close at four instead of seven,
thereby curtailing the noon lunch hours. Photographs were shown of his two sons and three
daughters—revelers in winter sports. With pride
he displayed medals awarded for his collection
of stamps, and one received at New York in 1936
as a judge at the International Philatelists Ex-

hibition. He has written a brochure on American stamps but at present is chiefly interested in collecting Mexicans.

"How many? Well, to date, about twenty books. It is an expense, yes, it is an expense."

The love of distant places was, we felt sure, the reason for the hobby. His eyes gleamed at mention of his ships.

Another expedition included Fantoft Stave Church and the House of Grieg. There is a record of a stave church built at Fortun on the Sogne Fjord about 1166. Hundreds were erected in the centuries that followed, but many were destroyed by fire. To-day only a score survive. Of these one of the finest has been removed from Fantoft and erected on a private estate near Bergen. We mounted through a forest of oak, beech, and fir to the knoll on which, shut in by trees, the chapel stands. Built, like the purely Norwegian country houses, of logs, like them it seems to be a natural growth from the soil. It is surrounded by a stockade fence with lich-gate, and inside the enclosure is preserved a primitive stone cross of the type used in Norway nine hundred years ago as meeting-places for worship. Stave churches were later erected, usually by a Viking for his family and retainers. Not more than eighty could be accommodated in the Fantoft church—none of these churches, so carefully preserved nowadays by annual coats of tar (which, however, adds to their

inflammability), is large. Warriors left their
weapons in the porches. Blackness formerly prevailed within, or shadowy candle-light. There was
a gate for lepers—there are still about twenty
lepers, all old people, in a hospital near Bergen.
The carved pews and well-preserved murals are
of the fifteenth century—that is to say, modern
innovations. It is the exterior that is more rewarding, with its high-pitched roof, shingles over-
lapping like leathery scales, and its fork-tongued
dragons with trailing sinuous tails. To Norsemen,
as to the Chinese, the dragon was spiritually
symbolic.

"There is a music seems to hover here unheard,
a presence rather than a sound." The lines on
Grieg occurred to me as we approached "Troldhaugen"—the Hill of the Trolls.

"He was a lonely man," said the official from
Bennett's who had brought us thither. "Frail,
and weak, and, like all geniuses, lonely. I once had
the honor to shut a train window for him. He was
a wisp of a being—that the wind might have blown
away."

In his day Grieg's lakeside habitation was the
only one in the region. Bergen was reached laboriously, by horse-drawn vehicle, before the
coming of the railway to Hop (Hope) in 1885.
To-day, with motors, the dwelling is readily accessible. Since the recent death of Madame Grieg
the place has become a national shrine.

The Studio of Grieg

Troldhaugen stands on a point of forest land high above Noråsvannet, a brackish lake connecting with ocean. A clearing has been made just sufficient to reveal views from the front windows of the white cottage, green trimmed and set in woodland of birch, pine, and fir. Murmuring of wind in zither tree-tops is no less apparent in these singing woods than at the Finnish home of Sibelius. Within, the house bears witness to the simple tastes of its owner, and also, I am loath to admit, to his lack of taste in house furnishing. There is nothing indoors that attracts the eye except photographs and other tokens: a painting from friends in Copenhagen, a chandelier from the ladies of Bergen, a Steinway grand piano given by admirers on the occasion of Grieg's sixtieth birthday. A signed picture of Queen Alexandra has been cherished, and on the walls hang familiar representations of Bach, Haydn, Mozart, Beethoven, and Wagner, as well as the beautiful head of the Master—not revealing his pitifully ineffectual form which, in the Bergen monument, suggests a caricature.

The elfin Grieg, naturally, does not reveal himself indoors. What were house furnishings to him? The moment we stepped into the forest and listened to the murmuring wind, the voices of his music spoke to us...those "wisps of living melody" he caught and put "behind bars on a white page."

Nina Grieg, herself a musician, may be seen singing at the piano in Krøyer's portrait of the pair in the National Gallery in Stockholm. She is buried here at Troldhaugen with her illustrious husband, their tomb set into a granite cliff beside the lake. Born in Bergen in 1843, Grieg died in 1907, and his wife not until 1935. They rest beside the pier, where they so often stepped into their boat, as though awaiting Charon's barge.

Another steep trail leads to the studio—a hut only large enough to shelter a table, sofa, and miniature upright. Here the lonely man found peace in listening to his voices. No timorous deer need have feared to pass this rustic cabin or to drink from the lake within its shadow. Shy forest creatures still frequent the place, lurking among the fronds of ferns, to scurry at the sound of

footsteps; and from a swaying laburnum is heard
a song reminiscent of Grieg's "Little Bird."

Ibsen came to this place. Here the two conferred. Echoes of Anitra's dance, trolls threatening the tormented Per, Solveig's song, haunt the
imagination. Here, at Troldhaugen, Grieg felt the
creative impulse in Nature given voice in his immortal "To the Spring." Thoughts fly to Flagstad's peerless rendition of *"Jeg elsker dig."*
Lovers of Grieg delight to remember that von
Bülow called the composer the "Chopin of the
North."

Edvard Grieg

The Lapp Encampment
at Lyngenseidet

Hammerfest

CHAPTER II

ABOARD THE *STELLA POLARIS*

BERGEN lay behind us, the North Cape ahead. Our maps were outspread upon steamer-chairs. How little association had I with all these names, how faint in retrospect, dimmed by an intervening quarter-century, were my Illustrator's boyhood remembrances of a former cruise.

"Molde, O Moldy!"—we used to joke about the name—"the strawberries were as luscious as those at Bergen.

"Hammerfest—it was after leaving Hammerfest that we saw a deep-sea fishing-boat towing a whale. The crew cast off the beast and fired a harpoon to show the technique. But the whale had been dead for days, and my father called it a large-sized smelt!

"Tromsö—I remember Lapps there...and Trondheim, I haven't forgotten it was spelt Trondhjem."

The names of the fjords rang in my ears like music—Hardanger, Sogne, Nord, Geiranger, Romsdals, Troll, Vestforden. Not yet did I know even the name of the one that, to my mind, surpasses the others in beauty—as did the cloak of Joseph—the north-of-the-Circle and nearest-the-Cape fjord, with the to me then unfamiliar designation, Lyngen Fjord.

Aboard the *Stella Polaris* we were now booked for ten days, crowded with excursions, from June eighteenth till June twenty-eighth, which would see us again at Bergen. How memorable they were to be lay as yet on the lap of the gods, and especially of the sun god. Our preparation consisted of receptive minds—slates wiped clean of extraneous notions, not entirely blank like our note- and sketch-books and kodak films, but like them, we trusted, sensitive enough to record impressions. We had saturated ourselves in the preparative of Scandinavian music, literature, and art; now Nature was to overwhelm us, make us willingly acknowledge the extent to which its Norwegian manifestation deserves what we had been inclined to consider overestimated praise.

Arrival at Romsdals Fjord was on the morning of June nineteenth. Snowfields checkered the peaks, green pastures were in vivid contrast, cas-

Åndalsnes

cades flung silvery tresses over shoulders of rock. We put to shore in one of the ship's launches, landing at the dock at the village of Åndalsnes —called by the natives Nes. The *Stella's* arrivals and departures, we were to discover, were always an excuse for milling crowds in its remote ports of call. There is nothing the descendants of the Vikings love as much as an especially svelte boat, and no vessel afloat, her passengers maintain, can surpass in elegance the twin-screw motor yacht *Stella Polaris*.

A caravan of forty cars, organized by Bennett, awaited the two hundred passengers. My Illus-

trator and I scrambled into an open Buick, joined
by another couple, but departure was indefinitely
delayed as we awaited the fifth passenger. He
proved to be an elderly gentleman, swathed in
hooded cape and leaning on a cane. Sinking heavily into the seat beside the chauffeur, this individual announced that he was like the old lady
who wished she had been created a rock and could
praise God merely sitting. At three o'clock we
were at last ready to set forth, and the ride, despite its whirlwind speed and brief duration (we
arrived at four thirty for tea at Stueflåten), initiated us into the mysteries that are Norway.

The Romsdal, into which our course at once
mounted, suggested to us our first love of all
mountain valleys—that from Luz-Saint-Sauveur
to Gavarnie in the High Pyrenees. The vegetation
was similar: in the lower reaches lush pastures
were starred with clover, scabiosa, bluebells. Ash-
trees, rowan in flower, birch, and aspen added to
the greenness of the lower levels, replaced as we
mounted by fir and somber pine. There were
orchards of apple and cherry, many frame houses
and red-painted barns, but as we left the more
settled regions, we came to scattered homesteads
fashioned of weathered logs, in the style of the
forefathers. From these came the pungent odor
of burning resin. Curls of smoke rose above the
turf roofs. Spring was in the air. Cowbells tinkled,
there was a smell of goats. A lamb frisked across

our path. Young children in frocks of red, blue, or green waved as we passed, tossing us flowers of welcome. Dun ponies, of Nord Fjord race, were harnessed to carts or painted hay-wagons. Snow-plows were, for a brief period, stranded at roadsides.

The Romsdalshorn, Norway's most popular mountain, suggested by its form the Aiguille du Dru at Chamonix. Although not of great height, only 5,104 feet, it has style not excelled even by the fjords, in this respect surpassing Norway's peaks noted for their glaciers. These Romsdalshorn does not possess; snow melts rapidly on its sheer cone and precipitous rock structure, but wisps of cloud often veil its barrenness and make it tower to apparently fantastic heights. The frozen harshness of the Trolltinder and Vengetinder, outdoing Romsdalshorn in altitude, seems to close the valley. There is, however, to the north, a gash cut by the furious Rauma through which both route and railway wedge. The Romsdal or Rauma Line, opened in 1924, connects Åndalsnes, via the Dovre Railways, with Oslo and Trondheim —each less than three hundred miles away, yet, formerly, more than a day's journey.

Cascades were dominant. Spray filled the valley. Not Alps nor Pyrenees could rival these. Ice-cold breath came on the wind from Mongefoss, thundering on the left; from Slettafoss, roaring beneath a rustic bridge like a rampageous off-

The Romsdalshorn :
Norway's most popular Mountain.

spring of Imatra; from Vermafoss, pouring from the white heavens its divine purity upon the darkness of wooded mountainside. As we sped ever upward, the roar of falling waters all but deafened our ears. Rainbows danced in bewildering profusion.

The climax to this valley, fine though the view may be, cannot compare with the Cirque de Gavarnie, climax to the valley of Luz-Saint-Sauveur. At Stueflåten, where lilies-of-the-valley may be gathered in the woodland, we thawed in the warmth of the bleak frame hotel. All others departed after tea, but where was our "Colonel"? —for so he was called. In answer to inquiries we found him, surrounded by attentive waitresses in costume, indulging in the purchase of an extra muffler. *Husflid* or cottage industries are more plentiful than toadstools in tourists' haunts.

The wind had risen during our brief stay at the inn, risen to a velocity such that, on the descent, eye-glasses were blown from noses. It roared and whistled about us, as we huddled in steamer-rugs, with a ferocity we were not again to encounter until the North Cape. The return —with views of the Bishop's Peak, Kongen and Dronningen, the distant toy-like train trailing past Vermafoss which drenches it with spray— moved with the harmony, the rhythm, of an ancient saga. It was, however, a race with time. We were aware that the *Stella* was sailing at seven.

Should we overtake our fellow-passengers? Suddenly we came upon them. Seven cars blocked the roadway. Our first thought was one of concern—perhaps there had been an accident! No, merely that one of the ciné-camera devotees felt constrained to take home a record of a solitary fisherman standing in a rowboat and reeling for trout. My Illustrator had hesitated to stop one car in order to snap Mongefoss!

Sailing time. Types we were soon to recognize and even to call by individual appellations clambered into waiting launches. But my Artist, where was he?

"Sketching, I suppose," said the Colonel, pleased, on this occasion, not to be the last.

"Oh, no, he must have gone in an earlier launch," said Bennett's factotum, with authoritative manner. "This is the last boat."

"Not without me," I assured him.

"But," said he, "there is no one left ashore, everyone has been rounded up."... He gave the signal to depart. At the same instant a nonchalant figure in ruddy tweeds issued from the door of a distant shop.

"Buying Christmas presents for your wife?" shouted the Colonel, through cupped hands.

The approach to Molde is dramatic. From the harbor is to be had one of the finest views in Norway, including, as it does, the Romsdalshorn, Vengetinder, and the aiguilles of the Trolltinder.

We were to see the distant panorama of snowclad peaks bathed in Alpine glow and, later, with resplendent half-moon peeping between the foreground masts of anchored fishing-smacks.

Most of the town's three thousand inhabitants —at least those below the age of thirty—were massed at the dock to welcome the *Stella* or came scurrying along the shore promenade. At nine o'clock we were sauntering through the sheltered town, where roses and fruit-trees on walls give the illusion of a more southerly latitude. We were to be reminded in Finland of the quiet dignity of this "Paradise of the North" when we visited Sortavala. Both are quiet, northern, remote, consist of low villas, and yet in appearance reflect the culture of their inhabitants. The Hotel Alexandra at Molde is a favorite resort, especially with amateur fishermen.

Gardens were gay with lupins, peonies, laburnums in flower. Old sea-captains sat at doorways. We made our way to the church: custom demands that tourists see the altarpiece, Alex Ender's "Women at the Sepulchre." Photographs were taken with success by my Illustrator after the hour of ten, supposedly the evening limit for this latitude. It was light enough to read when we boarded the *Stella* at midnight. Can any other day equal this one? we asked each other, and answered, Perhaps not. The rest will be variations on the theme of incomparable Norway.

Sunday. Reverend Andersen conducted a service in the lounge. As the chairs were in fixed positions, half the congregation offered backs to the minister! Prayers were said for the rulers of earth, with noticeable exceptions, a Lutheran chant was played by the orchestra, the Lord's Prayer and blessing followed in Norwegian and then in English.

After service we read the notice board:

DET BERGENSKE DAMPSKIBSSEBSKAB
[B. D. S.]
[BERGENSKE STEAMSHIP COMPANY]

The captain has just received a telegram from "Neptun," King of all Seas. He will meet all the passengers on the after deck where the orchestra plays—at 5:30 p.m. to-day.

A salute was fired as the *Stella* crossed the Arctic Circle. Instantly Father Neptune was seen clambering up a rope ladder, followed by his buxom "Queen." He was clad in yellow oilskins and was of phenomenal height—realists were to note his extra sole-leather and murmur, "The second mate!" Festoons of olive-brown seaweed, inflated bladders reeking of the sea, clung to him and to his trident. His hair and long beard were of stringy texture, but his "wife" had Gretchen braids and was powerful enough to lift a man—which "she" proceeded to do after the first triumphant ceremony of arrival, escorted

AT THE ARCTIC CIRCLE

by the ship's band. The captain and Neptune exchanged handshakes. Cymbals clashed. Neptune spoke. In thunderous English he announced that "As all of you have given tribute to Neptune on the North Sea,"—roars of laughter from the crowd—"you shall be rewarded!" Prodding the prettiest girls with his trident, the Sea King singled out those to be kissed and presented with a certificate signed by Kaptein Ellefsen of the *Stella* certifying that so-and-so had, on June twentieth, crossed the *polarcirkel*. The wife of a Jain, one of Gandhi's right-hand men, was chosen but modestly drew her sari about her, sending her imposing husband to be embraced. Never have I seen so many cameras simultaneously in action —huge ones with tripods, tiny Leicas, old-fashioned Bull's-Eyes. There was a sound as of locusts—motion-pictures in the making. My Illustrator complained during the entire cruise that he could not budge without tripping over some one changing a film or getting in the way of a lens, nor could he escape the endless talk on light meters, times, and apertures. I drew his attention to the fact that, in addition to water-color and pencil sketch-books, he carried two kodaks!

"You're very busy on your holiday," a friendly soul remarked to my Artist.

"Holiday!" the latter exclaimed. "It's no holiday for me!"

The friendly soul turned to the authoress for help. "Does he mean it?" he inquired, puzzled.

"There is a woman astronomer on this boat who *is* having a holiday," I told him. "She says that the only absolute rest for her comes with these starless daylight nights."

Midnight Sun

Our first midnight sun was due to appear. An unearthly light preceded the momentous hour. The steel-blue east to starboard was bright as midday. Overhead was fainter blue, while a Valhalla rock island was lost and reappeared, looming above horizontal mists like peaks in a Chinese painting. A rosy glow, as of Loki's fire, illuminated vegetation and rocks till the whole was obliterated by smoke-like cloud. Valhalla was destroyed, but next came an isle of the heroes circled by gulls. Engines stopped—otherwise land or fogs might mar our view. Even so will the mist cover rise unduly?

My Illustrator tells how, on his childhood cruise, the sun was seen at eleven-thirty but never at twelve. Arctic gulls soar tirelessly. There is a stir of lesser wings—Mother Carey's chickens? Along the western horizon hangs a fringed curtain of gray cloud, like smoke from a forest fire. The sun has unveiled his splendor. Although low in the heavens, he does not set. Horizontal clouds, angel-winged, hover above, and, at the stroke of twelve, a golden wake is flung like a magic carpet across the still gray water. Almost imperceptibly the orb rises, glowing with increasing intensity. The sky beneath turns to molten gold—gates to a golden Jerusalem.

The *Stella,* after the way of ships, had fired three salutes. The Jain had observed how different this sun was from the "upright" one seen at the equator. The ship's heart began once more to beat, and, aware of its familiar throbbing, we watched the midnight sun momentarily eclipsed by "the island of giants."

Our weary eyes saw suns on every hand—symbolic suns, redemptive suns enlightening the world, sun of the East, sun of the West, the North, the South, the real, the unreal...which reality, which illusion? We were changed. We had put on immortality....A new day, awaited by a wartorn world, another revelation of man's unity!

At midday following the midnight sun, tenders took a limited group ashore at Finsnes to rejoin the *Stella,* that evening at Lygenseidet. Earth, sky, and air conspired to make this a day of days.

Was not this the first time we had set foot ashore
in the Arctic Zone? Never should we have visualized it thus. Snow mountains bordered a verdant countryside. We drove past fields riotous
with dandelions and mammoth buttercups, past
cottages with roofs of growing sod. Friendly salu-
tations greeted us—as though we were royalty.
It is an event for these people to see anyone
from the outside world. Like all Norwegian country folk, they wore bright red or green or cobalt
blue, even to the boys' shirts. Men in the prime of
life, probably at sea, were conspicuously absent.
The women, bronzed and stalwart, were veritable
daughters of the Vikings—Norwegians being, to
my mind, the handsomest of the Scandinavians.

Linemen on telegraph poles were replacing
wires, destined, doubtless, with the radio aërials,
to be torn away by winter gales. Fences seemed
to us unnecessarily high, held in place by "wig-
wam" posts. After the farms came peat-bogs, a
sweep of heath open as Alaska. (We were reminded of the Colonel, who, we found, had brought
with him photographs of Alaska to prove that
Norway had nothing to surpass his country!)
Magpie nests carried our eyes to birch-trees. At
Malselv we crossed a swift current by primitive
ferry, the ferryman wading in boots to expedite
our launching. Mount Istindene with its snows
and glacier, as seen from the water, made us
yearn for a longer tarrying. Ingrids and Elsas

—if not Heidis—not yet grown, horses and foals, horned cattle, goats and kids with many-toned bells, enlivened the way, frequently obstructing our passage.

Near the Rundhaug Hotel at Ovrebygda we were to see our first Lapps—five men in striking regalia, lounging outside the country store. Inside the hostelry the gruff face of Ibsen looked down from the wall, also Björnson and the contours of local mountains. Via Bals Fjord we crossed the ridge to Nordsjosbotten, surprisingly near the Finnish border, where a halt was made for *lopsa,* pancakes to be eaten with *geit ost,* a sweet brown goat's-milk cheese for which I soon acquired the taste. The hostess welcomed us in English, saying her home was on the Columbia River three hundred miles from Portland. She had come back to this resort for her holiday. The "resort" was a rough shack, but in it we found not only waitresses in antique costumes but fine linen and good cheer.

Evening approached, but with it no threat of darkness. There was, however, a polar chill as we started the last and most dazzling stage of our journey. The road skirted the shore of Lyngen Fjord. Across the water rose the wondrous mountains...to me nameless, almost mythical in their nearness and Tibetan remoteness. I knew that I should never set foot upon them yet that they would be enshrined in memory with

the mountains the very thought of which forms
my doxology of praise—Fuji, the cloud-topped
hills of China, the Grand Cañon of the Colorado,
the Jungfrau seen near Mürren, the Vignemale,
and the Cirque de Gavarnie. The virgin snows
partly concealed the glaciers, but rocky structure
emerged clear-cut against the evening sky. A complete barrier against the outer world was this
range. It rose abruptly from the fjord's edge and
was, therefore, startlingly reflected. Adding a final
drop of beauty to our overflowing cup, the desolate shore along which we sped was occasionally
indented by coves where lonely dwellings were
festooned with fishing-nets. These mud huts were
primitive as that first built by Isak, in Hamsun's
classic tale. The high prows of dories and their
red-green banded hulls suggested Viking ships.
A solitary figure, surely once a seafaring man,
followed us with a long field-glass...motorists
are rare upon this road, and summer seasons
short.

The wind had risen. Skeleton-thin scarecrows
in flapping black coats with pairs of limp sea-
gulls for gesturing hands twirled in an eerie
danse macabre. Gulls, it appeared, not crows,
menaced these meager crops.

The *Stella* had preceded us to Lyngenseidet.
Before boarding her we had time to visit the
Lapp encampment. To one nurtured on the Santa
Claus legend the reindeer has sentimental value

perhaps above his just deserts; but no reindeer at Skansen in Stockholm or elsewhere in captivity can compete with reindeer nuzzling in a woodland close to their grazing-ground. We were in a mood where it would hardly have astonished us to come upon Eskimo igloos, and, as we walked up the mountain valley to the Lapp village, this is what we found. Not igloos, indeed, but mounds of sod, exaggerated ant-hills (we had seen during the day mammoth hills created by the toil of ants) with burrow doors. Dogs yelped at our approach, and children, replicas of parents, motioned us to the settlement where families had spread out tempting wares—horn paper-knives, belts, and fur-lined slippers, gaudy caps. It was these many-peaked jester caps, worn at jaunty angles, that most intrigued us, next to the wrinkled parchment of those imperturbable Mongolian faces. Tiny of stature as children, almost, they genially allowed us to peer into huts where, in pots hung over central bonfires, the evening meal was in preparation. Blue-gowned were the women, in cloth similar to that of their husbands' coats and similarly edged with scarlet. The men's snugly-clad legs, combined with jester caps and jerkins, gave them a strangely medieval appearance, a romantic appeal aside from that of their nomadic lives.

Ranging at will over the north of Norway, Sweden, and Finland, the Lapp follows whither his herds lead. The reindeer, we thought, were to this northern mainland what the gulls were to the sea—visible incarnations of the spirit of the place. With their sad eyes they gazed hillward, as if eager to return to upland mosses. Their branched horns were covered with soft fur, not yet rubbed bare. Whither would these strange creatures lead, whither the Lapps, now so comfortably grouped about their fires, follow? We envisaged the open plateau raked by the pitiless winds...the driving snow. In our minds' eyes we could see the deer, by nothing daunted, pawing, as reindeer do, with black hoofs in the waste of snow, unerring in discovery of sustaining lichen.

Hammerfest was our next day's stop—Hammerfest, the most northerly town in the world and a center for the preparation of cod-liver oil.

"Only seasoned travelers like Hammerfest," my Illustrator read aloud. "Perhaps that is why we do."

"Like is too mild a word," I added, ecstatic to be, for the first time in my life, in Arctic surroundings.

The harbor was crowded with powerful two-masted fishing-boats, their brown sails furled, their engines at rest. Every line of these stubby smacks spoke of strength rather than grace. They looked as though built to butt against ice barriers. We had passed the *Lomstinn* from Rosand as we entered the harbor. The men aboard had waved eagerly, as lonely Norwegians do, holding up samples of their catch. Bare hills flecked with snow backed the somber town—there are over three thousand inhabitants. Norwegian flags flew from boats, and an official swallow-tailed banner from a pole at what was perhaps the custom-house. Sunlight on rippling water reflected on the sterns of the massed craft.

To step ashore at Hammerfest is to feel the proximity of the polar regions. Spitzbergen, the most northerly settlement ever reached by cruise ships (rechristened Svalbard, its old Norse name, since the Treaty of Versailles), is only four hundred miles away. Spitzbergen was the name bestowed upon the archipelago by its discoverer, a Dutch explorer, in 1596. Henry Hudson reported on "the abundance of whales, seals and walruses" to be found there. Although Christian IV of Denmark and Norway claimed Spitzbergen, it was a no-man's-land until a mandate was conferred on Norway by the Treaty of Versailles.

Hardly has the voyager stepped ashore at Hammerfest before he is confronted by polar bears —not, indeed, in life, but incredibly realistically displayed to attract to furriers where eyeless skins of bears, articles fashioned of walrus tusks, and throw-overs of eiderdown form temptations to the vulnerable. A handsome silver fox sold for fifty dollars. Girls from our steamer reveled in

Every line of Norwegian smacks
speaks of strength

Lapp hats, becoming to flappers, and startled the dealers by asking for "slacks, you know, pants," showing disgust when they did not know.

We hailed an antiquated taxi, time being limited, to drive us—a twenty-minute walk—to Fuglenses to see the Meridian Column:

TERMINUS SEPTENTRIONALIS
ARCUS MERIDIANI
25° 20′

with the names of the rulers of Norway, Sweden, and Russia and the dates 1816 and 1852. It is in the form of a bronze globe showing the continents. So piercing was the wind that I allowed my Illustrator to penetrate alone to examine the towering racks of drying fish—to us suggestive of Gaspé. A hospital is seen from this point, for seamen disabled in these northern waters.

In words from various languages I attempted to converse with our fat troll of a driver. He was accompanied by a doll of a daughter, whom, from time to time, he would hug, and who, in response, would mechanically gurgle "Papa!" Their mouths formed perfect crescents. Next Sunday, the father told us, a group of fifty would be confirmed at the church. They come from the country districts three weeks in advance and remain for training. When we saw these young people conversing on the "old" (replacing one destroyed by fire) church steps, they seemed like friends. Norwegians, we decided, had stalwart, upright characters written in every line of their beings. We walked to the new church, with its well-tended cemetery and a bench where a young woman sat in meditation. This was a quarter of the town where tourists were evidently a novelty, yet signs reading "Shell," "Singer," "Golden West Virginia Cigaretta," made us feel almost at home.

As we gazed upon the seamen's graves, the recollection was borne in upon us of the nearness to Svalbard, whence, from King's Bay, in 1926, Amundsen's airship *Norge* flew across the Pole, landing in Alaska. From Svalbard, also, Byrd was to fly, in the same year, to and from the Pole. From the same spot, in May, 1928, General Nobile set out in the ill-fated airship *Italia*. Once a year, in late July or early August, the *Stella Polaris* and the *Prince Olav* continue the North Cape cruise to Svalbard and northward to the floating pack-ice, coming, sometimes, within about five hundred miles of the Pole.

Gazing from the *Stella's* deck, on our departure from Hammerfest, we should hardly have been astonished to behold Olaf Trygvesson's ship, the *Long Serpent,* emerging from the mouth of a fjord.

"Viking," says the Century Dictionary, "a Scandinavian rover or sea-robber of the class that infested the seas about north and west Europe during the eighth, ninth, and tenth centuries, making raids upon the coasts."

"From about the year 800 the 'Viking' and his ships became a familiar and dreaded sight, from Iceland to Gibraltar, and from there to Constantinople," writes Freda Lingstrom in *This is Norway*. "Their activities, as far as England was concerned, ceased when King Knud of Denmark united with Olav Trygvesson of Norway and Olav Skotkonung of Sweden and created a kind of federation of states of which Great Britain formed a part.... Their fleet of longships, manned by ferocious warriors, swept all before them.... The boats had a grim and pagan beauty, and were dearly loved by the Vikings, whose wild, rhythmic verse extolled them in terms of poetic and passionate admiration." In 852 Olaf the White was acclaimed King of Ireland, in 861 Pisa was captured, in 882 Paris was besieged "when 700 vessels with 30,000 men sailed up the Seine." In 900 came the colonization of Normandy. It is said that the Norsemen went most often to the British Isles, the Danes to Germany and the Mediterranean, and the Swedes to the Baltic and Russia.

Harold Fairhair was the first to reign as monarch of all Norway (from 872 until 930), having subdued his enemies in order to win the hand of the Princess Gyda. At the end, however, he made the mistake of dividing his kingdom among his twenty sons, so that the last state of the country was no better than the confusion of earlier centuries. The land was not to be again united until 995 under Olaf Trygvesson, founder of Nidaros, now Trondheim.

After Hammerfest our course lay northward sixty miles to the Cape. With Viking courage our captain was to steer his modern version of the *Long Serpent* within spying distance of Hjelmsöstauren—the Bird Rock. We felt, perhaps, like unofficial observers at the League of Nations—embarrassed by the very nature of our position. The observed, however, were not unduly disturbed by blasts from the *Stella's* foghorn. An officer assured us that the birds were used to the *Stella's* visits—in which case they have long memories, as these calls occur only five times a year. Thousands of gulls fled from their cavernous nesting-rock only to return, and an equal number of eider-ducks, pure white beneath with smart black coats, marked vividly as magpies. (Sibelius was to call our attention to the fact that Finnish crows wear dinner-jackets!) Their flight, unlike that of the Arctic gulls, was a rapid flapping of wings as squads scurried close to the water. Scouting eiders floated near-by, craning black necks sinuous as cormorants'.

At six in the afternoon we stole upon the Cape, familiar to many because of the Horn, a boot-like rock projecting from the cliff—as though the protruding appendage of a troll swallowed, as trolls

are said to be, by cliffs. Passing beyond the
promontory, we came to another, similar in general contour and mistaken by many passengers
for our destination. On deck was heard the usual
clicking of shutters. But we were to turn between
the headlands to attempt a landing on the slightly
less sheer wall of the Cape. From the deck we
could see a distant café and a red post-office. A
zigzag path led upward to a couloir of snow. We
congratulated ourselves on having seen the top,
as mists now blotted out the upper reaches. Many
passengers, at sight of the clouds, decided against
what might prove to be a futile shore excursion,
discouraged, too, by the roughness of the Arctic
Ocean.

The icy winds that blew through supposedly
impervious garments made us ready to believe
that, at the *Stella's* speed, the Pole was but three
days away. Launches were lowered. Passengers
made abortive attempts at debarkation to starboard. Swaying steps were let down to port. Tales
were told of how, often, it is not possible to go
ashore. Aided by two seamen, I leaped aboard the
tossing shell. My Illustrator tumbled after. We
were off! Never before had I lived in an open boat
upon an uproarious ocean. At one moment the sea
cradled us, at another we were lifted to the crest
of the wave. A solitary steamer towards the north
seemed headed for the Pole. All save masts and
stack would be lost, to reappear heading undeviat-

ingly to the land of the walrus and the bear.
Deep-blue waters rushed appallingly upon us,
breaking in drenching spray. From Norsemen our
thoughts turned farther afield to Gloucester fishermen.

"Winslow Homer!" my Painter shouted against
the wind. "We're living in a Winslow Homer."

Trondheim ✠ ☩ ☩
The Cathedral is the Pride of Norway

NORTH CAPE

CHAPTER III

THE NORTH CAPE AND AFTER

To LAND or not to land? It was an open question. Gulls peopled the rocky walls of Nord Kapp. A brown-sailed boat scudded by. The taste of salt was on our lips. To our relief the launch was skilfully brought to the landing-stair. On terra firma we got our breath in the shelter of the post-office, where North Cape and Nansen stamps were ready for mailing on post-cards to a waiting world. The success or failure of the expedition was still shrouded in a cloud mantle.

A mule could climb most of the zigzag to the heights. The altitude reached is a scant thousand feet, but so dramatic is the promontory, so Alpine its granite structure and frigid atmosphere, it gives the semblance of vaster height. Benches are provided for the scant of breath. Ladies and apoplectic gentlemen gain courage from them. It was with relief that we noted the Mississippian, whose physician had warned him against heart-strain, abandoning the project and returning seaward. Goat-like youths passed us. One called that this was the sixth time he had climbed the Cape.

"Must be a steward," someone murmured.

The lower reaches of the path were fringed with familiar buttercups, paler globe-flowers, and lank forget-me-nots. As we mounted, the sward, short as that cropped by sheep, was patterned with minute yellow violets. Higher, where melting snow disclosed rocky surfaces, crevices were cushioned with moss campion and anemone-frail dryas.

Overheated by our climb, we had stripped off our coats. Sunday's parson, Chicago-born of Norwegian stock, encouraged laggards—carrying their wraps. An officer of the *Stella* had lent an unwilling foreign girl a pair of shoes. He dragged her upward, repeating, "But you must see, you must!" to all the protests of the crude young creature. We looked down upon the silvery beauty of the *Stella,* remote now as though we had severed all our bonds. The time came when she, too, with all the world, was swallowed in fog. At this juncture a Norwegian seaman loomed out of nothingness...was he stationed at this point by Bennett? As a blast greeted our ascent, he motioned to my coat, holding it for me and turning up the collar.

"Cold vind," he muttered, pointing upwards.
An old stager pushed by. "You're half-way,"
he threw back over shoulder.

"Half-way!" I almost sank in my tracks.

"But you'll soon be on the top—the rest's on
the level."

Chilling fog... we had reached the plateau. We
hastened beside the guiding wires. At long last
voices were audible ahead. An apparition of dim
sun was vouchsafed... like the dying flicker of an
electric bulb it faded. The midnight hour was
nearing. Again the apparition flared, a diffuse un-
recognizable brightness. Our woolens dripped
moisture. No friendly bell of beast guided us over
this field of rocks. The voices grew louder. The
Refuge loomed. To what purpose had we come?
We stood irresolute, shivering in the wind's fury,
yet loath to abandon hope. Coffee was being served
within, and cards were to be had, officially signed,
testifying arrival at the North Cape... bizarre.
Tales of rain and fog prevailed—of skepticism as
to the captain's prediction that we should see the
midnight sun though the passengers left aboard
would not. "Nothing venture..." this son of the
Vikings had said to us.

Midnight neared. "Nothing venture..." I murmured, as the unbelievable happened, the pall of
fog inexplicably lifted. The door of the heavens,
set in azure, opened, disclosing an orb of fire in
a golden paradise. Like specters at cockcrow di-

aphanous cloud shapes fled to oblivion. There was no sunset. This was dawn! For the first time water could be seen undulating at the distant base of the cliff.

Sun-worshipers continued to arrive. A game grandmother, assisted by two sailors, was embraced by a daughter who exclaimed, ''I never thought you'd get here!'' Groups must be photographed before the monument marking the ascent of Oscar II. From the buffet came the smell of steaming coffee, and a chorus of students could be heard singing:

''Glory, glory, hallelujah!''

A distant gun fired three salutes. The *Stella*... we had all but forgotten the *Stella* and sailing-time.

When we returned to our ship, a collation was spread—such luscious strawberries and whipped cream and cookies as cannot be found save in Norway. And the hot chocolate!

''I never tasted such chocolate!'' I remarked to a friendly steward, who, with a wry smile, replied, ''But has Madame ever been before to the North Cape?''

Two o'clock found us still on deck. We could not bring ourselves to leave until, as the *Stella* steamed southward, the precipitous Cape was eclipsed by lesser promontories. Last of all to go was the just visible Refuge. A solitary girl in slacks, the tomboy of the boat, had remained with us, and, as seamen came to flush the deck, she cried, with outstretched arms, "North Cape, I don't want to leave you!"

North Cape, upright, erect, upstanding, symbol of Scandinavian integrity. If Gibraltar fall, no longer firm in the face of enemy planes (and dubious diplomacy), the North Cape stands.

Tromsö was reached next day. Situated north of the Polar Circle, Tromsö has been called the capital of Arctic Norway. "Polar traffic" (odd expression!) is said to start from here, as well as communication with Spitzbergen, last permanent settlement of the North. At Tromsö, too, is an observatory for the study of northern lights. How we wished that we might have seen the radiation of the Aurora Borealis!... silver and yellow most often, but sometimes crimson paling to buff and green. These manifestations are frequent in winter, but naught compensates, in the wintry sky, for the absence of the sun, which at the North Cape remains below the horizon from November eighteenth to January twenty-third.

In anticipation, Tromsö was a cold and barren place washed by a leaden sea. The Gulf Stream, however, is to be reckoned with. Its girdle of comparatively warm water is the salvation of Norway as a habitat for man. On account of the subterranean ridge along the coast, whose pinnacles form skerries, only the upper or warmest waters penetrate into the fjords, whereas farther

from land the Norwegian Sea has profound and
frigid depths. To our astonishment we were
greeted by a sun bathing Tromsö in midsummer
heat...it was indeed Midsummer Day.

Furriers, displaying skins of polar bears, form
the same characteristic note on the shopping street
as at Hammerfest. We made our way to Andersen's, where an affable shopkeeper demonstrated
how the reindeer gets his branched horns.

"In May," said this robust son of the North,
"the straight horns start to grow. At first they
are covered with fur, and in them so much blood
circulates that a broken horn, at this season, may
result in death. In August full growth is attained,
and at Christmas Santa Claus' reindeer are beginning to lose their antlers. How do they get the
branches? The reindeer kicks his straight horn
[by contortions the shopkeeper endeavored to
demonstrate], and where kicked it branches. Then
he rubs his cleft hoof on the spot and thereby oils
it! There's power in those little black hoofs!"

Skins, eider quilts, mittens embellished by geo-
metric design or stylized reindeer, tempted us;
but it was the walrus-tusk carving that proved
irresistible. Jensen both father and son, the Norwegians famed in this art, dwell at Tromsö. I
have before me as I write the bas-relief of a polar
bear upon an ivory iceberg.

The Arctic Museum displays a mother bear with
her young, a startling group by which to be con-

fronted. Above the stair are shown antlers of reindeer in both the velvet and bony stages. The Cathedral may be visited, but of greater interest is the tiny Catholic church with its modern Norwegian interior. The pews are veritable Viking ships for color—vivid green with scarlet tops. A gigantic fish in outline forms the appropriate ceiling design, while the altarpiece has an equal nicety of fish motif. Converts to Rome should be the reward of the decorators of this church.

The drabness of Tromsö is redeemed by the geniality of its people. Curly towheads gleamed in sunshine as did summer frocks. Cotton stockings were the only concession to thrift and climate. One student in especial seemed the embodiment of the coöperative spirit. We had asked him how to procure a taxi to cross the ferry to the Lapp village. Not only was he to find a taxi, but he volunteered to go along as interpreter, and not a penny would he accept for his services. He beguiled the way by telling us of the school system. First come seven years in the free lower school— the people's, corresponding to our public school; next, three years to the middle (high) school, whose pupils may be recognized by green-visored caps; followed by three years in gymnasium (college)—red caps—or, if the student be studying a profession, seven years at the University of Oslo.

Tents had been erected by campers who would celebrate Saint Hans not with fires of Saint Jean, as in France, but with smoke. Dancing there would be, around smoking pyres, dancing and joy—but not midsummer poles, as in Sweden.

Tromsdal was soon reached, a plateau loosely encircled by snow mountains. The Lappeleir consisted of some nine huts formed of birch staves covered with sod. The roofs had apertures in lieu of chimneys, and smoke curled above the tall grass that substituted for thatch. Of windows there were none. The inclined doors were closed, but on our approach one after another was thrown open. Each home was guarded by a yapping Lapp dog, akin to the Spitz (the latter was given its name not as a native of Spitzbergen, but because it was the breed taken there to hunt the fox). The men were off in the hills—all but a grandfather. The women with papooses peered from black interiors. These Lapps follow their grazing deer to Sweden in winter, others penetrate to Finland, but the majority of the members of this extraordinary race dwell in Norway in the provinces of Tromsö and Finnmark.

There was in the valley one Norwegian house, a *sportskafe*. Here students come in winter to ski. A portrait of Knut Hamsun hung on the wall, and one of Jonas Lie the writer (father of the American painter) who spent his boyhood at Tromsö.

To our astonishment, we learned, on boarding the *Stella Polaris,* that none of our fellow-passen-

gers had made the excursion to the Lapp village,
but all had instead walked the streets of Tromsö,
where distractions do not abound.

Troll Fjord

One of the advantages of cruising on a yacht
like the *Stella* is that she may go where ocean
liners are, by their size, debarred. Next morning
found us entering the Troll Fjord. Escaping an
apparently impassable barrier, the *Stella* penetrated into a crystal lake bounded by stupendous

cliffs. The first officer stood during the procedure
at the bow, ready to order the anchor dropped at
the least sign of wind. With a few other un-
wontedly early risers we had taken possession of
the extreme bow, where we were warned to remain
until the boat should leave the fjord. Late-comers
with coats or bathrobes—ill-disguising that they
still wore pajamas—crowded the boat deck. The
grim rock walls that narrowly closed us in, the leaping cascades, were distinctly mirrored. Eider-ducks
skimmed the water as though to remind us that
we were still north of the Circle. It takes daring
navigation to turn in such restricted quarters. The
feat accomplished, discussion ensued. Should we
go to breakfast or to bed? The latter offered
temptations after four nights of celebrating the
midnight sun. In this respect the record was exceptional, as often all the nights in the Arctic
Zone are overcast.

Thoughts of *The Last of the Vikings* lent interest to the Lofoten range passed after Troll
Fjord. Clouds, sunlight, and showers combined in
one vast glory. How like the *Seal* of Bojer's saga
that passing fairy-boat! With cod-fishing fleets
and snow mountains the Lofoten Islands offer the
splendor that is Norway.

Had we seen Svartisen Glacier en route to the
Cape or before unprecedented Lyngen Fjord, it
would have come into its own. Glaciers, like commodities, sometimes become a drug on the mar-

ket. Holands Fjord was reached in the afternoon, and parties set out afoot for the base of the glacier. Others had gone before us. The comments ran in this wise. The Englishman returning, swinging his cane: "It would be a nasty cold place to be left, what?" An American business man: "I call this frozen assets." A hitherto unknown woman: "There's one thing about it that's just too bad. We can't tell the folks at home about it, adjectives fail...." To me the remark was more poignant than she knew. I felt like saying, "Put not your trust in adjectives."

A ragged sky enhanced the looming quality of the massif. The glacier has poured itself into the valley, and, like Bossens, it may be seen by the pedestrian while threading his way between birch-trees. Jostedalsbreen is Europe's largest glacier, but Svartisen ranks second in Norway and is the only one to come down to a fjord. The size is guessed as two hundred square miles... limitless the glacier appears when seen from a steamer's deck. The purity and immensity of the topmost snowfields transcend all but a craftsman's pen. A fragmentary rainbow, a red barn, gaudy rowboats, added telling notes to the color scale.

Nowhere is the enchantment of distance more appreciable than with a mountain. Yet, even when we stood upon the glacier, we were entranced by the beauty of dripping ice-caverns creviced with sing-

The Svartisen Glacier

ing blue, dazzling icebergs borne downstream by gurgling waters. The tourists swarming upon the ridged moraine could no more mar the majesty of the whole than if they had indeed been ants. All of us seemed equally unimpressive in this supreme presence. As we turned boatward, clouds hung ever lower, heavier, and more ominous until Svartisen was extinguished ... glowing the brighter in sunlit memory.

Trondheim is a dignified town whose main street is primly lined with rowans. To appreciate the latter to the full it is necessary to have come

descends to the Brink of the Fjord

from the treeless North. To stand one day upon
the Svartisen Glacier—well within the boundaries
of the Arctic Zone—and the next upon the streets
of Trondheim, which might be Denmark or Holland, far removed from polar atmosphere, is an
experience in contrasts. My Illustrator had visited
Trondhjem—but not Trondheim. The latter is the
Norse designation revived since the *Landsmal* (or
country speech) was established by the law of
1930. The country folk are in the majority in Parliament and, claiming Norse descent for their
tongue, are doing their utmost to supplant the

Riksmal, the more literary Norwegian spoken in the cities, which, they claim, is a language impregnated with Danish, dating from the Danish conquest.

The young man who showed us through the King's Palace at Trondheim was irate on the subject. "The *Landsmal* is taught in the country schools around Bergen," he said, "and spoken by politicians who seek popularity. When I travel, to understand the notices in the trains I must read them several times. It is hard on city dwellers... really ridiculous. The Crown Prince is so democratic that he speaks both tongues. Do you know that his infant son, Harald, is the first heir to the throne to be born in Norway since the days of Olaf Håkonsson in 1370? The people went wild at his birth."

The King's Palace was built in 1770 by a Norwegian lady as a summer residence. Being the largest house in the town (perhaps the largest wooden building in Europe), it was bought by the Government for the King. It has no central heating, but is warmed, somewhat, with coke stoves. His Majesty resides here twice a year. The interior is very French, with white woodwork of the Empire. The crimson brocade of the paneled drawing-room and its crystal chandeliers reminded us of the White House, while other rooms suggested Trianon. The bathing facilities were, however, superior to Versailles! In the Queen's cabinet a couch covered by a polar-bear skin seemed ready to receive a Wagnerian diva.

To would-be visitors may I state that perseverance will enable you to find the right gate and the courtyard overshadowed by lindens where perhaps a maid with a mop will guide you, as she did us, to the portal where admission may be obtained for the sum of fifty öre. Obstacles in the way but add to the zest of conquest.

Trondheim, which now boasts a population of some fifty-seven thousand, was founded in 997 by Olaf Trygvesson, who christened it Nidaros—the mouth of the Nid. It was Olaf Haraldsson who compelled his people, at the point of the sword, to accept the Christian faith. Losing his life at the Battle of Stiklestad (near Trondheim) in 1030, the martyred King was later to be canonized as Saint Olaf. His nephew, Olaf Kyrre, established a bishop's see in Trondheim and built a cathedral to the glory of the Trinity and in memory of Saint Olaf, whose shrine was placed therein. Tales of miracles were recounted. Pilgrims multiplied, the offerings justifying the building of the handsomest cathedral in the Northern Countries. The Pope's legate, visiting Norway in 1152, raised the see of Trondheim to an archbishopric. The province included the Hebrides, the Isle of Man, and the Orkneys.

The Cathedral was ravaged by fire in 1328, and again in later centuries. The opening of the nineteenth century found it deplorably neglected. After the adoption of the Constitution at Eidsvoll on May 17, 1814, the Norwegians became aware of the importance of restoring their national monuments. The work at Trondheim began in 1869, and the interior was completed in 1930—on the nine-hundredth anniversary of the death of Saint Olaf. Here, in 1906, Håkon VII was crowned.

Having docked at the foot of Munkegaten, we had but to follow our noses to its far end where the Cathedral's spire rose temptingly. We had tarried on our way at the King's Palace, and on the market-place to admire the monumental gray stone Viking—Olaf Trygvesson, the city's founder. We entered the Cathedral at last by an ancient chapel. Girls were decorating the chancel for a wedding. The nave, we saw, was of transition period, the transept austere Norman. The white-and-gold Empire organ is the fourth in size in a European church—surpassed only by Liverpool and by two in Germany. Thinking we had completed the tour, we were surprised to be ushered beyond a partition blocking the west end and to find ourselves in a magnificent Gothic continuation of the nave. Only the walls of this portion are original, but the restoration of these pure Gothic arches is in itself an accomplishment. A rose window, designed by Gabriel Kielland in brilliant reds and blues, is the gift of the women of Norway. Soapstone quarries have been worked in this region down the centuries of the Cathedral's building. We visited the stone-cutters, where chips were flying, within the shelter of a western court. Hand tools are used. We were impressed by the continuity of tradition. There is reason why the Trondheim Cathedral has been called "the pride of Norway."

Five o'clock found us listening to the Lohengrin wedding march, grateful for this opportunity to hear the superb tone of the organ. Guests arrived in evening dress—ladies hatless and low-gowned. The auburn-haired bride was all that a bride should be. The established worldly position of the guests was evident. We had observed magnates stepping from Packard cars. It was only when the verger appeared with an overgrown key and explained that all doors would be locked until the departure of the wedding party that we reluctantly took our leave, being, for the nonce, Cinderellas irrevocably tied to a sailing-hour. Consolation was found, till the fateful time, at the Bakeri Wilh. Hoff Conditori, famed for its chocolate with whipped cream and pastry cakes—not to mention confectionery in the shape of sailboats or elves seated in the center of fairy-rings of toadstools.

"Norway, you've been to Norway," my inquisitive friend remarks. "What was the most beautiful place you visited?"

In Norway, as in Switzerland, there is such wealth of scenic splendor as to make the question unanswerable. I shall tell of one incomparable excursion.

"Saturday, June 26th:"—read the Bennett leaflet—"The *Stella Polaris* is due to arrive at Öie in the morning. Passengers booked for the shore excursion will be served breakfast at 7:30 A.M. Land by the ship's motor boats at 8:15 A.M. and motor according to printed programme—refreshments at Visnes—lunch at Videseter in the mountains—afternoon tea at Grotli and rejoining the *Stella Polaris* at Merok for dinner on board. Warm clothing is recommended."

Öie overland to Merok! Can it be that less than a year ago these words had no meaning for me? What visions rise before me now, visions of blue fjord and of stupendous cliffs, Niagaras of foaming waters; visions of harvesters in valleys, of mountain pastures, of friendly beasts and men, of zigzags leading to the heights, of eternal snows and glaciers of unimagined magnitude and proximity, of glacial ladders to the sky! All this lies packed, like crèche into a Christmas walnut, in the four pregnant words that give birth to a mental cinema: Öie overland to Merok!

Once ashore we chose an open Buick in company with a Southern belle and a diffident New England spinster. In the wild Novangsdal (*dal* being valley) a glimpse was had of dimly visible dwellings, submerged, like the legendary Ys; many lives were lost in the cataclysmic damming of the

torrent. Girls and men tossed hay to high racks
that seemed to surge like waves of green, bordering emerald water. Nord Fjord ponies trotted in
carts or grazed beside the roadway, stocky cobs
of cream color, a race prized in western Norway.
Stabbing winds brought icy auguries from glaciers
as yet unrevealed. Only the Boston spinster, in
tweeds, had come unprepared and must share the
rug of the beauty from Virginia.

The first halt was at Visnes Hotell on the Nord
Fjord. Next we mounted by the Stryn Route to
Videseter through a glacial valley ''an offshoot
from the Jostedalsbre,'' Europe's greatest glacier,
said our guidebook...fortunately actual guides
were never part of Bennett's equipment. Midway
we paused, I remember, upon a bridge to drink in,
with the elixir of rarer air, the wonder of the
gorge miraculously spanned. *Saxifraga cotyledon*
grew in unprecedented profusion, plumes of Na-
varre nodding from dizzy heights. By Videseter
we had left the scrub pines; a view as of Mont-
Blanc from Argentière met our gaze—Lodalskåpa,
crowning summit of Jostedalsbreen. Fortified by
salmon and edified by an English speech of welcome from our host, we continued to mount the
other two thousand feet to Grotli.

''You will remember,'' our innkeeper had said,
''this day. You will remember not only that you
have seen Jostedalsbre, the largest glacier in
Europe, but that you have had the unique experi-

ence (impossible a few years ago) of reaching as near as you wish to go by motor.''

"Everybody pleased but members of the Wilderness Club!" had muttered a Rotary Club devotee to his fellows.

The route to Grotli had been opened for the season in honor of our caravan. Drifts had been cut to let us pass. Snow bridges spanned streams whose brown margins had not yet burst into Alpine bloom. Boulders were in harmony with the scale of the valley. On the right hand Skytod Glacier towered—integral part of the vastness of Jostedalsbre. Europe's most stupendous survivor of the Glacial Epoch overpowers with its inhuman presence. Half-frozen lakes where miniature icebergs floated stilled the spirit of levity. Jostedalsbre, stark and barren, with no alleviating verdure or habitation, may stimulate the mountaineer to action, but to me it seemed a symbol of the inexorability of Nature's law. Here, for most of the year, unchallenged blizzards rage. As unrelated to man's routine is Jostedalsbre as the Mountains of the Moon.

Grotli! How happy the child Heidi would have been here, I thought, as goats jostled for salt at the hotel door. The sight and smell of the beasts, the jingle of their bells as the herd bounded to new pastures, gave color to our coming, which was simultaneous with the departure of a vanload of youths with rucksacks. Hot coffee was again pro-

vided by the unfailing forethought of Bennett—a
master of preventive precautions. Grotli inn is
constructed of logs, like most substantial Norwegian homesteads. Its dining-room was gay with
mirrors and painted dressers and warmed by a
hospitable soapstone stove. Crackers and goat's
milk cheese were offered, and an abundance of
coffee-cakes. Floors were scored by hobnails, for
Grotli is popular with Alpinists. Memories of
Swiss inns stirred at sight of a blackboard already
marked with calling hours.

After Grotli the descent begins. At Djupvas-
shytta we were astonished to find a tethered reindeer, but, having seen him, we were not surprised
when a pair of Lapps came into view as we sped
past the humble hotel. Cornices of snow melted
into the clouds. Gusts of wind brought showers in
their wake. Through holes of gray we caught
visions of glaciers descending from high heaven.
Snow swirled on the peaks, but our faces were
set towards the sea. By an astounding feat Norwegian engineers have linked these glacial heights
and the fjord by a ribbon of road. The ribbon has,
it is true, a "knot." At one place in the zigzag of
the descent the traveler is fearful that he will
lose the trail, so does the fillet turn and twist
upon itself... but only, miraculously, to reappear.
So slight an indentation does the roadway make
upon the cliff that from below it is unseen. Milk-
maids' huts were passed—swains come to the high

pastures of a Sunday—and at last, after a breath-taking steep descent, we beheld the few roofs of Merok. Our excursion's end brought us our first sight of the Geiranger Fjord, where the almost forgotten *Stella* had come to collect her errant passengers.

As though we had not seen enough for one long day, we were told, on going aboard, that the Bridal Veil (a fall resembling the one of the name in Yosemite) and the Seven Sisters would be visible to starboard shortly after the *Stella's* departure. The Seven Sisters is the most renowned of Norway's famed cascades. There was so strong a head wind that we did not linger on the upper deck but sought shelter at the stern. One of the sisters (assuredly the wraith of a bride!), wooed by the gale, had cast her veil to Boreas, who sought to drag her off. A foreground of foaming wake, of circling gulls, a background of rock walls, intrigued me less than a middle ground of an isolated farm in mid-cliff. That it was reached by man was proved by a dory riding at the mountain's base. It is on such farms as this, we were told, that babes are tethered.

Passengers, too, might be tethered to their advantage, we thought, observing the empty decks. Captain's dinner . . . a preparation of running baths, a chatter from cabins, a clicking of wardrobe trunks; and outside, to be seen from the damp deck, the Seven Sisters transcending Valhalla, a gradual transition from day to evening, a benediction descending gently upon us from the quiet hills—as once it had done upon the not dissimilar West River in China.

"Don't tell me you're still looking at scenery after all this time!" It was the voice of the Colonel.

"Don't talk to me of pretty pictures! I've seen all the pretty pictures I want to see," we had heard him remark to his wife, who had tried to lure him, one day, from starboard to port. His solace was in joining the Rotarians, fresh from an International Congress in Nice, who warbled daily in the smoking-room songs to the Rota*ree. Chaqu'un à son goût!*

Our arrival at Nærö Fjord, the most sensational portion of Sogne, was in a Scotch mist. High cliffs with their inevitable waterfalls bordered the channel. Disembarked at Gudvangen, the *Stella's* passengers climbed into waiting *stolkjerres* to mount single file, precisely as depicted in old prints, to Stalheim. Like the *calèche* in Quebec, the Norwegian *stolkjerre* is a survival from an era prior to horse-and-buggy days. Each cart seated two, with driver on rumble. Coachmen, shifting reins, leaped frequently to earth to walk up steepest grades. Our fellow, squint-eyed and genial, with gestures of whip, indicated, half-way, a beacon on the heights—the red line of Stalheim Hotell. Because of the steepness of the highway,

Nærö Fjord is the most

all *stolkjerres* were abandoned, and the able-bodied
climbed the last thousand feet.

The view down valley, seen from Stalheim, with
its famous Sugar Loaf Mountain, is classic. Despite scudding mists, at the time of our arrival it

sensational branch of the Sogne •

was revealed. On the descent, in order to obtain a
nearer perspective to Sivelfoss, falls notable even
in Norway, we left the roadway. A column of
spray blown from the cauldron where waters
churn is visible afar. Moisture has engendered an

almost tropical profusion of ferns clothing the hillside. I remember, as, after lingering, we followed the path to the highway, the gesticulations of a ship's officer.

"Come along!" he shouted. "I am responsible to see that no one is left behind."

Answering the summons, we were, at the same time, bidding farewell to the last high day of our cruise.

Balholm with its associations with *Frithjof's Saga* and King Bele, the village on the shore known as Balstrand, were reached late of an evening. Although Hans Dahl's studio and the modern *stavekirke*, erected by Church of England summer visitors, were seen, no square-rigged sailboat greeted us, nor did the snow peaks more than charily reveal their presence.

Bergen, running true to form, was to give us a showery, not to say cold, welcome. But, rain or shine, Bergen is Bergen.

Stalheim

In the Setesdal :
The Rygnestadloft.

STAVANGER

CHAPTER IV

MOTORING TO THE SETESDAL

A NORTH CAPE cruise should be augmented not only by a journey on the Bergen-Oslo railway but by a motor tour in southern Norway. No matter how many other fjords have been visited, Hardanger, at a convenient distance to the south of Bergen, should not be overlooked. The Hardanger Fjord comes rightly by its fame. At times of festival its women wear striking costumes. The Hardanger violin has more than a local reputation. It is, however, the grandeur of glaciers—Folgefonn and Hardanger Jökul—in combination with blue waters and verdant vegetation that gives this fjord an especial appeal. Fruit-trees in flower may be photographed against fields of ice and snow. Although Sogne, with its one hundred and thirty miles, is the longest of the west-coast fjords, Hardanger is a close second, measuring one hun-

dred and fourteen. In cascades it surpasses its
rival, possessing two of Norway's grandest—
Skjeggedalsfoss and Vöringfoss.

Our five-day excursion, with return to Bergen,
was made in a Plymouth driven by a student
of the University of Oslo, Håkon Svarstad, himself a native of the Hardanger. At Norheimsund
we were to see his home and the school where
Svarstad senior, now a member (Christian-Folk
Party) of the Storting, is teacher, a profession
for which Håkon is in training.

"We are seven children," said Håkon, the tall,
the fair, the silent. "All of us work with father
on the farm. There are ten buildings, and gardens."

The run from Bergen to Norheimsund was to
take us three hours. We passed barns whose walls
warded off dampness with a thatch made from
dwarf juniper. Later we came to a chaos of stone.
Sheds of pine logs saved the narrow route from
demolition by landslide or avalanche. Steep fields
were harvested by men staggering beneath their
loads. As we neared Norheimsund—a favorite resort is Hotel Sandvens on the fjord—the rude
huts, rustic posts roofed with slabs of layered
rock, reminded us of Aragon. Dragon teeth of
granite edged the precipice, fierce warning to
automobiles. Many were the "route wagons"—
jitneys and autobuses—that we passed. Silver-fox
farms were numerous.

The law of the Medes and Persians was no less inflexible than are meal hours at Norwegian hostelries. It was an irritation at Norheimsund, where we arrived at noon, and with a long ride ahead, to find it was impossible to procure even an omelet; in order to partake of food, we must wait until one-thirty, when doors would be unlocked and luncheon served us in company with a horde of excursionists.

The daughter of the house has been photographed in the elaborate bridal crown and embroidered trappings worn on wedding days. We have, vicariously, watched the merry couples following a fiddler and dancing on the dock of Sandvens Hotell. Yet, disillusioning as this may be, we are told that the "bride" may still wear the snug red bonnet, not yet having coiled her golden tresses beneath the white coif of the married woman. Her crowning seems to have been done for the benefit of tourists who demanded postcards of a wedding.

The hours from three to six were spent upon the ferry from Öystese to Ringöy. Having crossed the Hardanger Fjord, we were to motor along the upper reaches known as Sör Fjord to Odda. Scattered settlements bask in enough sunshine to produce luxuriant apple and cherry orchards. Seen from the highway, the fruit-laden trees and red church-spires contrast with the blue waters of the fjord or the snow-crowned glacier of the

Folgefonn. Odda, remembered as a resort by my
Illustrator, has become a disfigured center of car-
bide factories. After supping at Odda we still had
time to climb in our Plymouth over the Selje Pass
to a land of trolls, only to descend, in vertiginous
hairpins, to the inn at Horda.

Where but in Norway could such a twin water-
fall as Låtefoss, cutting the sky and thundering
through forest to highway, pass as a mere incident? Were we not en route for Telemark and
Setesdal? Both are famed for their ravines and
forests, their *sæters* or upland pastures, their
snow-clad peaks and passes. Lovers of the antique
cherish the folkways preserved in the Setesdal.
Of Norway's mountains it were monotonous to
speak as often as their worth may merit. In this
respect my Illustrator relieves me of sole respon-
sibility. To connoisseurs of mountain inns let me
heartily recommend the Hotel Breifonn, at Horda,
overlooking the Röldal Lake. Backed by the hills,
with other peaks seen across the water, this base
is ideal for those who would tramp both up and
down the valley. The place smacks of the best
Alpine tradition.

Although the month was July, we did not need
to translate Centigrade to Fahrenheit to discover
that freezing was the temperature registered at
the time of our early-morning departure for Grimstad by way of Telemarken. Still chillier was the
frosty air that welcomed us to the high pastures of

Haukeli, the Haukeliseter. Here a café, an adaptation of a *stabur,* has been constructed for tourist use. Without native woolens to warm the outer and frequent stops for coffee to warm the inner man, travelers would be less content, and praises of Norwegian holidays would be less unanimously sung. Before the coming of the railroad, before the birth of our friend Håkon, this had been the post-road from Bergen to Oslo—then Christiania. Grim tors reflected in half-frozen lakes. Large-horned cattle, of breed superior to those farther north, loomed beside the highway. Belled goats were driven by herdsmen who walked like flies upon the mountainside. Milk trucks were headed down-valley, while at cabin doors signs of *Geit Ost* (sweet goat's-milk cheese) tempted me. It is a taste well to acquire in Norway. Men and women passed were mostly afoot; they were not necessarily the tourists we thought them, because of their heavy packs, but perhaps merely natives on holiday or returning from their market town.

At Dalen we stopped for luncheon and to mount to a stave church, restored in 1727 and still in use. It stands amid graves ablaze with Iceland poppies. Curiosity led me to inquire the use of a long-handled wooden spoon. At time of burial it scatters "earth to earth." Masses of pansies clothed the hillsides, and, as we descended, forests of Norway firs, gloomy, with pendant branches, tops with clock-weight cones brown against the sky. In

Telemark, too, we saw our first *staburs*—granaries, ancient, painted red or unstained sepia.

Grimstad, upon the Skagerrak, nearer to Oslo than to Bergen, offers no sight of moment save the Ibsenapoteket. Apothecary jars are kept as when Ibsen was apprentice here. A bust of the dramatist stands among roses, and, on the house wall, a tablet announces that here *Catilina,* the first play, was written.

"Knut Hamsun is now sixty," wrote his translator, W. W. Worster, in the *Fortnightly Review* for December, 1920, at the time Hamsun was awarded the Nobel Prize for Literature. "For years past he has been regarded as the greatest of living Norwegian writers... but it was not until this year, with the publication of *Growth of the Soil,* that he achieved any real success, or became at all generally known among English readers." "Isak [the hero of the book]," says Worster, "stands out as an elemental figure, the symbol of Man at his best, face to face with Nature and life. There is no greater human character—reverently said—in the Bible itself."

To approach Norway without knowledge of this masterpiece of Hamsun's maturity would be to forego needed insight. Primitive man in the Northern Countries differs not greatly. Hamsun, like Kivi, has depicted a primordial Adam, an Adam whose humanity modern man might do well to imitate.

The chance of meeting the author of this book was, we knew, slim, yet it had brought us to Grimstad. "He sees no one," we had been told in Bergen, "makes no engagements, but take these letters and ring his doorbell."

A fifteen-minute run in the Plymouth brought us to Hamsun's country-place. How secure it looked, although upon the highway, facing a sheet of open water yet withdrawn behind iron fences and locked gates. The hour was almost ten of an evening—the sun at the horizon. Nine windows looked, like unwinking eyes, down from the second floor, and below were four to each side of the white-columned door. Cherubs in stone (were they from Italy?) stood guard over freely blooming yellow roses. Lights flashed in the dining-room as our car stopped. A burly figure—his own?—passed the window. Voices reached our ears. Håkon, as spokesman, disappeared to present credentials. Håkon had read the master's books and was elated at thought of meeting the author. We gazed wistfully after him, admiring the straight paths edged with violas, lilacs, and laburnums. A horse-chestnut in flower showed us we had come to Norway's south.

Håkon had been told to wait. We were parked dangerously on the curve. Autobuses veered to avoid us, passengers stared at the house as they swung around the corner. Håkon returned for his pipe. Will he miss the maid? Had we not been

told to call in Norway between one and three?
What a wild-goose chase!

The door was thrown open. He came, younger
and more virile than the impression given by his
photographs—an eagle, gaunt, quick, lithe, and
powerful. His voice addressed us—the voice of a
Viking...a Viking, as no doubt Norsemen had,
with a Scotch burr.

"Forty years since I visited America! I am not
a good American now!"

"But you are, you still speak well," we assured
him.

"I am so deaf, speak slowly and distinctly.

"You are from Pennsylvania. I was there. I
saw the oil wells... in Pittsburgh, yes?

"You will do a book on Norway? How does that
happen? You are not Norwegians? You were perhaps born in Norway and have come back? No, it
was your publisher suggested the idea. I, too, have
an American publisher, in New York. If I had a
copy of my new book from England, I would give
it to you, but I had only one and I gave it away."

(How characteristic of the man, we thought! "I
had only one and I gave it away!")

By now we were in the garden and Hamsun was
patiently signing a first edition of a book we had
brought. How firm a hand, anyone who saw the
signature would say. For thirty years the rugged
right hand has trembled, and the books have been
written laboriously, so laboriously.

"Mr. Oakley paints? He will enjoy the Setesdal. You say you will go to-morrow because it is Sunday, but the people wear their costumes every day in Setesdal...silver buttons, the women with white fronts...

"You, Madame, write? As I do."

"I wish it were as you do!" I exclaimed. We expressed our gratitude at being received.

"You do me honor to come," he said, "and you so young, so young."

Standing bareheaded in the garden, he pressed my hand with both of his. We talked of our trip on the *Stella Polaris* and thoughts of Isak at Bodö.

"And do they read my books in America?" he queried modestly.

He had signed the date, "7/3/37." "To-morrow," he recalled, "is your Fourth of July."

"And you said you were not a good American..." We remembered having heard that he had been, in the course of his hard and adventurous life, a motorman in Chicago.

Light faded. It was ten-thirty as we departed. Hamsun looked after us longingly. We sensed he would have liked to be full of life, also, of vigor to travel to far places. Did not the strength of his ancestry well within him? He waved his soft hat again and again—a friend, among old friends, it would seem. True, he knew Håkon's father who sat in Parliament. Our car started. Hamsun turned towards the house. My Illustrator stopped the automobile to take a snapshot. Our host came to the side gate and fired a parting shot to Håkon in Norwegian. In his native tongue he seemed less hampered by deafness.

"Since when," he called, "have they invented a way to take pictures in the dark? Does he do it with magnesium?" Again he waved, and we again, again.

"Adieu!"

"Adieu!"

At an early hour next morning we were to whisk past the place and to admire its well-established barns, its red cattle grazing in fields which resembled our native Pennsylvania. The house gleamed white in sunlight. A gray cat leaped from a window, where cacti blossomed, to chase an obtrusive terrier. No sign of the author of *Pan*—the well-groomed gentleman, the radical who has become actually benign. Fate held one other surprise—reunion in Oslo.

The Setesdal! A mountain valley down which rushes the uproarious Otra, spreading to a lake known as Byglands Fjord—thus far the railway comes. Approached from the south, that is, from Kristiansand, the valley extends almost a hundred miles in a northerly direction until at Bjåen it meets a barrier blocking union with the highway to Haukeliseter. Even as I write, this obstacle is being surmounted. A new road crosses the divide.

Autocars from Bergen will descend upon the
Setesdal. The inaccessibility that has preserved
local customs and extraordinary costumes will become a memory, but the grandeur of the mountains will remain.

Coming from the open marshlands, where cot-
ton-grass was profuse as snow on the hills at
Bykle, up-valley, we found delight in the sudden
change to somber gorges, dark with forests of fir
and pine. Setesdalens Sommerhjem on the lake
at Bygland amply deserves its name of Summer-
home, that is for those content with tramping
and trout-fishing. Nationalities were divulged by
flags on dining-room tables. Our host was for offering us an English flag, but this, we said, we
could not accept on July Fourth! The only American flag was in use by a couple who asked us to
join them. These Americans, of Norwegian birth,
were astounded to hear that Hamsun had received
us, and disclosed that their mother lived at Grimstad on an adjoining farm. Part of Hamsun's
manor, they told us, is very old. He bought the
place some fifteen years ago. His work is done in
a little white house on the hillside.

Church had let out shortly before our arrival
at Bygland, and women in the sumptuous costume
of the valley were casually encountered in the
neighborhood of the cemetery. The materials used
are of the heaviest, and it is a wonder that the
young girls are loyal to the native dress. They are

Costumes are sumptuous
in the Setesdal ✦

husky wenches, and indeed they need to be to support the burden of their skirts. These are extremely short, heavily pleated, the weight hanging from the shoulders, belted (over a bodice) with a wide girth of silver and leather. There is a skirt of white homespun, topped in winter by one of black ribbed cloth, while for a wedding a third of brilliant red is added. Every *stabur* (or storehouse) has its spinning-wheel. The man's costume is equally bizarre, as the trousers come almost to the armpits and are held in place by braces of leather. A large patch of the same material decorates the seat.

As we followed the Setesdal's only road, mounting towards the source of the torrent, our attention was arrested by groups of houses at Osa, at Valle, at Bykle. Like the barns, they were grass-roofed, weathered to a smoke-stained sepia. My Illustrator shows the wineglass form of the *stabur*. These depositories, whose upper floors are reached by ladders, are not merely the granaries we had supposed. How little we had visioned their interiors when, making inquiries from the son of the owner of the Vallarheim Hotell (an English-speaking student about to graduate from the University of Oslo), we were invited to inspect his ancestral treasure-house. Mounting precariously and ducking our heads, like geese entering a barn door, we found ourselves in a chamber where eighteen costumes hung—the trousseau of a bride.

(Our host's sister attempted to initiate us into the mysteries of tying the fringed head-dress. The result is a cone, shaped like a jelly-bag in the back, and in front a higgledy-piggledy tangle of fringe.)

Håkon, hard at our heels, was told that this outfit would last a lifetime, that is if the bride did not live too long! The groom's costumes, rich in silver ornaments and buttons, were no less elaborate. Chests were opened, quilts and rugs displayed. No moth, nor dust, corrupts the treasure of the favored Setesdal.

The men of Valle are woodcutters, workers in sawmills, and loggers. The first we saw in costume were felling pine-trees. In the forest we met an old fellow who by the cut of his garments and the quaintness of his hat might have stepped from *Mother Goose*. He accosted us and asked for a lift. But how to crowd him in? He would have been a most unusual hitch-hiker! A patch of embroidery embellished his chest, and bands of green edged trousers slashed at the ankle. Questioned as to whether there were any musicians in the valley, he produced a mouth-organ and began a capering dance.

"Are you rich in America?" he asked. "We are not, but we have food to eat and that is enough. We do not need to burn any surplus coffee and grain. What, can you tell me, is the news from madcap Spain?"

"A crazy old soul!" said the folk at Valle.

"Far from a Simple Simon," I thought,
"though stepped from a fairy-tale."

At Oveinang we visited the famous Rygnestadloft, a sixteenth-century log house built by a fugitive from justice. By means of tunnel and secret
closet the owner escaped capture, but bullets penetrated to his bed. The caretaker and his kindly
wife let us mount into their *stabur*. In addition
to the now anticipated splendors, we were confronted by lay figures on which hung the pair's
wedding finery—the crowned bride wearing several ancestral belts and rows of hand-wrought
silver ornaments. An equally fine display is to be
seen at the quaint Bergtun Hotell, where the
"bride" is laden with five hundred kroner worth
of silver.

The ravine widens after Valle, permitting
farms, but long before Hovden the land becomes
barren and too mountainous for cultivation. Once
more it was ten of an evening, but, on this night,
dark and overcast. Where were the welcoming
lights of the newly built hotel? Håkon had been
assured that the inn had opened the week before.
We were to come upon it suddenly—shrouded in
darkness. Explanations greeted us of a broken
motor, light off, water off. Supper, after prolonged
delay, by the light of a solitary candle, rooms
opening on a court where chauffeurs gathered,
short feather beds to cover weary limbs, interminable jazz, mosquitoes, no water ... a night of

Bykle : The barren

misery. Morning, still no water, no bells, no water, sour cream—no appetite.

Not until we had returned to Bykle did our mood change. At the hospitable wayside inn was Norwegian painted furniture, hot coffee, crisp bacon, honey, all the amenities of life not offered at the pretentious Hovden Höifjells.

Down valley I stopped to watch a silversmith at work outside his doorway with spirit-lamp and tools, fashioning coils of wire into glittering adornments. He gave me the address in Oslo to which he sends his brooches, and I, in my ignorance, had feared that Oslo supplied the Setesdal!

Osa! Soon were we to leave the heart of the valley, and no music, save the mouth-organ and

upper reaches of the Setesdal

the jazz, had we heard. My Illustrator stopped to sketch one more *stabur*. A fair woman, with diamond ring and unmistakably American bifocals, appeared at the house door.

"Is there no news of Amelia Earhart?" she asked, as though to a friend.

"You are American?" I said.

"Yes and no," she answered. "My husband is dead. We lived in California. Until I was nineteen I lived here in this house, yes, and wore the costume. Now I belong nowhere."

"Is there no music in the valley?" I inquired. "I have seen Hardanger violins in museums, but I long to hear one in action."

"Perhaps my nephew will play," she said, "if

he is not too tired, perhaps.'' With this she disappeared into the house and soon beckoned for us to follow.

A Hardanger violin, inlaid with mother-of-pearl, eight-stringed (four secondary strings to vibrate in overtones), was taken by its owner from its case and tuned with consummate skill. The first number was a, *Halling,* a folk-dance resembling the musette. What almost Oriental droning, unusual harmonies, and accentuated rhythms! The Basques have a dance, too, that ends with a leap in air. Next was another dance, this time of Telemark, and the third the *Skjalgmöi,* a dance of the Setesdal.

Modestly our violinist admitted to playing not only for festivals but over the radio, and he showed us his picture, taken in Minneapolis in June, 1924, as a member of ''Hardanger Violinist Forbundet of America.''

''Til Dreng Osa'' (To Dreng Ose), so his teacher had dedicated a composition. To Dreng Osa we owe the climax of our tour of the Setesdal.

After a cruise to the North Cape there is return to Bergen. In like manner after a motor trip to Setesdal there is apt to be a retracing of the way to Bergen. With the opening of the missing link of road the fashion will be to make a round tour through Telemark and Setesdal. Yet the southernmost tip of Norway, Cape Lindesnes, I trust will not be foregone; and also the balmy riviera of which Norwegians are proud as they are of the fact that from the sandy wastes of Jæren—an exposed province to the south of Stavanger—Leif Ericsson sailed to the New World.

Mandal, Norway's most southerly town, how remote a relative you are of northernmost Hammerfest! Kvinas Ridge, with highlands in the British, not the Norwegian, sense, with barren tors and an infinity of heather! Flekke Fjord! Stavanger itself, fourth city of Norway (after Oslo, Bergen, and Trondheim), paradoxical seaport—seat of a mellow Cathedral of Saint Swithin comparable to Winchester, its prototype, and known as "the finest monument from the Middle Ages in the whole of Norway, except the Cathedral of Trondheim"...yet a town with a hundred canneries, a world center in the preservation of anchovies and sardines! Stavanger, from which the Green Star steamer bears tourists, after happy holiday, towards Bergen, granting them a shadowy glimpse of the isle of Karmöy—known to the writers of the sagas. Than the little town of Kopervik upon barrow-studded Karmöy there is no older harbor in Norway.

Oslo ⚜ The Stave Church.
From the Hallingdal ✦

Oslo: Karl Johans Gate

CHAPTER V

OSLO AND THE GUDBRANDSDAL

THE BERGEN-OSLO railway is among the modern wonders of the world. Its construction, begun in 1875 and completed in 1909, is said to have cost about fifteen million dollars. Rising from sea-level, it reaches an altitude of over four thousand feet. Although thirty miles of track is above the tree limit, it is kept clear of snow, even in winter, by means of screens and sheds and rotary snow-plows of a thousand horse-power, each propelled by several locomotives. There are a hundred and seventy-eight tunnels—the longest, at Myrdal, over three miles in length—yet they interfere far less with the magnificence of the scenic glories than might be anticipated. The distance is only three hundred and seven miles, but the journey takes about twelve hours—hours that to the ardent traveler are all too breath-takingly brief. Hardanger Jökul dazzles with its vast ice-fields,

101

Finse tempts votaries of skiing the year round, while partisans of precipitous valleys will be divided in their allegiance between Flåm to the west and Hallingdal to the east of the mountain chain.

Another method of approach to Oslo is by its Fjord—eighty-five miles from sea to city. The first view of Oslo from the water is unforgetable —a spacious capital set between blue fjord and pine-clad hills. Ashore, grandeur is no less apparent. The Royal Palace, on an eminence at the head of Karl Johans Gate, dominates this airy metropolis which, for enterprise and modern planning, suggests the Washington of our day. The Vikings founded their Oslo in the year 1048. It was Christian IV, monarch of Norway as well as of Denmark, Christian the Builder, who hastened to the scene after the city's destruction by fire. He chose the present site, and his city was to bear the name of Christiania for three hundred years, from 1624 until 1924, when the former name was restored by act of the Storting, the Norwegian parliament.

Oslo, like Helsinki, is outstandingly modern, and because of the intellectual stimulus to be found here and the rare excellence of its climate, it would probably be my choice were I to take up residence in a Scandinavian capital. We had come from the chill of Bergen and the North Cape cruise. In Oslo the sun was not only warm but hot. We worshiped, at its shrine, and basked, as well, in the warmth of hospitality.

No less a personage than Mrs. J. Borden Harriman, our American Minister, had graciously received us; but our questionings were greeted with merriment. Mrs. Harriman, who had but recently arrived, insisted that we were to tell her where to go—although she admitted having flown sensationally over Norway's glaciers. The Embassy was built for a daughter of Alfred Nobel, in Italian style, and has ample gardens and forest trees, but not, as once it had, a view of the fjord, save from the housetop.

Madame Thiis, wife of the distinguished Museumsdirektor of Nasjonalgalleriet, we were able to tell Mrs. Harriman, had expressed unqualified approval of President Roosevelt's appointment of a woman. "So many people find it interesting," she had said to us, "to have a lady minister." Madame Thiis is herself an intellectual and is at present translating, for the first time into Norwegian, Thackeray's *Vanity Fair.* Her daughter had attended the same school as Kirsten Flagstad, whom Madame Thiis said was "always such a good girl." All Oslo had attended the gala performance given by Flagstad in the Frogner Stadion on the very day of our arrival.

The white mansion of the prima donna was a bower of roses, without and within, on the afternoon when her husband, Henry Johansen, received us. Bouquets of lilies, orchids, flowers of unfamiliar varieties, surrounded the inlaid piano, overflowed from drawing-room to library to hall and dining-room; but the lady of the manor had contracted a cold from singing in the open air. "Sir Henry," as his intimates call him—he being a potentate of the plywood industry—did the honors of his house.

Fresh memories of Flagstad's triumphs at the Metropolitan made us echo words we had read that morning in *McCall's*—bought for a krone at an Oslo newsstand, with cover design of Flagstad in helmet of a *Walküre*. "For her compellingly beautiful Brünnhilde in *Die Walküre* Norway-born Kirsten Flagstad, overnight, became a beloved figure in musical America."

"It was as Sieglinde, though, that I heard her first," I said, "and it was as Sieglinde that she made her début in New York. I hear it is her favorite rôle. But how compare perfections? Her Brünnhilde, Sieglinde, Isolde, are all so wonderful."

"Everything that she does is so wonderful!" exclaimed the lady's husband. We sensed that one of her finest rôles is played in Oslo...Madame Henry Johansen.

On a red-letter day we were to return to Tidemans Gate 6. Our host welcomed us in the hall, where hangs a collection purchased by him in Austria, during the World War, of one hundred

and one engravings of Shakespeare's characters
—a complete set of the period 1600 to 1650. (His
wife complains that they crowd into the dining-
room. She would like to restrict them to the hall
...but wives must give in sometimes!) From an
inner room stepped a more petite and youthful
Flagstad than we had anticipated. She gave a
slight curtsy of welcome. Her interest at first centered on mutual friends in America and that we
had lately seen Knut Hamsun, who is more or less
a neighbor of the Johansens at Kristiansand. If
we could see their country-place! Her garden is
near the sea. The plywood factory is on the water.
They were about to go there. Until this home-
coming she had not been in Norway for two years.
Does she get homesick! She goes about saying
farewell to every object, wishing she could take
it along in her pocket.

"And do you find any objects that interest you
in America?" I asked.

"Yes, the linen" (probably imported, I
thought) "and the Navajo rugs."

We spoke of her concert and the flowers we had
seen on our first visit.

"Many whose names were new to me," she
said. "It was hard to sing after such an ovation.
The King and Queen rose and then the audience.
I was given the blue-and-white striped flag of
Oslo and a laurel wreath, and by the journalists,
for whose benefit it was, this piece of Hadelands

Glassverv.'' She placed in my hands a massive hand-blown vase of Norwegian glass, engraved with a portrait of herself as Brünnhilde on the steed Grane and the music and words of the Valkyrie's cry.

Refreshments were served in the library, and when we admired a massive seventeenth-century armoire, "Sir Henry" opened its doors, disclosing a Phillips Dutch radio at which he listens when his wife sings in New York. Lifelike portraits of the pair hang beside the mantel. We were glad to be told that the distinguished couple will go together on the diva's coming tour of Australia and New Zealand.

The museums of Oslo are world-famous. The National Gallery, with an entire room devoted to Norway's, perhaps Scandinavia's, outstanding living painter, Edvard Munch, must be seen, as well as extraordinary decorations by the same master in the Aula of the University. The library of the Nobel Institute should be visited, with its fifty thousand books, mostly in English, and the committee room where the peace prize is awarded —the other Nobel prizes are given in Stockholm. We recognized signed photographs of Woodrow Wilson, Theodore Roosevelt, Jane Addams, Kellogg, Root, Nicholas Murray Butler, as well as Björnson, Briand, and many English statesmen.

Headquarters of the Norwegian Association of Home Industries assuredly must not be forgotten.

The Norwegians, in my opinion, excel other Scandinavians in carrying on the Viking tradition in the decorative arts. Blom's restaurant, belonging to the association of artists, with waiters in red vests and breeches, should be remembered, but my predilection in Oslo is for the café of the Grand Hotel. Not only is the food unsurpassed and served to the accompaniment of excellent music, but it is eaten in the presence of the most distinguished citizens of the city—present and to come. Portraits of past patrons look down from the murals. It is easy to recognize Ibsen glowering beneath his silk hat (he used to come daily for a glass of grog), also Björnson, Munthe, Munch, Jens Thiis with Milly Bergh. Hardly less interesting countenances may be observed during the dinner hour. Students of the university—Norway's hope these—rub elbows with professors and members of the Storting, while outside the plate-glass windows, open in summer and giving on the street, students surge incessantly of an evening, for Karl Johans Gate is to a Norwegian what the Cannebière is to a native of Marseilles. At the street's head, in front of the Palace, stands an equestrian statue of this same Karl Johan, once monarch of Norway and Sweden, elected heir to Karl XIII, but better known to history as the Marshal of Napoleon, Bernadotte.

Ships are no less a part of Oslo's life than of Bergen's. Liners, yachts, and fishing-vessels crowd the harbor. Pleasure-boats cluster about the Dronningen pavilion of the Royal Yacht Club at Bygdöy, reached in fifteen minutes by automobile or by ferry from Piperviken. The boat ride gives the wayfarer his best view of Akerhus, the ancient fortress and one-time royal residence—nowadays a rendezvous of pigeons. No one, however, should undertake the expedition to Bygdöy without first having lingered over the seductive collections in the Historical Museum. These include the Engebretsen portrait of Roald Amundsen, painted in 1921, and the collection of Eskimo ethnological objects brought by the explorer from Kaiser Wilhelm II's Land. The area immediately around the South Pole he named for King Håkon VII.

Poignant, to us, was a visit to Amundsen's home, preserved punctiliously as he left it on his heroic fatal last flight towards the Arctic in search of the *Italia*. "Svartskog," for so it is called, faces the water from its "Black Forest" setting in a manner similar to the house of Grieg. Sea birds hover near, while within may be seen a case of rare Siberian gulls. The explorer's bedroom is no larger than a ship's cabin, a resemblance which is emphasized by the fact that it has port-holes in lieu of windows. Upon a peg his blue-and-white bathrobe hangs, the material a polar-bear design presented during his visit to Japan. Amundsen lived in this house alone, watched over by his childhood nurse (who had a cottage of her own), the Betty for whom he named a peak. In his study hangs the picture by Millais that had fired his youthful imagination— the familiar picture of Sir John Franklin called "The North-West Passage."

Neither should the trip to Bygdöy be undertaken before scrutiny at the Museum of the wealth of objects unearthed with a Norse queen and her attendant in the Oseberg ship, discovered in a mound near Oslo in 1904, where they had lain probably since the ninth century. Sledges, a four-wheeled wagon, and carved bedposts reveal the consummate artistry of the time almost as much as the superb ship itself with its serpent-shaped prow and provision for thirty men—the ship now housed at Bygdöy with the only other extant Viking ships.

Having steeped ourselves in the atmosphere of adventure, having read Fridtjof Nansen's *Farthest North*, having moreover vivid memories of Amundsen's lecture heard in America shortly after his discovery of the South Pole in 1911 (he was later to cross the North Pole by airship in 1926), my Illustrator and I stepped with reverence aboard the *Fram,* now at Bygdöy. The architect who housed the ship has shown genius. From deck it seems as though the boat were about to slip into the fjord. What memories may not be evoked of Nansen and of Amundsen, who, first one and then the other, employed this vessel in voyages that stagger imagination! Norwegian successors to Leif Ericsson, both gave life itself endeavoring to aid their fellow-men. Nansen will be remembered not more for reaching "farthest north" than for his work as head of the Nansen office of the League of Nations. Under his leadership, between 1921 and 1928, homes were found for two million refugees, Russians, Armenians, Bulgarians, and Greeks.

Another attraction in the park at Bygdöy is the Norsk Folkmuseum. Had this collection not been later overshadowed by open-air museums at Lillehammer and at Stockholm, it would have made a more lasting impression upon us. As it was, I remember with appreciation the *stavekirke* from Gol in the Hallingdal and the fact that every building, even the *stabur* from distant Setesdal, had a native of the district in charge and wearing costume. It being Sunday, *Hallings* and other folk-dances were given with spirit on the stage of the open-air theater against a background of an actual hut and soaring Norway spruce-firs.

The train bore us to Lillehammer—over a hundred miles to the north of Oslo—where, without delay, we went to visit the Sandvig Collection on Maihaugen, a hill near the railway station. The open-air folk museum consists of eighty-five buildings—all from the Gudbrandsdal. It is now owned by a company of whom the president is a dentist, by name Sandvig, who has made the col-

Lillehammer ‡
The Per Gynt House

lection with his own funds over a period of fifty years. The anniversary of the founding has recently been celebrated.

The oldest house, built in 1440, has extremely low doors, in order, we were told, to make the stranger bow his head to the master of the house before making his entrance. A newer pastor's house, of the date 1600, had higher doors but not tall enough to admit a man upright. On the floor of farmhouses bits of fresh juniper are scattered, to give fragrance and catch the mud. Boughs of spruce serve as doormats, as elsewhere in rural Scandinavia.

One log house interested us because of associations. Bluebells nodded upon its turf roof. An eagle had been hung above the door and a wild goose on the gable-end, as though a huntsman dwelt within. The name of the former owner of this house was Per Olsen Hågå—Ibsen's model for Per Gynt. The house once stood on the Hågå farm near Vinstra. Ponds, by reflection, double the beauty of dwellings, primitive mills, and churches.

Sigrid Undset, creator of Kristin Lavransdatter, has dwelt at Lillehammer for twenty years. Eilif Moe, her lawyer, told us that she had recently made a broadcast to the United States, and that she had had a visit from her American publisher, Alfred Knopf, and by him sent her love to Willa Cather, the American author whom she most admires. Through Mr. Moe we were given an appointment to meet Madame Undset, but when the day arrived she was ill. So exhausted is she from overwork (she writes at night, aided by coffee and cigarettes) and the burden of family

SIGRID UNDSET

cares that the doctors recommend a rest...but she will not comply. Her house on the hillside is an ancient log one, brought from up valley, like those in the Sandvig Collection. A convert to Catholicism, a reveler in the pageantry of Norway's past, a passionate lover of plants and flowers, this diviner of men's souls has found

refuge between an orchard and a wild-birch fall
for which the place is named "Bjerkebæk." Many
are the literary associations with the Gudbrandsdal. Hamsun's humble birthplace is "Gar-
mostreet" at Lom, near Otta on the road to
Grotli. Johan Bojer spends his summers in Vinstra. The home of Björnstjerne Björnson and his
wife Karoline is preserved at Aulestad with all
their lares and penates. Those Björnson cherished most were busts of Grundtvig and of Goethe
as Apollo.

The Hotel Victoria at Lillehammer is an excellent place for headquarters. The abundance
and quality of its table especially recommend it.
A badger and a seven-foot brown bear—caught
forty years ago and realistically preserved—
startle new arrivals.

Our day spent in motoring into the heart of the
Gudbrandsdal, for lunch at Otta, was one of the
most rewarding in Norway. The valley is famous
for its fertility and prosperous farms such as
Heggerud Gård—of the type so admirably described by Gulbranssen and guarded for posterity
at Maihaugen. At Vinstra we were to see another
house of Per Olsen Hågå's (Per Gynt), moved
from his upland farm. At Kvam there was a
church built of logs with crude stone roof. Holiday-makers waved at us from banks of the rushing trout-stream or from bicycles; bronzed lads
stripped to the waist, girls making but scanty con-

cessions to modesty, formed a striking contrast to the young women of Vinstra demure in native costumes.

Lunching at the Grand Hotel at Otta, we fell in with a party of English folk, laden with rucksacks, who had come from Geiranger and Grotli by bus and had been tramping in the remote mountain region beyond Otta known as Jotunheim. In another direction beyond Otta lies the Dovre—whose notorious king is unforgotten by lovers of Ibsen. We were to have a tantalizing panorama of both these regions by mounting above the highway. The trip to and fro means an extra hour from Kvam to Rondablikk Höifjellshotell (High Mountain Hotel). From a cairn, Galdhöpiggen, Norway's highest mountain, and other peaks of the vast Jotunheim—Home of the Giants—are visible; while, in another direction, Rodane suggests the Romsdalshorn, which is, indeed, not far distant. Herds grazed upon the plateau, driven before our departure to grassgrown milking-sheds. I remember encountering a red bull upon the path, nor do I forget the springy feel of heath and reindeer moss. The sun was dramatized with interminable rays. Lightning was to play among the hills, and on our approach to Lillehammer we were to pass carts of gipsies —mothers clasping rain-soaked children. Halfdrowned picnickers made, nevertheless, a show of bravado.

Lillehammer: The Chapel from Isum

Our last day in Norway was spent at Oslo. We called at the office of the League of Norsemen. The manager told of how American high-school students of Norwegian descent are brought to Norway by the society for sight-seeing and a fortnight with relatives.

"Is there," the gentleman asked, "any service I may perform?"

"Would there be a possibility," I ventured, "of meeting Trygve Gulbranssen?"

"Of course," he replied. "I'll call his office. He is in the tobacco importing business."

Mr. Gulbranssen would call at our hotel—the Bristol—at four-thirty. Fresh from reading *Beyond Sing the Woods* and *The Wind from the Mountain,* we could have had no more welcome news.

The hour arrived and with it a fair slim man garbed, like all Scandinavians, in gray and wearing a soft black hat. Incredulous at his youth, we yet knew in our hearts that it was he. Gulbranssen advanced, and in turn we grasped his sensitive right hand with its conspicuous wedding-ring.

"I only look young!" he said, in reply to our exclamations.

Over a whisky and soda he chatted like...I was about to say, any other human being. (It is in the far corner of the lobby that Knut Hamsun is wont to linger, with pipe and outstretched legs, over his morning paper.) But did he indeed talk like anyone of our acquaintance? His English vocabulary seemed limitless, his pronunciation flawless, his accent more American than English, and yet this incredible man has never visited America and has spent but a week or so in England.

Brown bears are to be found within two hours of Oslo, he was telling us. On his father-in-law's estate there are elk in the forests. A young couple hunting there, during the four days open season, said they had seen the tracks of seven, but the dogs were distracted by the tracks of a huge bear in the snow.

"There is an old bear-hunter," he told us, "who sits by the chimney fire and tells me tales. Where? In eastern Norway, my country. I never tell where."

He recounted the following tale. A friend, alone in the forest, carrying two tins of berries, met a Large One who showed curiosity—as bears will. The friend, with admirable presence of mind, shifted his position slowly until, upon the wind, the smell of man would reach the bear. The strategy succeeded. The Large One fled. Later, when a bird whirred from the brush, the man dropped his cans of berries and he, too, fled, his nerves shattered.

We asked Gulbranssen if he knew the masterly bear story writen by Tolstoy when the author still hunted. It was the only one worthy to place with Selma Lagerlöf's and the bear story of his own in the opening of *Beyond Sing the Woods*.

I complimented him on the title and remarked that Sibelius had spoken of "the singing woods" at Järvenpää. He was pleased to hear that Sibelius had used the expression. The publisher had questioned the Norwegian equivalent of the word, suggesting "sound the woods," but the old head of the firm had said, "Let the boy have his way."

Minutes pass like seconds in such company. We were overjoyed to find that our visitor had come prepared to take us to dinner at Frognerseter, an

eminence above the Oslo Fjord. We walked past
the Nationaltheater with its statues of Björnson
and Ibsen to the only subway in the Northern
Countries. The restaurant was built some fifty
years ago, in the romantic style when dragon
heads were the fashion. Architects no longer use
Viking models. We dined on woodcock at a table
overlooking city, fjord, and islands. Skiers gather
in winter around this hearth.

There were postcards of Crown Prince Olaf
with his little daughters Ragnhild and Astrid, all
on skis.

"We begin young," said Gulbranssen, and
produced snapshots of his son, Per, and daughter
who with their mother were summering down the
fjord.

"Last winter," he said, "my son, aged three,
set out, unknown to his mother, with comrades on
skiis. She missed him... four hours went by...
and then, on a distant hill, she saw a figure no
larger than a fly crossing a snow-field alone—and
alone he returned. One must begin early."

"It is the fast downhill running that fascinates
Americans," I said I had heard from an expert,
and that "you must be relaxed, singing inside."

"In Norway," he said, "we have the most famous ski-run in the world. I shall show it to you.
Ski-jumping was introduced from Telemark about
sixty years ago. In the last of February or beginning of March the 'Derby' or international ski-

ing competition is held at Holmenkollen—the next station towards Oslo. Shall we walk there to take the train?

"Style and form, not height of jump, is what counts at Holmenkollen. It is a leap of fifty-five meters—while some places have ninety. There are enthusiasts who urge a hundred, but others care for safety. The King, the judges, and reporters are given places near the jump; the public sits on the frozen lake, while small boys hang, as I once did, from trees across the road."

Our host confessed to having gained experience in writing as journalist reporting the Olympics. Like many Norwegians he had never been to the North Cape. He had lately returned from Paris and Holland, where his three books had been first, second, and third best-sellers in December. His Dutch publisher had wished him to sign...my Illustrator and I differ as to whether it was fifteen hundred or fifteen thousand! In any case, he refused. We expressed surprise that he continued in the tobacco business, but he said he could not help wondering how long success would last. He grows weary of the sound of typewriters in the office, and composes, in the quiet of evening, pencil in hand.

Growth of the Soil he considers unequaled by any other modern work. "The Norwegian language question," he remarked, "must not be taken too seriously. It will solve itself. Such things cannot be forced." For years he and other writers have been using words from the country language that are more virile—making the literary language more Norse.

"The woods!" he said, as we walked downhill through the darkening spruce forest. "You do well to preserve them and to prevent floods by planting forests along the Mississippi. Without them all the little creeping, fluttering things perish. . . . President Roosevelt! how much I admire him, and your *united* States. Scandinavia also sets an example of understanding. England has helped to straighten out economic conditions, a good way, too. We must learn not only to tolerate each other, as nations, but to appreciate. It will come. It is the way of civilization.

"You will write to me if you have questions about Norway?" he said, at parting. "Some day I shall shake the hand of your colored man"—we had shown pictures of our factotum.

The descendants of the Vikings, I thought, as I looked into the deeply introspective eyes of our outgiving friend—had we not known him always? —have traveled far on the path of Wisdom.

Gud signe dig Norge, mit deilige Land!

Part Two
SWEDEN

Vadstena:
The castle of Gustavus Vasa

Göteborg

CHAPTER VI

GÖTEBORG AND GÖTA CANAL

IMPRESSIONS of Liverpool pale after a stay in London, as do those of Glasgow when Edinburgh has been visited. So it is with Göteborg, the west-coast industrial shipping town, when Stockholm is remembered. Yet salient were those impressions— my first of any Scandinavian shore. Coast lines of Norway may possess more grandeur, Denmark more familiar Old World quality, Finland more free open forest spaces, but for sheer Scandinavian character—not overlooking Stockholm with its eye-enchanting archipelago—Göteborg bears the palm. *Par excellence* Göteborg remains the Vikings' port.

It was from Göteborg that the *Kalmar Nyckel* and the *Fågel Grip* sailed on November 29, 1637, carrying the first Swedish settlers to America. Peter Minuit, their leader, had been commissioned by the New Sweden Company to found a colony on the west side of Delaware Bay. Land was purchased from the Indians from Cape Henlopen to the Falls. Pennsylvania (the only state to be originally settled by the Swedes, whose national colors it bears) was appropriately represented by its chief executive, Governor George H. Earle, in Göteborg, on November 29, 1937. Commemorative tablets, presented by the people of Pennsylvania to the people of Sweden, were unveiled. In the following spring the three-hundredth anniversary of the arrival of the ships on April 8, 1638, was celebrated by Delaware, Pennsylvania, and New Jersey.

Thoughts of these early wayfarers were in our minds as the American Scantic liner bore us towards our destination. Perhaps it is symbolic of Swedish fortitude and steadfastness in the face of, to others, unsurmountable difficulties that the coasts of Sweden, and especially the west coast, should be of such rugged and uncompromising stone. It would not be in keeping with the character of the Swede to build his house upon the sands. He has builded the mansion of his advanced civilization, no less than his actual architectural achievements, upon the living rock.

Clouds scudded across a wind-torn sky. Sinuous sea-serpents of surf curled and hissed along the hard line of reefs and skerries. Gulls encircled our boats, lighting on masts, soaring on the wind, or, transformed to harpies at sight of offal in our wake, swooping with raucous cries, rapacious as Vikings.

Hardly less numerous than gulls were the launches, flying the Swedish colors—sky-blue and sun-yellow. As the workers of the United States depart in Ford cars, the toilers of Copenhagen on bicycles, so, at the day's end, the workers of Göteborg—and those of many Northland cities— scurry homeward by water. Wooded shore received many, bare gray rocks on coast and skerries harbored others, while some puffed by us merrily waving welcome...headed for unknown destinations. Sloops with swelling sails—white, green, or red—tacked against the wind, while tall-masted yachts rode at anchor.

The fortress of Nya Älvsborg, no longer formidable, marks the entrance to the long approach to Göteborg. Our lungs are filled with the cool salt air of the Northland. The long afternoon permits the sun to shine with warmth, though day be waning. Light gleams on vermilion-patched hills, as we penetrate farther and farther into the heart of the city. Floating docks are numerous. The shipping of Göteborg, as behooves that of a Viking port, is such as could not disappoint the most exigent. Lesser craft, dark-sailed fishing-smacks fresh from assaults upon herring, hulls

♛ ♛ ♛ The Masthugg Church

laden with lumber and produce for England, foreign boats flying flags of distant nations, svelte
liners, the *Kungsholm,* pride of the Swedish Line,
at dock discharging passengers, airplanes whirring—such is the approach to Göteborg. Two
ancient strongholds come to view, and the time-
ball of the mariners' monument. The town is
dominated by that rock-rooted masterpiece, the
Masthugg Church, pride of Lutherans. They tell
how, after a century of peace, they dared to build
this modern temple, which the Government stipu-
lated—because it stands as such an easy mark—
must be demolished in case of war. Even though

dominates the Harbor of Göteborg.

Norway be your first view of Scandinavia, I defy you to arrive at Göteborg without thoughts of "fair-haired giants" and "Valkyrie women," for this is the coast of the Vikings.

Thoughts of Gustavus Adolphus, champion of the Protestant faith, came to mind as we landed, for, on the site of a trading-post, this hero of the Thirty Years' War, after ceding Älvsborg to his enemies, constructed Göteborg according to a careful plan. Strindberg described the place as he thought it must have been in those days: "almost circular in shape and surrounded by ramparts and moats, with rectilinear streets of equal length intersected by canals ... so that it resembled greatly the cities of Holland.'' This was in no way strange, as the ''Lion of the North'' had imported Dutchmen to lay out his town. Even in our own time, two of the tree-shaded canals (one sometimes used for parking in winter!) remain to give a certain Dutch flavor.

Next to its shipping, Göteborg is outstanding for its magnificent parks and, like most Scandinavian cities, for its adequate housing. It possesses the handsomest post-office in the North; an Art Museum (dating from the nineteen twenties, when it was constructed as part of the Göteborg International Exhibition) housing works of art originally in the old East India Company's building as well as a remarkable collection of sculpture by Carl Milles, whose renowned Poseidon fountain stands upon the plaza; a notable Arts and Crafts Museum; but the pride of Göteborg is Slottskogen, a natural park.

Our first act ashore was a bus ride. The castle garden closes at four to automobiles, but owing to the late arrival of our ship, its passengers were granted a special permit. It was a unique experience, that of driving at snail's pace, the only vehicle, through avenues overrun with humanity. Even the most humble were clean and well garbed, the majority couples or families with children. The former were headed for the open-air theater, while many of the latter, like ourselves, took the direction of the deer-park to see what our conductor called (it had a cockney sound) "the rinedeer."

"There are," said he, "no beers in the beergarden"—indicating not what the name implies but an empty bear-pit.

After a night's rest at the Hotel Göteborg, last word in modernity, we set out to see the model dwellings for workmen. Many flats have but one room and kitchen, only twenty per cent have baths; but so widespread is the custom of repairing to the sanitary bath-house, so infinitesimal—in comparison with our own—is the cost of living, so clean and attractive the slumless town, so accessible the week-end cottages, that Göteborg seems a foretaste of Utopia. In case of illness model hospitals are at hand, pensions await the aged. No gulf exists between the most lowly quarter and the ladder-steep drive known as "angels' way" with unpretentious residences of the rich bordering the sea—the "castle" of the "rollerbearing king" and the "palace" of the Socialist governor.

Göteborg and Stockholm, Sweden's second and first cities, are joined by what is popularly called the Göta Canal, although the name applies more especially to the route (known as "Göta Canal proper") after Lake Vänern has been passed on the way to Stockhom. A writer in the *Edinburgh Review,* speaking of the canal, says, "as a piece of engineering work it is a long way ahead of the Suez Canal.'' The idea of a waterway from the west coast to the capital obsessed many minds for centuries. In the year 1525-26 work was actually begun on a project to connect Lake Roxen with the Baltic. Under Charles IX a portion of the Trollhätte section was completed, but in 1755 its continuation was swept away by the breaking of a dam. Not until 1800 was the route from Göteborg to Vänern (Trollhätte Canal) finally opened, followed by the completion in 1822 and' 1832, respectively, of channels through the Västergotland and Östergotland. The waterway is not more than one third man-made in all its three hundred and forty-seven miles of lake, river, and canal. Twenty-five locks are to be mounted on this giant's causeway from the North Sea (or rather Kattegat) to the highest altitude (reached between Lakes Vänern and Viken), and thirty-nine are to be descended before one reaches the Baltic.

Our journey began where the Göta River pours itself into the Kattegat—the point chosen for the foundation of Göteborg. Bohus Castle was soon passed, a ruin of one of the most massive strongholds of the North, built originally by Norway to guard its one-time border (the Göta River) but belonging to Sweden since 1658. Some trace the origin of the word Göta to *göt* or rapids—those at Trollhättan, passed on the first day, are renowned. My Artist could but lament that he came too late to see them as they once were, rivaling Imatra; while the more practically minded relished the fact that the amazing power-station at Trollhättan generates some 190,000 horse-power.

Idyllic are the scant three days and the two brief nights spent aboard a Göta Canal boat. The trip has distinctive quality that differentiates it from canal trips in other lands, although my thoughts went often to Scotch experiences. Half its charm, we decided after deliberation, is the caliber of the country itself, so varied, so essentially Swedish, so dissimilar even to other parts of Scandinavia. The other half is the unparalleled experience of a cruise (aboard a liner minute, it is true, but perfect as to the last detail) one might almost say on dry land, so intimate are the opportunities to peruse the open book of rural life. Like a scroll the canal lies unrolled by day, a silvery part dividing the valley's sea-green tresses ...by night a gleaming moon-path to receive *Diana*, the name of our enchantress.

The spice of life being not only variety of action but variety in taste, it amuses me to get reactions from best friends and from perfect strangers. It is the latter, flashing like meteors across space, that are apt to see eye to eye with the author. Göta Canal is the one trip made by me that has not called forth the remark, "Oh, but have you seen Kinchinjinga, Mecca, Timbuktu?" as the case may be. Not even those who have journeyed

Idyllic are the days aboard

up the Nile to submerged Philæ raise their voices. There is an *esprit de corps* about Göta Canal travelers—an unspoken word that this is incomparable. So strong is the bond that our reaction, in greeting a friend returned from Sweden, is almost sure to be, "Did you do the Göta Canal?" If he "did" it but in part, and tries to persuade us that what he missed did not matter, our hearts go out to him, for we know that it is as a balanced whole that the trip is valuable, no one part outweighing another. There is, too, an inner circle of the elect—those who have, in addition, included a trip to that isle of fay, Visingsö. An exception proving the rule that the canal must be traversed came from my most scholarly friend conversant with Scandinavia. His highly original remark— which he was later, indeed, to qualify to include

the Göta Canal Boat ✦

Dalarna and Värmland—was, "In Sweden spend *all* your time in Stockholm."

Our voyage lay through an inland sea, Vänern, largest lake in Europe save Russian Ladoga and Onega. Next we passed through romantic Viken, with shores mantled by forests, and came at last to Vättern, second in size but, to my mind, first in beauty of Sweden's many lakes—and I do not forget lovely Siljan, the "blue eye of Dalarna." The *Diana* brought us to the very moat in which reflects the castle of Gustavus Vasa. Lacemakers, busy with bobbins, sat beneath the shade-trees on the historic quay. The architecture of this stronghold is known locally as Early Vasa. It has been called "Sweden's most beautiful Renaissance monument." First mention of Vadstena dates from the year 1303, the year of the birth of Saint

Birgitta, founder of the Bridgittine Order of Our Saviour, whose abbey church still stands at a short distance from where our boat lay moored. Less fortunate was the fate of the monastery of Alvastra, demolished in order to provide stone for Vadstena Castle, built by command of Gustavus Vasa.

To those aboard a Göta Canal boat there must be choice between visiting castle or convent. We chose the latter, lingering on the plaza of Sweden's most ancient town hall, enraptured by the peace of the convent garden with its bees and pear-trees—first of the Bergamote strain; visiting its cold, ruthlessly restored conventual church, where Saint Birgitta is said to be interred, with its "door of life and death," through which nuns passed upon taking their vows and again after death. During their lives they worshiped from the balcony—not being permitted to enter the body of the church. They could not even obtain a view of the altar. Confession was made by means of a tiny window. A living death...and in the name of religion!

Born on a farm in Uppland, the youthful Birgitta was married to a knight, Ulf Gudmarson, to whom she bore eight children; a daughter, Katerina, was to become the first abbess of the cloister of Vadstena. The pair went on a pilgrimage to Compostella in Spain, soon after which Ulf died in the Monastery of Alvastra. Birgitta, believing that visions had been vouchsafed her, recorded these "revelations," which were translated into Latin by the canon of Linköping. The founding of the mother house of her order was made possible by an endowment from King Magnus II and his queen. In 1350 Birgitta visited Rome, where she remained, save for pilgrimages, until her death in 1373. She was canonized in 1391 by Pope Boniface IX. The Bridgittines, an order of Augustinian canonesses, had such a part in spreading culture in the Northern Countries that the house at Vadstena was not suppressed till 1595. At one time there was a total of eighty Bridgittine convents. Several still exist on the Continent, and one, Syon House in Devon, boasts "an unbroken conventual existence since pre-Reformation times."

Associations pressed upon us as, at a later date, we returned to Vadstena to visit the interior of the castle. Having determined to do so, we were nothing daunted by the demeanor of the guardian, who informed us that lunch was lunch and no visitors would be admitted between the hours of two and three. Finding that we took this in good part, he welcomed us on the stroke of three and showed us, for our pains, something not seen by all, the dark tower approached through the gloom of casemates. Most worthy of remark is the Church Hall with its Gothic vault, where, in 1552, Gustavus Vasa celebrated his marriage with his third wife, Katarina Stenbock. Many parliaments have met at Vadstena. Here the patriot Engelbrekt forced his bloodless revolution upon Erik of Pomerania who had taken up residence in Denmark, and whose Danish bailiffs oppressed the Swedes. Here, in 1501, Hans of Denmark lost his throne. Here, at Vadstena, Gustavus Vasa was proclaimed regent in 1521 upon the overthrow of the tyrannical Christian II of Denmark.

Now that we find ourselves lingering at Vadstena, it might be well to make the detour that, whether it be by boat or motor, should, if possible, be included in a Swedish holiday even though it be necessary to make a special trip, as my Illustrator and I did, from Stockholm and Kalmar. I allude to the region of Gränna, with excursions to Jönköping and the island of Visingsö.

Lake Vättern guards its secrets well. Why, in this northern land, it should possess a Mediterranean charm has never been divulged. The view from that cosmopolitan hostelry the Golden Otter might be that from Sorrento—with Visingsö its Capri.

Lunch or dine at the Otter as you will, and then, for a stay at Gränna, decide whether you prefer a cottage on the country estate the Otter affords or whether, and this was our choice, you prefer the Old World, Victorian hospitality to be found at Grand Hotel Ribbagården. This rambling mansion nestling among orchards, shadowed by mam-

Gustav Vasa

moth elms, is choked with massive furnishings,
porcelains, baronial portraits. Its hostess welcomed us as we stepped into her rose-garden.
Wearing the costume of her husband's province,
even to starched head-dress and red stockings,
this English lady to the manner born explained
that she had adopted Swedish dress in order to
set an example to her domestics. Our host, Baron
von Duben, had lived in England for over forty
years. Then came the World War and the con-
fiscation of grain-mills in Russia whence came his
livelihood.

"There was no alternative," the Baroness told us, as she placed a floral arrangement in her drawing-room. "We returned to my husband's native Sweden, to this house that he owned. At first I felt like a peacock in the costume, but one becomes accustomed.... I am too old to learn to pronounce Swedish, but I tell my maids that I can see, hear, and feel as they do."

"What a pity that you could not exhibit your gladiolus in London!" I exclaimed.

The Baron, robust son of Viking sires, had joined us. He asked if we had observed a statue in his garden, and when our reply was negative, he led us to where it stood.

"It represents a duel," he said, "between Vikings. In those days wives carried burial sheets when they accompanied their men to a feast. These men, as you see, fight with blood-stained weapons. They ask each other, 'How much can you stand?' One indicates with his thumb half the blade, the other brandishes the whole knife."

"Those were the days!"... Startled by this voice behind us, we found that Carl had joined the group. This irrepressible Swede, a product of Langley Field, not as yet having enough hours in the air to qualify as pilot of a passenger plane, was willing to drive us about Sweden. "It's a holiday for me," was the way he put it. Having graduated from the University of Uppsala before his American experience, Carl could speak impeccable English, but he delighted in racy Americanisms. He had dropped his broad *a*, wishing to be thought a "regular fellow."

"Can Denmark be imagined with Hamlet left out?" my Illustrator had once remarked, "or Sweden without Carl?"

The hour had struck when we were to start for the island of Visingsö, and Carl had come in search of us. The motorboat *Hebe* awaited.

"Over Lake Vättern rests a grandeur of line and a light openness which is seldom met with elsewhere in Sweden," says the poet Verner von Heidenstam, who compares the moods of the lake to those of a temperamental woman. Only one other sheet of water in all the land has, to my mind, an equal allure, and that is the water that surrounds the mystic island of Öland. Alike in this, the two isles float barely above the surface of the water, and when the mirage plays upon shimmering sky and lake, the actual and the imagined merge. At Visingsö whispers from the past seem to hover, as at Öland, within access of the human ear.

That one sees what one wants to see and hears what one wants to hear may be illustrated by the following episode. Gränna boasts the ruined Brahe Castle, home of the lovely Ebba, who, despite love-letters (preserved in archives), never wore the bridal crown for her suitor Gustavus Adolphus. At Visingsö we were to see the golden

Kumlaby Kyrka

crown and hear that Ebba wore it for another,
finding Gustavus was ruled by his implacable
mother. Brahe church, Visingsborg—the castle
built by Per Brahe the younger, grandson of Per
the elder, raised to the peerage by Erik XIV...

but where, we asked, is the observatory of Tycho Brahe? We addressed our question to the driver of a velvet-cushioned travesty of an Irish jaunting-car. The driver looked as though he had kissed the Blarney Stone. His watery blue eyes lighted up at the words.

"Tycho, that's what I call the off horse," said he, with a flick of the whip. "I am driving you to Kumlaby Kyrka, and from the top of the tower Tycho Brahe made his observations. It's bright the stars look from there of a dark night. It's not white nights all the year even in Sweden."

Carl, who had come as interpreter, drew my attention to the fact that our cockney driver dropped not his *h's* but his *r's*—after the fashion in South Sweden. Arrived at the church, Indian file, driver, Carl, and I climbed in total darkness the spiral to the belfry. I felt, for the nonce, unduly like a snail. Not only was my pace snail-like, but I was shut in by suffocatingly close walls, guided by a rope hand-rail which, as another tugged, barked my bare knuckles against masonry. Encouraged at last by light ahead, we finally came to day, and mounted, breathlessly, uneven steps to view the bells and clockworks and, then, attain the tower top.

"A fine observatory!" gasped the driver. "See this peg used by Tycho in experiments."

Far below my Illustrator lingered with sketch-book among archaic tombstones.

Unfathomable as the Mystery of Carnac is the

Brushing cobwebs from my garments, panting, I was, none the less, filled with satisfaction at standing where the greatest of the Brahes had once stood. I recalled the lines the poet attributes to this aged astronomer: "I have loved the stars too fondly to be fearful of the night."

Not until we reached the Brahe church was I to hear from a well-informed verger, apropos of the incident, the ominous words:

"What nonsense! Tycho Brahe was never on this island. His astronomical observations were made on the island of Ven."

"And the horse?"

"The horse was named on the spur of the moment."

History that surrounds the Stones of Nässjä.

Visingsö was indeed famous long before the advent of the Brahe family. It was considered the heart of Sweden in the legendary past. In the Middle Ages the courts of the Sverker kings were held here, and here Magnus ~~Tadulås~~ reigned and died. It was at Omsberg, between Gränna and Vadstena, stronghold of the Sverker dynasty, that Alvastra and his queen founded Sweden's first monastery—that Alvastra cloister at which the husband of Saint Birgitta died, razed for the erection of the castle at Vadstena.

Unfathomable as the mystery of Carnac is the history that surrounds the stones of Nässjä on the east shore of Vättern between Gränna and Vadstena. Under the shadow of the pine-crowned

LADULÅ.

hill of Omsberg stand prehistoric monuments, pre-Viking without doubt, yet known as "Viking Stones"—as those in Brittany bear the title "Druid." It was in search of these at Nässjä that we drove, past fields of clover, to a remote farm-house. The "oatmeal" bell was sounding the noon hour. Beyond the house an unmarked, almost untrodden path led to the place we sought. Immense they were, these lichened hulks of stone, dwarfing mere humans. They formed a circle—as though of judges—in the center of which rose an oak-tree monarch. Wooded lanes led forestward, aisles in this prehistoric sanctuary. A brooding silence hung over all... broken only by the distant lowing of cattle. Underfoot was a carpet of heather, emphasizing the similarity of this setting to that of other far-distant menhirs.

Within stone's throw of the same clover-fields we had passed lies Lake Tåkern. Its sapphire surface was sprinkled, on the day of our visit, with flecks of snowy white, gleaming like miniature icebergs.

"Swans!" exclaimed Carl, "wild swans... it is the season."

No lane led to the margin of the lake, but from the road we obtained a nearer view of swans in thousands floating upon the water or flying in formation across the marsh.

At Omsberg we were to visit the Strand, lake-side home of Sweden's noted feminist, Ellen Key.

Since the death of its owner the Strand has become, in accordance with her wish, a holiday house for working women. The building nestles against a hillside with an orchard at its back and a lake view that, on a clear day, includes Visingsö.

In *The Century of the Child* Ellen Key wrote of the "promised land." "My school will not come into existence while governments make their greatest sacrifices for militarism." The promised land, she said, will never come "until mothers implant in the souls of their children the feeling for humanity before the feeling for their country." "As the twig is bent the tree is inclined" she supplanted with a conception which does not extinguish personality: "The new ideal is that man, to stand straight and upright, must not be bent at all, only supported."

On the walls of the entrance hall at Strand are painted Goethe's words, *Memento Vivere*—"Remember that you shall live," a paraphrase of those on Cæsar's chariot—"Remember that you shall die." Ellen Key respected the motto not alone for herself; her vision was a more abundant life for all mankind. So misunderstood was she by her countrymen that at one time she left Sweden determined to end her days in Italy. A friend sent her a banner at Christmas that, Ellen Key used to say, turned her homeward. On a deep-blue ground (the banner is preserved) Charles' Wain hangs over a double row of fir-trees and below the words

of Leonardo: *Non si volta chi a stella è fisso*—
"Who is linked to a star does not waver." Ellen
went home and built this house, where she lived
until her death in 1926.

Jönköping—a name known to users of Swedish
"superior safety matches" from the words "Jön-
köpings and Vulcans" on the familiar box—is
situated at the south end of Lake Vättern beneath the shadow of Mount Taberg. The Swedish
match industry, founded here in 1844 by a native,
J. E. Lundström, inventor of the safety match,
has weathered the gale of the Kreuger debacle.
One-third of the world's matches are produced
under the company's control in its Swedish or
foreign factories. It has been estimated that a
match a day—which should keep darkness away—
is manufactured by this organization for every
human being on our planet. Despite the suicide of
the arch-swindler Ivan Kreuger, the Swedish
Match Company has remained solvent.

Söderköping, a spa to be seen from the deck of
the Göta Canal boat on the morning of the third
day; Norrköping, as dingy and unprepossessing a
town as may be found in Sweden, a survival of
the Dark Ages in comparison with the New Day
of Finnish Tampere; Linköping, with its truly
magnificent Gothic cathedral, built by Bishop
Bengt, the brother of Birger Jarl—these as well
as Jönköping recalled to our minds the "chip-
pings" of England—Chipping Norton, Chipping

Sodbury, Chipping Campden—most comely of Cotswold towns. It is indeed said that "köping" and "chipping" are derived from the same root.

Having made our jaunt to Jönköping at the far southern tip of Lake Vättern, we must discontinue this detour (actually made later in our stay by motor with Carl) and return to our Canal boat at Vadstena if we are to arrive at Stockholm. At Motala many noted the conspicuous tablet marking the grave of Baltzar von Platen, engineer of the canal. We were more elated to observe, in the rushes of Kungs Norrby Lake, that wild swans were nesting. This was before the "staircase" of locks by which our boat was to descend from the highest point on the canal to Lake Roxen. Its slow progress gives the passengers an opportunity to visit Vreta Cloister, mysterious for us because of the late twilight hour. Founded by Carl Sverkersson, the sanctuary contains tombs of kings and queens of the Sverker dynasty and the mortuary chapel of the Douglas clan—as famed in Sweden as in their native Scotland. This part of the canal is perhaps the most idyllic. Holstein cattle stand in lush clover, mountain-ash and silver birches confidentially interlace their branches along the banks, while dim farmhouses turn the more glamorous as, one by one, lights shine forth. The peace and quiet of an age unlike our own constitute, perhaps, the unique charm of the Göta Canal.

"Peace and quiet!" my Illustrator exclaims, as

he reads my manuscript. "Do you remember our trip on the *Pallas* headed for Göteborg? Did you consider that night peaceful and quiet?"

"Must all the truth be told?" I query.

"A perfect rest for frayed nerves"...so the prospectus of the steamship company had read.

In the wee small hours of the night we had been awakened by a sound that in my voyaging around the world I had never heard, a sound unmistakable to the slowest wits, a rasping, grating, disintegrating sound that I had hoped never to hear.

"Aground!" I had called to my companion, who also had sprung from his bunk. It was obvious from the impenetrable rock wall almost within touch of our open port-hole and against which the boat knocked in vain that we were in the bottom of a formidable lock—that little stood between the floor of our stateroom, in the lowest region of the boat, and the rocks on which we once more excruciatingly scraped and ground. We had lurched to port, Stygian darkness prevailed, no sounds were heard on deck, the patter was not of padding feet but of my heart. There came a gurgle of rushing waters...heart-stopping for the nonce, for surely we were stove in...a lurch to starboard. Then, on an even keel, the valiant *Pallas,* clouds having blown from the moon, to whose goddess her sister was dedicated, lifted herself like an unwounded swan, flapping wings of praise to have escaped dire peril. Our fears were washed away by moonbeams, gleaming like beacons to indicate the narrow path.

"Did you know we almost ran aground last night?" the dentist from Brooklyn had remarked to the long-jawed woman doctor from the Bronx, within easy earshot of our chairs.

"You bet I did!" she had responded. "Thought all was up!"

"I didn't hear it," had continued the newsmonger. "First I knew of it was when I heard the folks talking. They said one of these boats sure went aground this month—not in a lock either."

"I bet you wouldn't have heard even that," had said the lady. "You'd have been left to go down with the ship... It didn't go down? That would have been just your good luck."

"Except the Lord build the house, they labour in vain that build it." These words—in another tongue—have been placed on a marble tablet on the wall of the canal at Mem, where the Göta Canal joins the sea. We have come to the Baltic with its thousand isles, some sheltered (these are wooded), others washed by wave and wind, bare as icebergs, home of seal and gull. Again we turn inland, passing Södertälje with its cargo-laden ships. A canal was opened here in 1819 to connect the Baltic with the Mälar Lake. Here lumber from central Sweden and iron ore from Bergslagen meet. We have reached Mälaren, and arrival at Stockholm must wait for another chapter.

The Stockholm Town Hall

CHAPTER VII

STOCKHOLM, THE QUEEN OF MÄLAR

WOULD you have glamour of Venice, beauty of Paris, substantiality of London in one and the same metropolis, go to Stockholm. A paradoxical blending of Italian skies and waterways, Parisian parks and boulevards, with clubs, museums, and home offices of far-flung corporations immediately suggestive of London—all this, as well as the purely indigenous, awaits you in the Swedish capital. Art and industry united, slums and shabbiness abolished (if indeed they ever existed), a florescence of ultramodern apartment houses abloom with awnings and window-boxes, model flats for laborers, a king's palace housing an unpretentious king, a vivid juxtaposition of tidy quay and well-groomed boulevard, a wedding of land and sea (for the city embraces a dozen islands), are out-

153

standing characteristics of the most romantic capital of the North.

The view from the Grand Hotel, or indeed from the Strand, suggests the Grand Canal. Sunsets, which in summer are not competely obliterated until dawn, reflect in still waters, as do a myriad craft—dark-sailed barges, cutters and schooners carrying firewood from Finland, Vaxholm boats, not to mention palatial liners, such as the *Kungsholm,* afloat in Strömmen within hail of the Palace. The quarter of the Opera House is most Parisian, with its statue of Charles XII and King's Gardens in French taste. Kungsgatan, the major shopping street (a portion blasted from the gravel ridge, its viaduct flanked by skyscrapers), is more suggestive of Chicago, as are the masses of high-power American cars parked on Gustav Adolf's Square, but London is recalled in such surroundings as the headquarters of the Swedish Iron Masters Association.

Nature has blessed Stockholm. The approach to the city, whether by Lake Mälaren or from the Baltic, is unparalleled even in Scandinavia. To come by train is to lose opportunity. It was an August morning when we first entered the archipelago from the Baltic. The city is so placed as to be both Queen of Mälar, on the west, and of the Baltic, on the east—through the waters of Saltsjön, the Salt Sea. A red moon had set, and, shortly after, the sun pierced clouds. By four o'clock it rode high in the heavens. The approach to Stockholm is a matter of hours, and of pilots for bar, islands, and dock. The first pilot leaped like a Viking raider aboard our Scantic liner. He was in his element where wind-driven surf assaulted outer reefs. Gulls circled overhead with raucous cries, and far-sighted passengers spied seals on lonely rocks. A silvery light played on water rippling between the isles. How suggestive of islands off the coast of Maine! We passed a fort, a castle, and, as we neared the capital, residences of prosperous citizens on wooded shores or islands. The villas had a similarity—painted a rich red, each with its own flagpole and every one its private dock with slim-sparred boat or launch, the sole means of communication with the outer world. Humans were still abed. Masts, even of cruise ships, formed convenient perches for the omnipresent gulls poised against the blue, a striking emblem of Scandinavia. We were to dock far from the heart of the city beside the port of the hydroplanes. Throughout our stay in Stockholm the ocean-soaring gulls and their darting hooded brothers, with arresting cries, casting shadows hither and yon, formed the *leit motif* of Stockholm's quays and bridges.

On arrival the visitor has his choice of three ways to obtain an impression of Stockholm—not to mention the bird's-eye view from the air which becomes increasingly popular. One is by open car

Stockholm

Venice of the North. ✦

(taxis are useless), another by train to be had at
the Opera House, marked Ringlinje (Circle of the
City), and the best is by motor-boat that weaves,
a swift shuttle, beneath seventeen bridges, a route
known as Waterways of Stockholm. I made the
latter circuit in company with a Swede now living
in New York. He pointed out the Military College
where he had received his early training. He used
to sail to wild islands where now apartments crowd
and to ride on bridle-paths near the estate of
Prince Eugen. What he considered sordid to me
seemed a clean and legitimate business quarter.
The last lap was rural. Ducks scurried to right
and left. As we brushed past, swaying sea-grass
rustled. Cordell Hull has done much for American
foreign relations, this Swede volunteered. He had
hopes that Roosevelt would better the housing
condition of America's poor. "You know he has
Scandinavian blood. Some of his Colonial ancestors were of Swedish extraction."

"Apotheosis of Stockholm, the City on the
Water"—the title of a fresco in the Blue Chamber
—might well serve as a designation for the Stockholm Town Hall. " 'Stadshus,' 'Town Hall' or
'City Hall,' 'Hôtel de Ville,' 'Palazzo Municipale,'
'Rathaus,' are the names in common use for a
building devoted to the requirements of municipal
functionaries," writes Ragnar Östberg, architect
of the Stadshus. "It forms the very seat of honour
of the citizen.... One would fain see the Town

Hall stand out as the right new tune to good old words.''

To this end Östberg has employed a style both romantic and indigenous, both ancient and modern, both traditional and yet highly original. Completed in 1923 and opened on Midsummer Eve on the four-hundredth anniversary of the coronation of Gustavus Vasa, the Stockholm Town Hall bears the distinction of being a palatial edifice erected, and at immense cost, by the people and for the people. Its building took place under a Socialist government and at a time when most of Europe was at war. A consensus of opinion places it first among architectural achievements of our era. The district finally chosen for the site was Kungsholmen, ''a quarter which arose during the seventeenth century when Sweden was a Great Power.'' On three sides the garden is surrounded by Lake Mälar.

The impression made upon me by the Stockholm Town Hall was so vivid that it changed my entire attitude towards things Swedish. Nurtured in a more conservative tradition, I was at first sight stunned by the sumptuousness of the Golden Chamber, but, on second thought, I acclaim the ''Queen of Mälar,'' presiding, Medusa-haired, with pagan beauty of a sea-goddess, over this banqueting hall. The painter Einar Forseth is responsible for the designs of the mosaics which, on an incredible background of scintillating gold, line the walls from floor to ceiling. The enthroned Mälar Queen, monstrous as Burmese Buddha, receives contributions from representatives of East and West. To the west may be seen the American flag and symbolic skyscrapers, English ships, the Eiffel Tower, while to the east are shown Russia and the Orient. "Brilliantly designed," Östberg says of the mosaics, "with youthful freshness" ... a remark which would apply no less to the work of Östberg's own maturity. Seven hundred and fifty diners can be seated at table in this astounding chamber. Should they not be garbed as for a presentation of *Arabian Nights?*

The Blue Hall—paradoxically red!—is hardly of less moment. Here the people may dance, more than a thousand strong, upon the smooth stone floor. Here is the largest organ in Scandinavia. Breath-taking as a Gothic cathedral is the Council Chamber, with open-truss ceiling, more than lofty, remote, almost, as sky. Hangings of crimson brocade (of Swedish design but made in Italy) give regal splendor to the "throne" of the Chairman of the Municipal Council. There are a hundred men (why no women?) almost evenly divided between the Conservatives and Liberals of the Right and the Socialists, with a few Communists, of the Left. The same thirst for civilization, beauty, learning, that compelled Queen Christina to seek solace in Italy manifested itself in popular interest in the building of the Town Hall.

When, owing to a war in which Sweden had no part, costs rose unprecedentedly, the citizens of Stockholm poured out their treasure in order that the copper covering of the people's palace should be completed. While Rheims was being shattered, the Town Hall of Stockholm was blooming from the fertile soil of Sweden.

The rough red bricks employed in its perpendicular surfaces find culmination in a tower of unsurpassed dignity named, for one in the former palace, "the Tower of the Three Crowns." Seen from a distance across the water, the golden diadems gleam, while a lesser Moon Tower presents a glimmering crescent, reminiscent of Constantinople. Upon the summit of the Great Tower, facing the east and in the direction of the ancient city, are inscribed these significant words:

Glory be to God, in Heaven, peace on earth and good will toward men.

Practicers of Christianity, coöperators, sharers of opportunity, are the Swedes. "By their fruits ye shall know them."

Stockholm is noted for its churches, both antique and modern. Perhaps the most outstanding example of the old is Storkyrkan (Saint Nicholas' Church), in the "city within the bridges," built in 1264 and since 1721 the coronation church of Swedish sovereigns. (We attended a crowded Lutheran mass there one Sunday at eleven, departing at twelve forty-five when it seemed to be

GVSTAVVS ADOLPHVS
D·G·REX SVEC· GOTH:ET
VAND·MAGNVS PRINCEPS
FINLANDIÆ DVX· ETC·

getting well under way!) Riddarholm Church, on
the island of the name, mausoleum of the Swedish
kings, including Gustavus Adolphus, upholder of
Protestantism in the Thirty Years' War, stands
beside a statue of Birger Jarl, founder of Stock-

holm. The Engelbrekt and Högalid churches are extraordinary examples of modern ecclesiastical design. The twin spires of the latter symbolize the Law and the Gospel, while the main entrance is the Gate of Life. The former, in distinction worthy to be mentioned in the same breath with the Town Hall, is, characteristically, not named for a theologian but for a Swedish national hero—founder in 1435 of the first Riksdag or parliament.

Writing in 1928, Henry Goddard Leach, editor of the *Forum,* called Sweden "the most *civilized* land I know." He would have no reason to change his opinion to-day. "The Incredible Swedes," Hubert Herring entitles a recent article in *Harper's.* He points out that blocks of modern apartments have been built in Stockholm as the result of an alliance of private capital and government subsidy. "Sweden," he says, "has gone into business. Sweden is in the power business, Sweden is in the railroad business, Sweden is also in the telephone and telegraph business. Stockholm boasts more telephones, its population considered, than any other European City.... A Swede is certain that he owns his country and controls his destiny to a degree not true of the Englishman, Frenchman, or American."

The extraordinary success of *Sweden: the Middle Way* in the United States is undoubtedly not alone because of its readability but because of a profound interest among Americans in "a controlled capitalism that works." "Sweden has prospered," writes Simeon Strunsky, "and has remained a democracy." Capitalism has been wisely controlled in industrial Sweden. Says Marquis Childs: "One-third of all retail trade and more than ten per cent of wholesale trade and manufacture for domestic consumption are carried on by coöperatives without profit; and the implications of this, in low prices and high quality, reach out to the entire consuming population." The practical Swedes do not acclaim Mr. Childs for writing his book on their "middle way." Far from it. They prefer blunt truths to anything that smacks of exaggeration. "The book is too flattering," they say, "to be accurate."

The first consumers' coöperative was founded in Sweden in 1850, modeled on lines of the Society of Equitable Pioneers of the British Rochdale weavers. Almost half the population of Stockholm is said to belong to Konsum.

Seventy per cent of the inhabitants of the city live in flats of two rooms and kitchen...which means, of course, overcrowding; but to offset this rather startling condition, due in part to the rapid growth of the city, the Government has financed the construction of cottages in which ten thousand citizens live—ninety per cent of the cost to be amortized in thirty years, the remainder by work of the owner. Stockholmers, because of the city's situation, may in a half-hour reach the forest by bus or steamer. Not only the well-to-do but laborers commute in summer to wooded islands. On the outskirts of the town, as in other Scandinavian cities, the garden-colony allotments are sure to be admired by the most casual observer, especially of a week-end, when their occupants will be at work tilling the soil. There are over five thousand of these plots, rented for a mere song. Each has a cabin with running water, a flagpole, vegetable patch, probably a fruit-tree and flowers. Of a Saturday or Sunday many enthusiastic families stay overnight.

Birger Jarl, in fortifying the junction of lake and Baltic and thereby founding the city of Stockholm, had in mind the "padlocking" of the fertile shores of Mälar against Esthonian pirates. The immense Royal Palace stands in the oldest quarter of the town, having for neighbor the Storkyrkan, not far distant from the Stortorget (Great Square) where Christian II, the Danish King, perpetrated the massacre of eighty-two Swedish bishops and noblemen. In the labyrinth of medieval streets may be found Den Gydene Freden ("The Golden Peace"), a tavern dear to the poet Bellman. The descent to its old tap-room, still in use, is down a steep stone stair, and beneath it, in the bowels of earth, probably the old wine-cellars, barmaids in frilled caps serve, by candlelight, some of the best food in Sweden. Bellman and his boon companions, could they return to-day, would recognize the tavern doorway on the side street—through which they must often have reeled.

Stockholm's restaurants are numerous as they are famous. Opera Källare, in the building of the Opera House, offers windows overlooking Strömmen with its Sunsinger monument to the poet Tegnér. Smörgåsbord included, on the day of our visit, such tidbits as pickled eel mixed, by a substantial waiter, with egg, capers, and other ingredients, eaten with *knäckebröd* (crisp rye bread), to be followed by lobster, veal with the inevitable *grönsaker* (peas, carrots, potatoes), and coffee. Luncheon ends abruptly in Sweden without sweet, savory, or fruit. The diet, if continued, would soon, we feared, provide us paunches equal to those of the rotund waiters. Two other restaurants not to be overlooked are Hasselbacken and Gondolen ("The Gondola"), beside Katarinahissen ("The Elevator") at the traffic center of Slussen. Longfellow used to come to this terrace on Södermalm, the quarter of Katarinakyra, to dream his dreams. To us, established at Gondolen, the place seemed like a plane of Imperial Airways. We could imagine ourselves floating over Stockholm as once we had done over the English Channel. Bellman frequented the shade of a mighty oak in Hasselbacken garden. Remnants of the tree live to shelter his statue. Dinner is served in the open among the Regal lilies, and served to

Stockholm: ♪ ♪ ♪
The Finnish wood boats dry their sails.

the strains of a string orchestra. The stroll homeward, through moonlit and illuminated streets of Stockholm, is a fairyland warranted to give palpitations to the most prosaic.

"Home" to us was the Strand Hotel—less overrun with Daisy Millers than the Grand, and in all respects above reproach. The windows of our suite looked out upon the Finnish wood-boats and, in the immediate foreground, upon a bevy of little steamers—white ganders on whose backs Stockholmers are borne hither and yon. I remember with especial pleasure a certain dinner served in the pink glow of the mirrored restaurant at the Strand. The dusky Marian Anderson was at the table next... in the midst of a brilliant tour. I recalled having met the contralto in Philadelphia, her home, and the success of a recital at the Academy of Music when she had sung compositions by Sibelius as well as Negro spirituals. The friend who dined with us was a woman journalist resident in Stockholm.

"Look about us," she said. "You don't see many Swedish women. Sweden is a man's world. Despite their feminists and advanced laws, the wives remain at home. You think the Swedes phlegmatic? Then you are wrong. No people are really phlegmatic, and certainly not the Swedes. They are like the Scotch. They do not show their feelings. Look at those people on our right. They have lifted their glasses in the solemn *skål*. Now

we can have no idea if they are telling witty
stories...no voices are raised, there is no change
of expression. You think them complacent? Well,
that I am willing to admit. They do not care if
foreigners come. Indeed, many American tourists
are objectionable. They pause for a day en route
to Russia and go home and write ridiculous articles.

"What," she urged, "is your most outstanding
impression of the Swedes?"

"That they are descended from mermen!" I
replied, laughingly. "To-day's comic supplement
advertises children's day at the Stadium by means
of such vulgar, fleshy, green-haired and green-
tailed mermaids that I intend to stay away. Milles'
sculptured two-tailed sea-maidens—I am told such
creatures actually existed—affect me less unpleas-
antly, and I have come, after the first shock, to
admire the personification of this sea-obsession,
the Queen of Mälar in the Town Hall. In New
York such a conception would be unthinkable.
Here it is all in the tradition. This full-blown
nation does not stem from a Madonna lily, but
from a water-lily entangled in sea-grass. Its is a
fishy background personified by the Mälar
Queen."

"How odd!" my friend exclaimed. "And do
you think the people fishy, too?"

"I am not yet prepared to say," I answered
her. "There is a seal-like quality about some!"

On the dock near the Katarinahissen stands a lowly monument with ring for mooring boats. It is by Carl Milles, Sweden's most noted sculptor, and represents a rotund two-tailed sea-god and a mermaid in embrace. I have heard it called obscene... but it is, rather, grotesque and entirely in keeping with Swedish humor.

Carl Milles has a studio-residence at Herserud, on the island of Lidingö, a distant quarter of Stockholm. The gate is opposite the restaurant Villa Foresta—known to drivers of taxicabs. This shut gate, impossible to crash, opened with a "*Var so gud*" on the day of our appointment. Milles spends most of his time nowadays at Cranbrook, near Detroit, but returns for summer holidays. On this occasion he had left for Italy, but his niece, Miss Folcker, who lives here with her mother, was a gracious hostess. I was awed by the beauty of the terrace—a second Naples, Amalfi. Standing among monumental statuary and red—not stone—pines, we looked down upon a sea of Mediterranean blue. "Susanna Surprised at the Bath" stands near two mighty bronze boars. The villa itself, with its outside stair and lily-pool, is essentially Italian. I was led to the playing fountain, a dolphin with four tritons—the same may be seen with Europa in Chicago. Against the house wall stands Folke Filbyter, sung by Verner von Heidenstam, the grandfather on horseback searching for his son's son, who is Birger Jarl.

GOD

This gnarled, I was about to say wattled, old man is shown here in bronze head and part of torso; indoors there is a plaster model of the whole. One in the quest, the horse searches with his rider. This monument we were to see in happy setting at Linköping. Portraits there are—the spirit of our friend Erik Wettergren emerging from a block, the composer Hugo Alvén, lately married at sixty-five. Obviously our hostess' favorite was a mermaid riding astride a monstrous dolphin. The girl dwelt on the beauty of the rounded lines ...yes, sensuous curves, pagan, fish-like, true to Scandinavian myths.

A huge but headless model of the Sun-Singer displays its manly beauty against blue of sea and sky. Near-by towers a column from the old Swedish Opera House. Milles tiles, with imprint of spring wild flowers, lead to covered terrace with chairs whose carved backs were once horse-collars, now entwined with the names of Olga and Carl (Milles). Boxes there are for birds and brown squirrels, and within the dwelling not only a Pompeian gallery of sculpture but other treasures—two Swedish bibles, one printed in 1540 ... this came as an anonymous gift some twenty years ago when Milles had completed the majestic Gustaf Vasa for Nordiska Museet. On a piano, brocade covered, lies an open atlas where visitors are requested to sign names near their "home towns." Little room remains on the map of U. S. A.

Orpheus in green bronze, with lyre aloft, stands, appropriately, outside the modern Concert Hall. Eight listeners have returned from the doors of death while Orpheus lulls three-headed Cerberus. Milles understood his problem. The fountain calls for playing water, animation on the steps or upon the plaza of a market-day. Poseidon, on the square of the Göteborg Art Museum, has caused no greater stir than Orpheus. A bronze study of the central figure of the Concert Hall fountain has been given to the Yale Gallery of Fine Arts by the sculptor, upon whom the University conferred the honorary degree of Doctor of Humane Letters. The war memorial at Saint Paul, a thirty-six-foot Indian god with peace-pipe, was executed on condition it might be a monument to peace. This year the Milles fountain, "The Wedding of the Mississippi and Missouri," is to be unveiled in Saint Louis. The Art Commission is divided between praise and condemnation.

Days we spent in the galleries of Stockholm: the National Museum, with its wealth of material (we noted with especial interest a bust by Anders Jönsson of H. M. Konung Gustaf V, taken in 1934, and other portraits in bronze by Carl Eldh of the Crown Prince, Crown Princess Louise, and a leonine head of Strindberg); the Thiel Gallery, of no less interest, with its paintings by Scandinavian artists such as Liljefors, Larsson, and Prince Eugen, and arresting etchings by Zorn—

portraits of notables, many with familiar visages, perhaps none more touching than a weary Renan. Having read the confessions of Strindberg in tortured mood, we were astounded, on being confronted by the subtle beauty of a landscape, to discover it was the work of the playwright. Thiel Gallery was constructed as a private house. It is situated on the most beautiful part of Djurgården Island (Stockholm is served by ten ferries, supplementing bridges) not far distant from the estate of Prince Eugen. The approach is rural. We caught a glimpse of water, hay drying on racks, secular English oaks. Statues by the Norwegian Vigeland, back of the museum, are surpassed, to my way of thinking, by Rodin's "L'Ombre," a man's figure, strong shadowed face with head somewhat bowed. This bronze is superbly mounted on a low pedestal which in turn stands on a natural granite boulder tufted with grass and bluebells. The sun, having won his battle with the powers of darkness, shone in triumph. After days of rain, Nature rejoiced. Brown squirrels, brandishing plumes of black, bounded from oak to oak. At the request of Erik Wettergren of the National Museum we were permitted to visit the private gallery of modern paintings on the estate of the King's brother, Prince Eugen. The collection includes a room of his own sensitive landscapes. We had already admired murals from his brush at the Town Hall.

Mr. Wettergren was our patron saint throughout our stay in Sweden and especially in Stockholm. This was, of course, as it should have been, for Erik is Stockholm's patron ... had we not seen the medieval form of Saint Erik looking down upon us at Town Hall, in the Assembly Room of Aldermen?

Foremost among our saint's benefactions was the procuring of an opera box for a memorable September first when his wife (the Metropolitan Opera star Gertrud Wettergren) was singing the rôle, always in Swedish at the Royal Opera, of Amneris in *Aïda*. It is rare that one singer combines beauty of voice, person, and presence with power of acting, youth, and magnificence of costume. New Yorkers who have heard Wettergren's Dalila, Brangäne, or Carmen need not be informed. The lady's husband told us that after her friends saw her as Carmen, they said to him, "Is Mrs. Wettergren like that?" Erik Wettergren has been connected with the Museum since 1909 but with two years off as actor and six years as director of the Royal Dramatic Theater. He was the first to present *Green Pastures* to Scandinavia.

The shop where Greta Garbo once sold hats was pointed out on the Haymarket, opposite the Concert Hall—not far away at 8 Sergelgatan lived Fredrika Bremer, Sweden's premier feminist; Fritze's Booksellers to the Court—here may be had Zorn etchings (a shop where we were recog-

Skansen

nized after a year's absence!). The Nordiska Company is a department store where the language question has been solved—interpreters wear the flags of the nations whose languages they speak. Orrefors glass was sold by a Russian who in addition to speaking fluent Swedish wore the flags of the United States, Great Britain, France, Germany, and the Russian flag of the old régime... so kind of the Company to allow it, she said with the enthusiasm characteristic of the high-born Russian. The modern Law Courts should be seen; the headquarters of the Match Industry; the City Library, with its clumsy tower, where enthusiasts stand to read the newspapers, as does the populace daily at noon in the Palace court to watch the change of guard and hear the military band; the House of Nobles—the building survives though the institution has been abolished.

Nordiska Museet (the Northern Museum) and Skansen, on the island of Djurgården, are said to constitute the foremost museum in the world devoted to the cultural history and ethnography of one European nation. The collections were begun by Dr. Arthur Hazelius, a man of vision, in the year 1872. Skansen is the open-air section, and in no other country has a finer group of native dwellings been assembled. Our first sight of Öland windmills and of Swedish girls in provincial costume was at this combination of folk exhibition and zoölogical garden. Near a Lapp hut, freshly roofed with turf, reindeer were eating greedily the "moss" or lichen known by their name. Polar bears were handsomer by far than those which languish in southern climes, while brown bears erect on hind legs, with naught but trenches between us, begged beseechingly. At the restaurant hot chocolate and waffles were to be had in lieu of tea. I remember returning on another occasion to dine—the airy terrace gay with parasols and blooming clematis, the music pavilion harboring performers who played in overcoats and slouch hats. Cold winds were forgotten when we heard the strains of Sibelius' "Spring Song." Windmills loomed against a darkening sky. In a vista of the city, boats and buildings were later to scintillate with lights.

Reluctant to leave Stockholm, we were nevertheless thankful to be able to take whole skins with us. How many a time we came within an inch of eternity! We risked our lives each time there was an artery to cross, so headlong was the surge of trams and buses, trucks with lurching trailers, of bicycles innumerable. Scant opportunity is given the pedestrian. No omnipresent police, as in London, to protect, yet traffic is, as in England and contrary to the custom in other Scandinavian lands, devastatingly to the left.

Beyond the city two excursions are outstanding, the one to Drottningholm, the other to Gripsholm. The first is reached in twenty minutes by motor, the second by a longer ride or, delightfully, in about three hours by boat. The summer palace, Drottningholm, remotely suggests a Versailles and is filled with a collection of paintings of crowned heads of whom a depressing number have lost their crowns if not their heads. A guide dwells lingeringly on the self-evident characteristics of massive tables, chests, and bureaus. The present building was begun late in the seventeenth century from plans by Tessin the elder and was finished by his son, designer of the palace in Stockholm. The garden shows lack of imagination—a sameness of pink rose clusters. The English park dates from the reign of Gustavus III, the first European monarch to recognize the independence of the United States. It is the Theater, begun in 1764, with its wooden waves that roll if they do not toss, its stage thunder, its absence of curtain (it was not considered respectful to drop a curtain in the Royal Presence!), that probably lures the visitor to Drottningholm. It is worth a longer journey.

Gustavus III erected the "Cavalier's Wing" at Gripsholm and added to the Queen's Wing constructed by Hedvig Eleonora, widow of Charles X.

The builder of Gripsholm was a nobleman, Bo Jonsson Grip, who died in 1386. It was Gustavus Vasa who began the collection of paintings, chiefly portraits of royal personages, which now numbers in the neighborhood of two thousand. (We were shown a press filled with damask cloths, the patterns illustrating biblical stories. On a bride's chest was carved the parable of the prodigal son —an odd choice!) The quality, as well as quantity, of the works of art is high, but even if this were not so, the towered castle, mirrored in moats, has power to outwit time. On June 19 and 20, 1937, a brilliant jubilee was held to celebrate the four-hundredth anniversary of the founding of Gripsholm.

Stockholm
Kornhamnstorg

Örebro Castle.

Mårbacka

CHAPTER VIII

POETIC VÄRMLAND

SEPTEMBER! the month of months for a tour through rural Sweden. Carl Högstadius, with a battered Reo borrowed from a friend, was at our disposal. To an aviator this must have been a tedious means of transportation, but Carl entered into the spirit of our quest. The week's round trip from the capital proposed by our Stockholm-loving friend in America was instantly seconded by Carl. It was too late, he admitted, for Gotland, but for Värmland and Dalarna, no better season could be found. They were, in his opinion, the high-water marks of the Swedish countryside. Mälaren, Vättern, Vänern we knew, but not yet the Fryken Lakes and Siljan, the "Blue Eye of Dalarna," likewise included in the Swedish Lake District.

Örebro was our halt for the first night. Its island castle, around which river swirled, delayed us on the bridge. Interest in its martial round towers was divided with flaunting poster announcing that on September twenty-second Marian Anderson would be heard in Örebro. The program included "Didn't My Lord Deliver Daniel?" as well as Händel and Bach. Laudatory words were quoted from the New York *Times* and from Mrs. Roosevelt. We were to leave Örebro with reluctance next morning, lingering in the park to see a red log cabin, Kungsstugan, bearing the date 1617 and believed to be the oldest timbered building in Sweden. On Stortorget stands a statue of Engelbrekt, who, from Örebro, led the war of liberation from the Danes. Two years later, in 1437, he was assassinated as he set out on his way to Stockholm. It was in Örebro that Marshal Bernadotte was elected, in 1810, Crown Prince of Sweden.

Karlskoga is in the region of notorious Bofors with its arsenal and munition-makers said to possess Krupp's secrets. We were told the company no longer is permitted to sell arms to Germany. Nobel factories and cellulose works stand at Uddeholm and Billerud. A more amusing excursion is from Kristinehamn to Södra Råda, "Old Church," where the Judgment Day is depicted in frescoes. The dead have risen, naked but crowned. Souls are weighed by angels, but a devil tilts the scale to his advantage by adding the tip of his own tail. An ancient bearded man with the key warned us—as though we could not see for ourselves—of tar dripping from roof and ladder. Once a year, at midsummer, a service is held here.

Through pine woods, a commonplace in Sweden, we were to drive via Kristinehamn to Karlstad, the capital of Värmland. On the outskirts of the town we were to pass the rough commemorative stone from which emerges an idyllic head of the poet Fröding, successor to Värmland's Tegnér. How he loved this spot where, in his day, barefoot girls picked violets! It is not far from the place of his birth. "The Lovers" and a child pursued by a fantastic troll form the base of this monument beneath the birches.

At Karlstad no wood-nymph was to trail across the square, as in the narrative of Gösta Berling; but the Stadshotell overlooking the northern shore of Vänern, where, from the river Klara, logs floated lakeward, fulfilled our expectations. It was a rallying place of Sweden's magnates. Ironmasters all, we thought, looking from one to another pompous group, *skåling* in solemnity within the shelter of the somber dining-hall. I felt as though staying at a man's club.

Filipstad was omitted from our schedule, being to the north of our route. Many visit the tomb of that naturalized American John Ericsson, the first to apply the screw to steam navigation and inventor, in 1862, of the turreted ironclad *Monitor*. This son of Värmland was born near Filipstad in 1803 and died in New York in 1889. He is buried in a monumental tomb of Swedish granite on which an American eagle has alighted. His coffin is draped in the Stars and Stripes, as when his remains were sent from the United States aboard an "ironclad."

Karlstad not only is the capital of Värmland, but it possesses interest because situated but sixty miles from the Norwegian border. It was the meeting-place where, in parliamentary fashion, the union between Norway and Sweden was dissolved. Under the leadership of Björnstjerne Björnson Norway had expressed its desire for independence and a king of its own. This the Swedish Riksdag, convened by Oscar II, was willing to grant under certain conditions. It was agreed at Karlstad that Norway would discontinue the building of fortifications along the Swedish border; a neutral zone, where no military operations would be held, was created, and a compact entered into to present future disagreements to the tribunal at The Hague.

Karlstad stands at the confluence of the Fryken Lakes and the fertile farms of Värmland. Fryksdalen the valley is called, and to readers of Selma Lagerlöf, once and forever, the Gösta Berling Country. Into the heart of its hills and

dales the trusty Reo bore us, with Carl's steady
hand at the wheel. Our start had been inauspi-
cious. Following a night of stars, day had dawned
drearily. Karlstad was blanketed with fog, and it
took, we thought, an aviator's powers of divina-
tion to keep our chugging charger upon the road.

There had been no opportunity to postpone our
ride, as we had but the required two hours from
Karlstad to the time of our appointment with Dr.
Lagerlöf—so we had been warned, before leaving
America, to call her; for the lady is not only an
avowed internationalist but a Swede to the core.

In preparation for our visit we had reread *The
Story of Gösta Berling* which had brought its
author fame as the winner of a prize contest and
(with *The Wonderful Adventures of Nils* and
other works) international repute in 1909 as the
first woman and the first Swede to win the Nobel
Prize for Literature. Later, in 1914, she was to become the only woman member of the august group
of eighteen that forms the Swedish Academy.
In this capacity she journeys winterly to Stockholm to deliberate with her fellow-judges upon
candidates... in 1930 the choice fell upon Sinclair Lewis, who presented himself in Stockholm
to receive the award. *Harvest,* we had acquired,
rich fruit of maturity; as well as the trilogy,
Mårbacka, Memories of My Childhood, and *The
Diary of Selma Lagerlöf.* The Nobel Prize, ap-
proximately $40,000, Dr. Lagerlöf had used for

the purchase of her ancestral estate and to enlarge the homestead. The move to Mårbacka
entailed administrative responsibilities. At Christmas several score of retainers and "crofters" are
entertained by the Lady of the Manor. This we
learned from the reading of Hanna Astrup Lar-
sen's brief biography.

"Into this dreary atmosphere" (of the period
of Strindberg, Brandes, Ibsen), writes Miss Lar-
sen, "came *The Story of Gösta Berling* with its
faith in God, its faith in man, its zest for life, its
love of beauty, strength, brilliance, happiness. . . .
In her interpretation of spiritual things she is a
mystic, in her treatment of bygone days she is a
romanticist, and yet she is a realist in her grasp
on actualities."

Could it be that we were about to see the author
who, with H. C. Andersen, has meant more to
world-wide readers than any other Scandinavian
writer? Could it be that we were to touch the hand
of the woman who had created Gösta, who had
written so tenderly of Sweden's first feminist,
Fredrika Bremer, as the "last old mamselle" of
Sweden? Could it be that we were to hear the
voice of the genius who had written a short tale
which, like Henry James' "Turn of the Screw"
in *The Two Magics,* is almost too haunting to be
borne—the tale called "Peace on Earth"? "Such
remarkable things could happen in the olden
times." So it begins. The stage is set for the

Gösta Berling

mysterious events inherent in the Värmland of bygone days. Characteristically, too, the tale ends with the unexpected—the omen of the obliterating snow.

Cousin to Esaias Tegnér is Selma Lagerlöf, cousin to Gustaf Fröding, and, in her own right, a poet, though her medium be prose.

While our car was still an hour's ride from Mårbacka, Carl asked the direction of a peasant. "Oh," said he, "the house of Selma Lagerlöf!" Imagine, we thought, a like reaction in the United States!

By the time we were near enough to spy signposts pointing to Mårbacka (the estate—there is no village), the magnetic sun was dissipating mists. The house, with its orchards, was easy to recognize from the roadway, although turning a cold shoulder to publicity. Hundreds come in summer hoping for a glimpse of the chatelaine. In August a road chain deters the more brazen.

Almost the first words spoken by Dr. Lagerlöf, on welcoming us, had to do with magic— "Erland's circle." We had admired the portraits of four generations of Lagerlöf ministers and their wives gracing the walls of the salon. The first, she told us, was Daniel, born in 1651, minister of the church at Arvika. Erland was, I remember, the fourth.

"Erland was a saintly man," his great-granddaughter told us. "It is said of him that when forest fires raged, he rode around the area, and within the circle the fire ceased...the same is often said of holy men in the countryside... the people still speak of 'Erland's circle.' It is unusual,'' said this scion of ministers, with justifiable pride, ''in any except noble families to have four generations of portraits.''

A central table in the drawing-room was laden with books in sumptuous bindings sent to Selma Lagerlöf as member of the Nobel Prize Committee. A grand piano stood open. We remembered having seen pictures of our hostess taken at the piano. We spoke, then, of our visit to Sibelius and heard that she shared our admiration for the magic of his music and had also made her pilgrimage to the Master in Finland, a treasured memory. Although her first allegiance is to literature, has she not called music ''the way between heaven and earth''?

(On her seventieth birthday she attended a performance of *I Cavalieri di Ekebu*—based on *The Story of Gösta Berling*—at the Royal Opera House in Stockholm. The saga was successful as a play, produced at the Royal Dramatic Theater in 1936. The first motion-picture featured the youthful Greta Garbo, in the rôle of Ebba Dohna. November 20, 1938, is the date of the eightieth birthday.)

It was not until our hostess left the room in search of a photograph which she was to auto-

Selma Lagerlöf

graph that we observed her slight lameness. In her absence we noted a portrait bust of herself by Grönkvist, the Psyche from the Naples Museum, signed photographs of the late Queen of Sweden, "Victoria"; of "Louise," the Crown Princess;

and of our hostess' especial patron, the Crown
Prince.

When Dr. Lagerlöf returned, she laughingly explained that the open book she held in the photograph—in which she was dressed in the same rich
browns as we now beheld her, with tortoise-shell
beads at her throat—was not one of her own! We
produced snapshots of summer and winter at our
country-place in Pennsylvania.

"It is Sweden!" she exclaimed. "Haymaking;
and you have snow, too!"

We hastened to say that on arrival in Värmland
we had simultaneously remarked, "It is Pennsylvania!" "New Sweden" our state had been christened by its earliest settlers. I had done my best
to discover at least one Swedish ancestor in honor
of the tercentenary of the Swedes' arrival... but
without avail.

"Did you really?" she said, much amused. She
felt I should be satisfied with English, Irish, and
Scotch.

"Värmland does not reveal herself to everyone," she told us. "You have done well to come
in September—our most beautiful month. Have
you seen the berries on the ash; the fields with
sheaves like soldiers marching? Värmland is
fickle. It is a good omen that, for you, she has
withdrawn her veils."

We were shown the view of the orchard from
the dining-room, and our hostess disappeared into

the pantry, returning with a Chinese plate piled with translucent apples.

"Astrachans!" I exclaimed, fresh from the reading of *Harvest,* remembering how the present owner of Mårbacka had written that she must regain the place "in order to be able to eat, once more, its apples."

"Take those with medals, like those worn on breasts; they are sure signs of merit." We were to discover, as, after departure, we sampled the luscious fruit, that those with overripe patches could be peeled with the fingers, were sweet as honey and juicy as peaches. Magic is in the very soil at Mårbacka.

At Sunne, the nearest village, the Hotel Gästis is the inn where Gösta had been found drunk by his parishioners. No word of English was understood. The front of the white building was, I recollect, aflame with woodbine. Our overnight stay gave us opportunity to visit the near-by sites of Gösta's adventures, masquerading under other names than those known to us—for Sunne is none other than Bro, Gösta's parish; and ~~Rotternos~~ is ^Rottne^ Ekeby; half a dozen may be seen from the observation tower overlooking the Fryken Lakes. After a visit to East Ämtervik, the church attended by the Lagerlöfs, where their monumental tombs stand in the churchyard, we drove to "Ekeby." Iron-works no longer predominate, "cavaliers" no longer make merry in the "wing" of the bachelors, but a major's wife still upholds the tradition of hospitality. An avenue of birches, commensurate in size with the grand tradition, leads toward the valley where, in former times, stood the furnaces. At the entrance is a parking-place to accommodate autocars. What one woman has started!

"How peaceful," Selma Lagerlöf had said, "before the coming of the automobiles, was Värmland."

Ekeby

Dalarna ‡

Costumes are gay at Leksand

The Mounds at Old Uppsala

CHAPTER IX

RUSTIC DALARNA

SUNLIGHT played upon golden birches, mountain-
ashes were conflagrations of berry and scarlet
leaf. Before saying farewell to Värmland for the
North we were to pass "Gurlitta Cliff" of bear-
hunt fame. What reader of Lagerlöf would dare
to mount, unarmed, its steep alluring trail? After
the bear mountain came bogs, a monotony of peat
drying on hurdles; old barns and staddled granaries, rust-red, of morticed logs; a few last habita-
tions; potato-diggers stolid in earth-brown fields.
Already our thoughts had lost themselves in the
deep forest we were about to enter, the forest in
which provinces of Värmland and Dalarna merge.
Fantastic mushrooms, food for beast and man;
cone-tipped firs, bearded with moss; reindeer
lichen; assuredly trolls.... Carl broke in upon our
thoughts to announce we were entering Dalarna.

The village of Vika, with its midsummer pole and log houses dwarfed by racks of hay, resembles the early Mora, where Anders Zorn was born. Leaving the forests behind us, we drove at length into his native town. Although Zorn dwelt at Mora, he was forced to seek material in the villages— as well as in the wide world. More than that, he brought the village to the town, founding an open-air museum. In the Gammelgård, furnished even to a collection of costumes, Zorn painted and often relaxed beside the fire. The hearth is, in so cold a province, the center of home life, and Dalarna, the very heart of Mother Svea, is called "the Hearth of Sweden."

The church is apt to be the focus of interest in Swedish towns, and especially is this true at Mora. Zorn's rustic house and studio (Madame Zorn continues to live here) may be seen from the churchyard in which the master was buried in 1920 in a tomb of his own designing. A grave, recalling Viking mounds, with bronze bas-relief by her son, immortalizes the mother of Zorn. Examples of the painter's virtuosity hang in the school—renowned renditions of himself and also of his wife; while in the court-house is an early portrait of the King, in evening dress, young and svelt and, almost to a fault, elegant. In the court-room the picture of a woman of Dalarna grieving beside the prostrate form of her husband should move the stoniest judge to mercy. "Anders Zorn,"

Mora: Zorn's Gård

says the judicious author of *Sweden, the Land and the People,* "was intoxicated with materiality, and sweepingly dedicated his tremendous powers, his inexhaustible facility, to depicting that materiality.... It is impossible not to ponder over the paradox of a genius wholly absorbed in sensuous externals achieving such intangible immortality."

Zorn the sculptor is less well known than Zorn the painter, Zorn the etcher, but no one can fail to notice, on leaving the church, the statue of Gustavus Vasa, in the dress of a son of Dalarna. In translation its inscription reads: "Here where Gustaf Eriksson spoke to the peasants of Mora in 1520, Dalecarlians have raised this monument in 1903. The work of Zorn."

Gustaf Vasa came of a noble Uppland family. His father having been put to death in the Massacre of Stockholm, on the occasion of the crowning of the Danish Christian II as King of Sweden, Gustaf, disguised as a peasant, endeavored to arouse the people of Dalarna to throw off the foreign yoke. The Dalecarlians were, however, incredulous of his tidings. Knowing the emissaries of the king were in pursuit, the fugitive sped towards Norway. It was not long before his tale was verified, and ski-runners were sent to overtake him. So it was that new pages of history came to be written. At the termination of the War of Liberation, in 1523, Vasa was crowned King of Sweden—one of the ablest who ever ruled in Scandinavia. Vasaloppet is the name given the long-distance ski race (fifty miles) from the village where the future king was overtaken, Sälen, to Mora. The event is held annually on March sixth.

Sweden can count on a midwinter display of polar lights in her northern province until the end of March. In the region of Stockholm, where lakes and bays are frozen, the aurora is eagerly anticipated—in contrast to its appearance on January 25, 1938, in southern Europe, where, according to French scientists, it had been unknown since 1709. In France, Italy, Spain, and Portugal, fearing they knew not what, the peasants knelt in prayer.

Midwinter and midsummer are both excellent times to visit Mora. The skiing brings no greater crowds than does the observance of Midsummer Night—with dancing on the green. Not only do the Dalecarlians celebrate the festival with abandon, but owing to the costumes still in general use in the province, the ceremony has an Elizabethan rusticity.

Each of the trio of Dalarna towns, Mora, Rättvik, and Leksand, presents an equal appeal. It is important to plan a visit at time of festival or of a Sunday, when funerals are held. Beyond Mora lies Färnås, a red town, glowing for us in the rays of the setting sun. Its ancient cabins beside the lake were huddled as though in conference. We were to spend the night at the Hotel Persborg at Rättvik, than which Sweden possesses no more admirable inn, unless it be at Båstad. The bewitching costumes of its waitresses, the English country-house informality of its bountiful breakfasts, its distinguished clientèle, are things not soon forgotten.

Sunday morning found us speeding to Leksand. Beautiful was the procession we came upon on arrival. To the tolling of a bell a cortège of mourners, flecked with sunlight, filed beneath the avenue of birches. The garments of the women included striped aprons of brilliant yellow over much-gathered black skirts and basques edged with scarlet. Girls wore bonnets fluttering with ribbons, while matrons' head-gear was topped by white kerchiefs. The coffin, drawn in an open cart, was banked with flowers. At the church gate the minister awaited, a quaint figure in short gown and tall hat. The ceremony called for the brush of a Zorn, as did that within the edifice, with worshipers seated in cobalt pews. Our return to Rättvik's church was planned to see the exit of its congregation. Here not only do the women flaunt skirts with apron-like panels, red stockings, and peaked caps, but men and boys stroll nonchalantly in tan breeches, tassels dangling, and coats of antediluvian pattern. A hundred or so "church" stables crowd beside the water...for Rättvik *kyrka* stands upon a promontory.

Our arrival at Falun was joyous. We had prevailed upon Carl to ask a question at the railway station—the address of the ~~Skrogs~~. *Skoks*

"Just ask at the station," my aunt's Swedish nurse had said to me, of her family not seen for half a century. Following her thought, I had supposed Falun to be a village instead of Dalarna's chief town with fifteen thousand inhabitants.

"~~He~~ will think I'm kidding him," said Carl, "for you know ~~Skrog~~ means Wood and Sweden is full of woods! It's like looking for a special log in the river."

Carl returned from his quest bubbling with mirth, a habit acquired in the U. S. A. "The man wouldn't believe I was serious," he said.

Dalarna : † † †
Sunday at Rättvik .

The cashier at the hotel showed us the telephone book. None of the Skrogs seemed to be the retired engine-driver we sought, nor yet his school-teacher sisters.

"What else do you know of them?" the girl asked, and on hearing of the aged mother's recent death, she exclaimed, "Of course, the ~~Skrogs~~ at Slossen!"

Not for a good deal would I have missed our visit to this estimable family, ending their days in comfort, in a ten-room house, on pensions provided by a paternal government. It is of the Skrogs I think when Falun is mentioned, of the view of the lake from their windows, of their yellow cat and polished kettles rather than of the famed copper-mine. At present the chief product of the mine is sulphur ore, used in sulphite-cellulose plants and in the making of the red paint that dyes farm buildings in rural Sweden. Bergslaget, the oldest company in the world (it dates from 1288), includes to-day not only the mine but iron- and steel-works, paper-, saw-, and pulp-mills.

After teaching at Landskrona, Selma Lagerlöf retired to Falun, where she and her mother lived for twenty years before the return to Mårbacka. Carl Larsson was a neighbor at his country-place, "Sundborn." Here Larsson lived and painted his wife and children in nooks and corners of the cosy interior which is strangely familiar to admirers of the artist's work. Here he added a paneled room in honor of a visit from Prince Eugen.

The President of Jernkontoret had arranged that we should visit the steel-works at Sandviken. Viktor Magnusson, a vice-president, was our host. Talk turned to Finland. Mr. Magnusson had no patience with Finlanders who refuse to learn Finnish. "If they must speak Swedish," he said, "let them return to Sweden. They would not complain of speaking English if they lived in your country." He spoke of the United States of America and said that he would like to see a United States of Europe.

Sandviken's motto is, "From the ore to the watch-spring." The furnaces are small in comparison with the American because the fuel used is charcoal—prepared in the forests of Dalarna. A high percentage of Gillette blades are made at Sandviken because of the superior quality of its steel, but not those, we were told, for the United States Army or Navy!

Sandviken had lately celebrated its seventy-fifth anniversary. Over four thousand men are employed, and, said Magnusson, "We are 110 per cent busy—working all time and 10 per cent to fill next year." Whiffs of whale-oil—in which the steel is drawn—reached us as we were shown an ultra-modern cold rolling-mill (one of the world's largest); the annealing is electric. An exhibition of products included airplane profiles for wings

Sandviken Steelworks

and circular and other saws. A building has been erected especially for the manufacture of saws. "To compete," said our host, "with Disston!" We were not permitted to leave until we had seen the workmen's chapel and crematory (designed by the architect of the Engelbrekt Church) and the cemetery with its shaft of light burning to the "unknown soldier" of industry.

The last pause made in the sweep of our circuit was at Uppsala, before we returned, now but forty, miles southward, to our base at Stockholm. We stayed at Stadshotellet (to the frivolous suggesting not *the* State" but a "little" hotel) on Drottninggatan, favorite parade-ground of students.

Uppsala, capital of the province of Uppland, a university town with over thirty thousand inhabitants, is likewise the seat of the Primate of Sweden and possesses the largest cathedral in Scandinavia. Its Gothic spires dominate the plain, accenting the resemblance to rural England.

Our first view of the huge pile of the castle, begun under Vasa, was made poignant by the fact that we had seen the alluring Garbo in her humanly appealing, if historically false, picture *Queen Christina*. (The Swedes are proud not of Greta's box receipts but of her artistry.) Bourdon's portrait of "Kristina"—as the Swedes write the name, despite the fact that she spelled it with a *C*—shows her a striking figure on horseback, with falcon and page. It was in the Audience Chamber on June 11, 1654, that this brilliant though erratic great-granddaughter of Vasa and daughter of Gustavus Adolphus abdicated. The courtiers refusing to remove her crown, Christina was obliged to perform the act for herself. A reviewer of Margaret Goldsmith's psychological biography, *Christina of Sweden,* suggests that "perhaps only this post-Freudian age can fully understand her." All Sweden was horrified when this daughter of the savior of Protestantism in the Thirty Years' War adopted Catholicism and was ceremoniously welcomed to Rome by the Pope.

The Cathedral, begun in the thirteenth century, majestic within and without, contains the tombs of many notables: Gustavus Vasa and his three wives; Oxenstjerna, the "practically omnipotent" chancellor; the botanist Carl von Linné, professor at the university, known to the world as Linnæus; but, in the year 1938, the one causing most remark is that of Emanuel Swedenborg, scientist and mystic.

Swedenborg was the son of Jesper Svedberg of Falun. Although in the United States better known for his writings on religion (he did not establish the church that bears his name), in his native land his contributions to science are especially stressed. Author of two hundred books, authority on steel and iron, on the human body, Swedenborg was the first to conceive the nebular hypothesis, the first to place psychology on a rational basis. It has been said of him that he stretched out "intellectual tentacles from the tangible to the intangible, to interpret the cosmos as a divine creation." On January 28, 1938, world celebrations on the two hundred and fiftieth anniversary of the birth of Swedenborg acclaimed the philosopher as foremost Swede—the "Aristotle of the North."

Like Gustaf Vasa, Carl had spent years at school at Uppsala and at the university. He pointed out with pride the house of the Värmland Nation, designed by Ragnar Östberg—of Stockholm Town Hall fame. "Nations," he explained, are the clubs of the undergraduates from the different provinces—perhaps to be preferred to fraternities in American colleges. There are over three thousand students, a fair proportion of them girls.

The University Library possesses six hundred thousand volumes and rare manuscripts. There is, for example, the *Codex Argenteus* from Prague—the Gospels in fifth-century Gothic; Snorre Sturlasson's *Edda*. We remarked a missal by a nun of Vadstena, the signature of Nicholaus Copernicus, dated 1524, letters by Celsius, Swedenborg, a poem by Linné to his fiancée, a song by Bellman, the Finale of Mozart's *Magic Flute,* Andersen's manuscript of "The Fir Tree or the Snow Queen," a letter from Andersen's adored Jenny Lind; but of letters from living celebrities I remember but one, signed by the woman who is year in and year out the most popular author in Sweden, Selma Lagerlöf. Upon the publication of *The Wonderful Adventures of Nils,* in 1907, the author was given an honorary degree by the University of Uppsala.

The King of Sweden (unlike the King of Norway) may confer titles of nobility. I am told the last time he has done so was in 1902, when a title was granted to the explorer Sven Hedin. In

Uppsala we were to have the privilege of meeting a youthful namesake, Sven Hedin Hörner, son of an adaptable American and Docent Nils Hörner, author of *Resa till Lop*, geologist on Hedin's unprecedented Asiatic expedition.

No one should leave Sweden without a visit to Gamla Uppsala, with its tumuli of the Iron Age popularly known as the mounds of Odin, Thor, and Frey—"the city where the Svea Kings of legend and fable held their court."

Rättvik

The House
of Zorn

The Isle of Öland :
Windmills of ancient days

The Towers of VISBY

CHAPTER X

KALMAR AND THE ISLES

As the globe-trotter is pressed for time to circle
the torrid portions of earth's sphere in the "cold
weather," so is the summer tourist to the Northern Countries compelled to hasten in the warm
weather. To those of us who on a first tour have
left undone the things that we would have done,
Scandinavia still beckons. No need is there to
apologize for a second visit to Stockholm. Our
former arrivals had been by the Baltic, by Göta
Canal, by motor from Uppsala, and now, to see
Gotland and Skåne, we had arrived by train from
Oslo. Carl was in waiting, returned providentially
from the Spanish war-zone.

The preliminary dull ride from Stockholm to
Nynäshamn was soon behind us, as was the hour

of waiting, in company with harbor mosquitoes, until arrival of passengers by train, the night journey aboard *Angaren Drotten,* the approach to a crescent of land with Visby in its center, medieval walls and unroofed churches cutting the sky.

Gotland, largest of Swedish islands (it measures eighty miles by an approximate thirty), is washed on all sides by the Baltic. A wealth of prehistoric weapons and other treasure is preserved in the Gotland Archæological Museum at Visby. During the Viking period Gotland's sons, Goths, like their brothers on the mainland, voyaged to distant lands and returned to enrich the place of their birth. Greek coins of the sixth century as well as Arabic have been discovered. According to the ballad: "The swine [at Visby] ate out of silver troughs, and the women spun with golden distaffs."

The first fortification of the harbor was erected in the eleventh century whereas the city walls were begun a hundred years later. Visby was to become one of the most important cities in the Hanseatic League. Here Germans and citizens of other Baltic nations foregathered. "Visby maritime law," it is written of this time, "held good in all waters from London to Novgorod." The city minted a coinage of its own. Then, at the height of its power, in the summer of 1361, the town was attacked by the Danes, led by their monarch Valdemar Atterdag. The most furious fighting was with the country-folk. Buried where they were slain, eighteen hundred of them, many still wearing coats of mail, the peasants are unforgotten. A circular cross of stone with worn Latin inscription tells how on July 27, 1361, the Gotlanders fell at the hands of the Danes before the gates of Visby. What the monument does not tell is why the burghers within the walls refrained from sallying forth to aid or from opening the gates to their fellow-Gotlanders. That the town was not utterly destroyed was probably because the citizens complied with the commands of the marauders. According to Hellquist's painting, the Danish king watched from the market-square while the distraught natives poured their jewels, gold, and silver into vats. Never did the town regain its unique position among Baltic cities. In the century that followed it was supplanted by Lübeck. Pirates were to infest Visby; Denmark was to contest its ownership. Since 1645 the island has been once more a part of Sweden.

Mariners of old, it is said, were wont to steer by the gleaming eyes of the carbuncles in the rose-windows of the Church of Saint Nikolaus. Wrenched from their accustomed setting by pillagers, the gems brought misfortune to the vessel that carried them toward Denmark, so the story goes, and from Baltic depths the twin lights gleam, luring men to death.

Sea-foam and roses, roses and sea-foam, nightingales and gulls, ruins, gulls and nightingales—

there you have Visby. Like Melrose, Saint Catherine's should be visited in the "pale moonlight"
—the ruin is reminiscent of Sir Walter's abbey.
Once a convent of the Franciscans adjoined the
church. Both buildings, and many others on Gotland, fell into disrepair at the Reformation. These
walls that remained unshaken by Valdemar's triumph can be oblivious to the hordes that besiege
them on arrival of a cruise ship. Twelve hundred,
we were told, had come ashore on the day before
our visit—half of them from the *Kungsholm*. Passengers from the *Reliance* were scurrying to
launches as we watched of an evening from our
balcony at the Stadshotell. At eight a warning
blast had sounded, but not until nine did the three-
horned monster creep, almost imperceptibly, from
sight. Two Swedish destroyers and a vicious-look-
ing mine-sweeper rode at anchor while their
superb officers quickened the hearts of damsels in
the restaurant of our hotel. Roses lined the terrace where couples wandered between dances. In
the dining-room bowls of daily-cut blossoms—
roses alternating with sweet-peas—lent fragrance.
Standards of freshness are as exacting for
flowers as for fish in Scandinavia.

Carl led us to the Church of Saint Nikolaus,
where performances were to be given, on July
27-30 and again in August, of *Petrus de Dacia*.
The story is of Christina av Strommeln, beloved
by Petrus, in Rome, whom she could not wed for

he was a Dominican. He was to become the head of the Order (this is his church) and she a saint. A chorus of "nuns, Dominicans, soldiers, and folk" was rehearsing; stage-hands were erecting an altar, and Gotland crosses—to conceal floodlights. The principals were to be from the Royal Opera of Stockholm. We lingered in the close. Perhaps as old as the church itself are the fruitful mulberry trees.

A hundred churches still stand on the island, but the sixteen at Visby, with the exception of the Cathedral, are in ruins. That edifice was consecrated in 1255 and has survived the centuries' vicissitudes. At its portal we were to come upon a wedding. Although it was only five o'clock, the guests were in evening dress. Townspeople lined the carpeted path. Topping the bride's tulle veil was a perky crown of smilax.

"She wears a crown!" the woman next me remarked with satisfaction. I echoed the Swedish words, as best I could, and, I trust, passed for once as a Swede.

The walls of Visby seen from the North Gate recall those of Carcassonne. From the hillside a dozen of the thirty-seven surviving towers are visible, and a stretch, not, indeed, of the Pyrenees, but of the sea. The town's situation surpasses that of Aigues-Mortes or of Avignon. The mazes of the streets support the comparison, as do not the open spaces, the omnipresent roses.

✠ Gotland ⁑

Bronzed young Swedes (it is a paradise for brides and grooms) are to be found in numbers at Snäckgårdsbaden with its cliff restaurant (one of Sweden's best) and cabins in pine woods. A sandy beach is its chief reason for being.

On our second morning we drove by way of the villages of Bro, Tingstäde, Lärbro, and Rute to Bunge. Most Gotland villages boast thirteenth-century churches. At Bro, in addition to a medi-eval tower, there are bas-reliefs—bits of sculpture

The Walls of Hanseatic Visby

still older than the present edifice—set like hall-
marks high on an outer wall. Leather-bound
prayer-books, my Illustrator discovered, had been
in use over a hundred years.

Carl pointed out a sign by the roadside—a
large M. "That," said he, "is a meeting stone
(where cars can pass), and so say the girls and
boys!"

At Tingstäde one of these meetings had culmi-
nated in a wedding. Birch branches still formed a

nuptial arch before the church. "There are no windows here to the north," said Carl. "A saying in the country is, 'All evil things come from the North.'"

My Illustrator agrees that one of the most picturesque open-air museums is Kulturhistoriska Museet at Bunge, owned by the State, with Th. Erlandsson as curator. There is the Stone of Hammars, engraved over a thousand years ago with the saga of a legendary lady. Windmills there are of unusual design; but interest centers in the farm buildings from the near-by island of Fårö. Shaggy-roofed houses, thatched with rush, are grouped about a wooden cross, where it was the custom for the farmer to lead prayers. The sheep of Fårö are black, as are the wild ponies of Gotland.

Before leaving Gotland we were to see the remains of the Cistercian cloisters at Roma; and Kallunge, where a naïve madonna gazes from her niche upon the traditional "leafy groves." A memory comes to me of a place that bears no name—none is given on the government sign which reads: *Märkligt Fornminne Skeppsaltning* ("Marker in Remembrance of Ship-Stones"). Outlined by boulders, this grave, in boat form, of a Bronze Age mariner stands in the forest off the highway in the region of Tofta. We happened upon it quite by accident. Silence enwrapped this last haven of one of Gotland's heroes.

Kalmar, to which we sailed from Visby, has preserved her castle known as "the Key of Sweden." The fortress dates from Viking days, but its ramparts, bastions, and towers were added in 1337. Until the reign of Charles X Gustavus, Kalmar guarded a frontier. Modern flour-mills contrast with castle and town gate passed on the way to the cathedral square, with its Old Town Hall and, in many ways, admirable Stadshotell. There my Illustrator had written "Mr. and Mrs." in the hotel register. A solemn English-speaking factotum appeared shortly after at our rooms. It was not allowed, said he, each name must be written separately. But place and date of birth for both had been clearly given? No matter—it was the law!

The Swedish provinces cannot be said to welcome the stranger within their gates. On arrival in a dining-room the new-comer stands indefinitely, no waiter or waitress condescending to throw a glance in his direction. At last he sits, in desperation, but then, inevitably, is told that the table chosen is engaged. The people of Småland, in which Kalmar lies (the province is the size of Belgium), are not, indeed, so different from their neighbors in Östergotland to the north. In the words of Bonnier's *Sweden:* "The inhabitants...are especially noted for their placidity and strong self-esteem, but they are friendly and hospitable. 'I am born in Östergotland, thank God!' is an old saying."

Kalmar Castle:

Kalmar has given its name in history to the Kalmar Union by which Sweden (which included Finland), Denmark, and Norway became united, in the year 1397, under one sovereign. It was here that Queen Margaret wrote her Letter of Union and here that Erik of Pomerania was crowned. The federation endured, at least in name, until the year 1521.

Slottsvägen leads to the Town Park, where children congregate about a duck-pond. I found myself disinclined to leave this spot, where baby

one-time Key of Sweden.

coaches assemble and old gentlemen feed carp, even though the outstanding collections demanded my presence within the castle. Next to the fortress the most memorable sight at Kalmar was a torch-light procession of students as seen from our balcony giving on the market-square.

Through Erik Wettergren, who has written a brochure on the subject of Orrefors glass, we lunched with the associate director and his wife to meet Mr. and Mrs. Hald, he the artist designer and, since 1933, director of the Orrefors Glassworks. The estate consists of twenty-five thousand acres of farm and forest. Wood-pulp is sold to paper-mills and firewood used by the company. Orrefors was, between 1726 and 1916, noted for its iron, but in 1898 glassworks were added. It was not until the advent in 1916-1917 of Gate and Hald that the manufacture began of artistic engraved and tinted Graal-glass. Two hundred workers are employed. First we were shown a blower with lumps of molten glass, passing to the next man, who also turns and blows, to next who shapes, and next who takes. The bowl then molded, its top sheered off, is blown to size and heated in flaming oven. We passed beneath whirling belts and among twirling blowpipes. We watched annealed articles emerge from tunnels after half-day coolings. Gossamer shreds of glass hung like skeins from oven doors. The fires burn with ferocity night and day save for a period before Christmas when ovens are repaired. In 1925 Orrefors was awarded the Grand Prix at the Exposition of Decorative Arts in Paris. Next to Sweden the United States is the best customer. Orrefors show-rooms are to be found in Rockefeller Center and in Los Angeles.

Having come so recently from Gotland, we did not travel, as we had done the year before, from Kalmar across the sound to plainly visible Öland. The King's gardens at Solliden had called. As the castle and cathedral on the mainland had receded,

the chalk ridge which forms the backbone of the
otherwise sea-level island had grown plainer, and
primitive windmills had whirred a welcome.

It was a motor ride of eighteen miles to Solliden, which stands beside the ruins of Vasa's
castle, Borgholm. As we approached and asked
our way, peasants pointed to ill-defined tracks
across the moors. A mere trail led us to the gate
with the initials VRS of the late Victoria, Queen
of Sweden. It was she who came to Öland in
1902 to visit and the following year built Solliden,
which gave her a semblance of the south. The
last years of her life were, for health's sake, spent
in Italy. An ancient mill stands upon the King's
property and is embellished by a finial of a crown.
While Carl went in search of the gate key, we
gazed over granite, carpeted with bluebells; over
heath and juniper scrub, aromatic in sunshine, to
where magpies flashed. A Scandinavian crow,
frocked in black and gray, looked wise as a parson. A glimpse of glassy sea emphasized the likeness to Brittany.

After long delay the gate was opened by a
mighty key, and, without sight of human being,
we followed the road to the King's favorite
August residence. The royal flag was flying as we
approached the Italian villa, but, we were to hear
from the King's first marshal, His Majesty was
indisposed, housed despite the beauty of the day.
His representative wore a monocle on a ribbon,

a monocle which—whether by its wearer's intention or not we could hardly decide—was constantly jumping off. The manner of the Baron was just what it should have been for an official of a democratic, but not too democratic, court.

A lackey was called to show us the grounds: a marble head of the late Queen; the Italian rose-garden, with clipped arbor-vitae hedges; the Dutch garden (its plants presented by Wilhelmina of the Netherlands); the impeccable croquet-court against a background of English oaks. Here the King plays daily at three; and here the players have tea while listening to world news from a loud-speaker on a tree.

Our departure was made by another still less pretentious gate. No sentries guard Solliden. "There is no need," said Carl. "Our King leads the life of a private gentleman except when he is required on ceremonious occasions."

Isle of Öland! with its romantic stones from Viking and prehistoric days; its reigning king; its queen's garden, hidden between sea and moor; its glassy replica of Mediterranean waters; its mysterious brooding quality of Morgat, Camaret, Iles aux Moines; its mills... was this not a dream? Öland is incredible... surely no such island can exist in the matter-of-fact kingdom of the Swedes.

Gustaf V
King of Sweden

Vittskövle : 🍁
One of the most harmonious of Skåne's Castles

Ystad: The ancient Court

CHAPTER XI

CASTLES IN SKÅNE

"Our castle's strength will laugh a siege to scorn," cried Macbeth. So, in the Middle Ages, might have shouted Jens Holgersson Ulfstand to his men when in 1505 he completed Glemmingehus and, looking out across its moats, realized he had naught to fear. Lordly owners of Torup, Skarhult, Vittskövle, later in the century, must have felt no less secure. Other names crowd the memory, but as times grew less perilous in Skåne, keeps and towers of feudal strongholds gave place to more gracious mansions; yet moats were retained, at first as essential to safety but later to complete the harmony.

It was not until I had seen a picture map in color of Skåne that I determined to visit this southernmost of Swedish provinces. Only the northern portion, dotted with blue lakes and rich in pine forests, connects with the rest of Sweden. South, east, and west, as my map shows, are bounded by cobalt sea. Sprinkled profusely, as grain at seed-time, over the paper surface, castles are indicated with enticing suggestion of pepper-pot towers, Renaissance turrets, Danish roofs, ruddy or white façades. The only answer to such a map is to step into an automobile.

The route chosen by myself and my Illustrator, with Carl at the wheel, was that from Kalmar. We slept at Kristianstad, and as sleeping is essential even on tours, we saw at a glance that Ystad, Malmö, Lund, and Båstad would all offer welcome domicile before we had satisfied ourselves with an adequate impression of Sweden's château country. That is to say, starting with the east coast, we should visit the south, then the hill-ridged center, and finally the west coast to Båstad on the northern border. Thus it was we visited prehistoric mounds, Viking stones, churches, agricultural colleges, seaside resorts, as well as Malmö and the University of Lund; but when fertile Skåne is mentioned, first and foremost come to mind rural dwellings, whether hospitable farm-houses and manors or more formidable medieval castles.

The nobility of Skåne is a survival from another age. Unlike those of neighboring Denmark and modern England, the immense estates have

not been to any extent divided. The landed gentry
is true to its traditions and rarely marries beyond
its own charmed circle. Counts and barons dwell
on the property that has been in their families
for centuries. "Saurians which have survived
their epoch," one of their own kin calls them in
an admirable article on life in Swedish country-
houses in the *National Geographic*. "Foreigners,"
says this Swedish writer, "think our nobility
stiff, reserved or sullen and haughty but they are
really shy and awkward. They shrink from im-
pulsive gestures or emotional language." To some
of us used to the more spontaneous ways of Latin
peoples these reticent sons and daughters of the
North present a problem. Scion of New England
and of the South, of England but also of Ireland,
I find my sympathies often conflict. Perhaps their
self-contained English cousins better understand
the Swedes and Danes.

Skåne once bore the name East Denmark. The
English version is Scania or Scandia—identical
with the southern portion of Sweden and traditionally supposed to be an island settled centuries
before the northern portions of Scandinavia had
risen from the sea. Scandia was probably the first
center of Scandinavian civilization, and it has
given its name to the tall fair peoples of the
North, which, racially, should include blond North
Germans. Linguistically the language spoken is
grouped with Danish rather than with the Swedish

spoken in other parts of the country. Skåne did not become an integral part of Sweden until 1658, after Charles X had dared to lead five thousand men with their artillery across the frozen Belts, taking the Danes unaware.

To return to our castles, of the twenty-odd visited none pleased me more than Trolle Ljungby. Our arrival was on a Sunday and during a typically Swedish downpour. One by one the pleasure-seekers in other parked cars, discouraged by the weather, chugged away. For us there was to be no morrow in northeastern Skåne. We gazed through the curtain of rain to where the castle rose in austere dignity of ancient brick above the pelted surface of the moat. Oak, horse-chestnut, and beech—the Scandian Graces—bending and soughing concealed the nobleman's chapel. There came the sound of a tolling bell. Drenched bicyclists passed, each bearing a wreath—in rural Sweden there is a veritable cult of the dead. When the mourners had departed, we decided to take refuge in the chapel. Portly twin sextons were about to lock the doors. Similar they were as Tweedledum and Tweedledee. They spoke mumblingly as Danes, together but not in unison. Carl, from the North, found it doubly hard to understand and to translate their words.

"They say, for example, 'Loond' for Lund, which I call 'Lunde.' It sounds so funny," he said.

"No one knows," they told us, "whether the castle dates from the twelfth century, but the chapel does." They called attention to a shield bearing the coat of arms of the Coyet family (whose descendants we were later to meet at Torup), owners of Trolle Ljungby in the seventeenth century and ancestors of its present owner, Count Trolle Wachtmeister. In the chapel hung a painting of a minister surrounded by his off-spring, the personification of middle-class respectability. It was astonishing to be told that one of these prim-looking daughters had become the mistress of Charles XI.

"Did you notice," said Tweedledum, "the boulder on the road to Kristianstad?"

"It stands beside a house," said Tweedledee.

"Well, this stone, it's a way they have," said Tweedledum, "had moved on a Christmas Eve, hundreds of years ago. The Lord of Trolle Ljungby (a Coyet) was riding that way, and he saw a light. The trolls were having a party. You should have seen the gems!"

Tweedledee took up the story, looking in his rotund eagerness not unlike a troll. "The Lord of Trolle Ljungby braved them all. He helped himself to what he wanted—the Horn and the Pipe. You've heard of them, I dare say."

"The trolls were hot in pursuit," said Tweedledum. "They got only the horse's tail as the nag leaped across the moat." (How like Tam O'Shanter! we thought.) "With that the trolls put a curse upon the house. Three times should it burn."

"It's true as the gospel," said Tweedledee. "Trolle Ljungby has burned twice and the third time...well, there will be a third time. The Pipe and Horn bring good luck to the family, and they must never be taken from the castle."

"And have they brought luck to the present owner?" I asked.

"To be sure they have. The Count is young, he has forty-four thousand tunnland (a thousand for each year of his life!), a wife, and three children ...what more could he ask? They are all at the seashore now, at Falsterbo."

Beneath dripping umbrellas we hastened to an archway adjoining the stables. The head groom had likewise taken refuge there. He looked like an Irish squire.

"Pity you came to-day," he said. "Now if you'd been here on Midsummer Eve....At one of the Wachtmeister estates there was a feast for six hundred farmers—sixty calves were killed, and there were plenty of drinks, I can tell you."

As we listened our eyes fell on a sign: "The Pipe and Horn are not to be seen. The public must not cross the drawbridge."

"Never mind that," said the groom. "If the Count was home, he'd ask you in. That's not meant for you. The trippers try to break the panes."

Fate had smiled upon us in the person of this lusty Swede. Even the shower ceased, the sun broke through, the better for us to admire the swans, the date, 1636, the espaliered pear-trees... a certain ground-floor window. There they were, tempting the passer-by: the Pipe, a curved ivory whistle, and the Horn, a tiny drinking-horn embellished with silver.

A maid in blue calico emerged. "You may see the gardens," she said, "anywhere except where it is marked *Privat*."

"The Swedes do not abuse such privileges," we thought as we entered the vast garden. "Trollenas, Trollenholm, Trolle Ljungby," I remarked, dwelling on the names, "how great a family, how powerless the trolls!" Our eyes were upon the storied castle's russet walls whose diamond window-panes blazed like gems in a fairy-tale.

Due south of Kristianstad is Vittskövle, one of the most harmonious of Skåne's castles. The house stands near the road, and, after the fashion of the land, its grounds are open to the inspection of the public.

"No strangers admitted," said a loafer at the cross-road where we parked our car.

Carl demurred. "The lady is a widow," he said. "When she hears about the Book, she will let you see the interior." He reckoned without knowledge of the inhibitions of the Swedish nobility, to whom publicity is anathema.

On his way to ring the doorbell, Carl met the lady. She told him that she was busy with guests and could not let us visit the castle. "She didn't even say she was sorry. I think the trouble is she doesn't speak English and is ashamed."

This conversation took place as we stood in front of the towered glories of Vittskövle, which with Torup and Skarkult has been called the best preserved and most characteristic of the sixteenth-century castles. If any changes have taken place in Vittskövle's medieval exterior, they are not apparent. In addition to formal gardens, a mist bush of immense proportions and ruddy in bloom had been planted with an eye to emphasis of the castle's color scheme.

Another automobile was parked beside our own, and to this car the Countess escorted her guests, waving farewell and returning slowly castleward. She had almost to brush our sleeves in passing. Did she so much as glance in our direction? She did not.

"These provincials!" murmured Carl, under his breath, for Carl, be it remembered, was of Stockholm. "When we get a Skåne station on the radio, we click off."

Skåne seen from the air gives the impression of a vast unevenly marked checker-board—grain of all kinds, rye, wheat, oats, and barley, alternate with clover, potatoes, and beets for the sugar-mills. Thus did it appear to Nils Holgersson

Glimmingehus

perched upon the back of the young gander who had joined the wild geese in flight to Lapland. *The Wonderful Journey of Nils,* Selma Lagerlöf's next best seller to *Gösta Berling,* has immortalized Glimmingehus. This fortress, untowered and unturreted, a stark five-storied "stone-house" with stepped end gables, is being restored to serve as a museum. Begun by Jens Holgersson Ulfstand in 1499, it was completed in six years. A bas-relief

over the entrance depicts Jens (who was a Dane
from Gotland) standing in medieval guise between
his first and second wives. A crude stone figure
of a wild man with a club is said to have stood on
the roof, a sentinel to affright trolls. Dungeons
there are worth peering into, but it is Riddarsalen
or the Knight's Hall with its adjoining chapel that
transports the beholder to a long-gone age.

To north and south of Glimmingehus are outstanding Viking stones—Stenshuvud and Kåseberga and, near the former, Kivik, an immense
prehistoric mound, discovered by a farmer in 1748
and in 1932 opened to permit entrance to the
sarcophagus, which in its antiquity and similarity
of symbols recalls the tombs of the Egyptians. It
is said to date from 1500 B.C., the same date as
Tutankhamen's tomb at Luxor.

Kåseberga, like Stenshuvud, is beside the sea—
in this case the Sound. The fishing village with its
tidy cottages, its display of nets and copper pots
in windows, was reminiscent of Devon. The children looked as though English would be their native tongue. Boats dried their sails inside the
breakwater, and a man indicated the direction of
the cliff in response to shouted inquiries. To the
top of the hill we trudged, wading through sand.
Along the marginal way we wandered. A lonely
cow lamented, we surmised, a lost calf. Swallows
of the land and sea swallows darted and circled as
though our approach were an unprecedented dis-

Gårdlösa: Site of Lindbergh's ancestral home ✦

turbance. Dramatically the stones emerged, un-announced, in perfect ellipse, the tallest towering above the height of any man. The earth at their feet was carpeted with a protective tangle of con-volulus. Unmarked, unmarred, virtually unknown, frequently obliterated by mists from the sea, stand the ageless sentinels of Kåseberga.

Gårdlösa, a name become familiar to Ameri-cans, is not far inland. It was from this farm of twenty-five hectares that Olaf Månsson, the pa-ternal grandfather of Charles A. Lindbergh, turned towards America. Four times a member of Parliament, Månsson, like his heroic descend-ant, was a pioneer in transportation. His projects for increase of the existing railways of Sweden met with opposition. Månsson, obstinate almost to fanaticism, defied public opinion and was not returned to Parliament. Soon after the birth of his son, Colonel Lindbergh's father, Månsson decided to begin life anew in Minnesota. It is said that this decision was made at the suggestion of King Charles XV, with whom he was on friendly terms. Like many others Månsson changed his name to one offering fewer difficulties.

Although Americans are beginning to seek Gårdlösa, they do not find the original buildings. The present house was not erected until 1871, following a fire. The affable owner, Johan Jönsson, regaled us with details of a movie made here and shown in Sweden. In 1928, said he, Herr and Fru Lindbergh flew from Copenhapen on their way to Stockholm and circled over the property. On their return from the north they landed at Landskrona and motored to the ancestral farm.

The month being July, my Illustrator and I decided to stay at Saltsjöbaden, the bathing resort on the outskirts of Ystad, rather than within the town. A fifteenth-century group of dwellings— half-timbered and with ramshackle balconies, built around a court—flew at the entrance the cross of Thor, flag of Hitler's Germany. We asked the explanation and were told that it was headquarters for young fascists. My Illustrator pointed out the fact that, according to the wisdom of the East, this banner should bring misfortune to its adherents, for its symbol turned in the same direction as the hands of a clock, contrary to the swastika hallowed since prehistoric times in the Orient and in America.

Motoring one Sunday near Malmö, we noted a dance in the open air. At the corners of the enclosure were flag-poles flying Swedish flags, while on another, as tall as the other poles end to end, fluttered an immense red banner. Carl's terse comment was: "The Communists are giving a party." He assured us that, like the Conservatives, they are a negligible minority, the vast majority of the Swedes being Liberals.

Sunday at Ystads Saltsjöbaden was to us surprisingly Continental for a Lutheran country. The gayest dance of the week was held, with an orchestra singing occasional jazz songs in English although Swedish folk-dances were equally popular. The custom that any youth is permitted to choose as partner any girl made eating almost an impossibility for pretty lassies. It is a rebuff injurious to self-esteem (of which Scanians have an almost Danish amount) to refuse without an excuse at least as valid as a sprained ankle. Many friendships are made in this fashion, but the girl need not recognize the acquaintance afterwards.

The beach at Ystad faces the open Baltic. Falsterbo, a more fashionable resort, is situated on the extreme southeastern tip of Sweden. The Falsterbohus, on dunes beside the sea, is crowded from May to September with families from the neighboring châteaux who come for swimming and golf (there is an English professional in residence) as well as to tan themselves on the beach, gay with canvas chairs and brilliant parasols. An American-born countess complained to us of the incessant wind and chilly water.

Skåne is said to have been cultivated for ten thousand years. As in Jutland, a wealth of Bronze Age treasures has been unearthed. The Phœnicians are known to have come to the Baltic for amber and for furs, and, in all probability there was direct intercourse with the Mediterranean a thousand years before the Christian era. Beowulf tells of the prowess of the people of Svea in the sixth century, and we know that culture began in the south centuries before the settlement of northern Sweden. The author of *Things Seen in Sweden* states that there are three hundred Danish (once the language of Skåne) place-names in Lincolnshire and that the dialect of Yorkshire is seventy-five per cent Norse...in all probability from Skåne.

Knowing the antiquity of the district, the traveler from overseas is dumbfounded, on arrival at Malmö, by the absence of mellow age. Neither is Malmö—unlike Oslo, Göteborg, Stockholm, and Helsinki—a pioneer in modern experiment. Drab and nondescript as a town can well be is this third city of Sweden. Indeed, the only reason for our two visits was to use the admirable Hotel Kramer as a base from which to motor to Torup, Dalby, and Östarp and, on another occasion, before taking the ferry to Copenhagen.

Of all the castles visited in Skåne we found none more rewarding than Torup. Unlike castles of the British isles, châteaux of France, or even strongholds of northern Sweden, the homes of the nobility of Skåne, like the counts and countesses that inhabit them, are at first sight not especially impressive. My Illustrator and I first visited Torup in 1936. Finding ourselves in Malmö, we made the twelve kilometers one Sunday afternoon and were permitted to walk beside the lake.

On our return to Sweden we again visited Torup, trusting to Carl's good offices to get us within the walls. "The butler was formidable," said Carl, and so, he surmised, was the dog, for this is what the man said:

"The Baroness Coyet is resting. On no account is she to be disturbed, and at her door sleeps the dog."

Our interest in Torup waned. "There are other castles far finer" was our attitude.

"Name one!" a Swedish friend retorted. "You haven't been in the courtyard. You haven't seen the collections made by the 'Queen of Skåne.'"

After an intermission in which we had visited many castles, armed with an invitation for a definite day and hour we attempted to take Torup by storm. So sure were we of the exactness of

the time and the assurance that the Baroness
would receive us that we dispensed with Carl.
The butler was stocky, the butler was stolid as
only a Swede can be, the butler had no tongue
but Swedish, in which he gave us plainly to understand that the Baroness was not at home. Our
cards were glanced at and firmly returned. Impossible to admit anyone in the absence of the
Baroness.

"But we have an appointment," I said, "made
personally with the Baroness by so-and-so."

"I have no orders," mumbled the factotum,
about to shut the door in our faces.

At this juncture a little girl scampered across
the courtyard.

"Do you speak English?" I called. She shook
her head.

"Parlez-vous français?"

Did she? Did she not go to school in Paris? She
was here with her grandmother only for the holidays. She would call her sister.

Marie Louise, a few years older, received us
with quiet dignity. Two long braids of flaxen hair
were the only points she had in common with
Faust's Marguerite.

"I remember perfectly that grandmother said
you were coming," she told us. "Grandmamma
will be *désolée* that she forgot and went out to
tea."

"Shall we wait for her return?" I queried.

"Oh, but when grandmamma goes out to tea she stays for dinner!" said Marie Louise. "I shall do my best to show you the castle."

It seems to me, in retrospect, that had the "Queen of Skåne" been at home, we should not have seen or heard as much as we did under the auspices of our punctilious guide and of her seventeen-year-old sister, who joined us at a time when we were standing beside a Zorn portrait of her mother—a full-blown replica of herself. The girls explained that their parents were not dead, only in South America.

The front walls of Torup, hoary as its towers, measure three meters thick. The ancient rooms form a unique setting for modern, not modernistic, paintings. One of the forest of Torup is by Prince Eugen, a frequent visitor. The Baroness, we could see, was a knowing collector of paintings, books, and *objets d'art,* as well as of plants for her garden—one of elusive beauty. A screen was covered with silhouettes done from shadow-pictures of her guests—the King, Prince and Princess Bernadotte, the former Kaiser. In a tower room hung portraits of our guide and of the younger sister: "Ingeborg och Diana"— Diana being a French poodle.

"Diana sleeps outside grandmamma's room," the girls told us. In the hall I noticed leashes of every color of the rainbow.

"Have you a dog for each?" I asked.

"They are all Diana's! It is the custom to get a new one whenever we are in Paris."

A signed photograph of Svinhufvud, ex-president of Finland, stood near one inscribed to "Etta Coyet" from Selma Lagerlöf, who has stayed at Torup. A youthful likeness of the Baroness has the *finesse* of a French marquise. In the drawing-room hangs the portrait of the Coyet, magnificent in uniform, who purchased Torup from the State (Sweden having taken it from Denmark) and gave it to his nephew, Ingeborg's grandfather. Portraits of Charles X and Charles XI, leather murals, chairs covered with tapestry of the region, graced the baronial dining-hall. Over the mantel is a painting of "Fru Gorvel Faders Datter til Giedske," the builder of the castle. She and her third husband are buried in the cathedral crypt at Lund.

In the library we were shown many editions bearing the *ex libris* of their owner, but prized above all a manuscript volume, lifted from a glass case, in which the Baroness has recounted the history of Torup. Written in a large free hand, sumptuously bound, the volume is illustrated in color and pen and ink with copies of portraits, coats of arms, and engravings. Torup is shown in all stages of its development.

How intimate a picture we had been given of life in this château, probably the most elegant in Skåne! With what new eyes we looked out upon

Torup Castle

the garden where Diana picked her way between hedges clipped no less precisely than herself! How well we understood the adept placing of the Milles bronze mermaid disporting her two tails against the water of the moat! A glimpse into the life of another age had been vouchsafed us, a precious glimpse of an order of society destined to pass away.

In the neighborhood of Torup the farm of Östarp nestles among undulating hills. Pigs still wallow beneath the horse-chestnut at the entrance to the court, but, within, the house is preserved as a demonstration in the field of the open-air museum at Lund. This survival from Danish times is complete as to hand-painted furniture, home-woven tapestries, and even a room filled with cheeses. A table is set with wooden blocks for plates and horn spoons with which to dip into a common dish. A primitive oven is shown, and straw beehives against the plaster wall—timbered and topped with moss-grown thatch. Östarp haunts the memory, as does Dalby Church, dating from 1134, the oldest building in Skåne.

Restoration at Dalby may be glossed over because zeal has not been an instrument to destroy what it set out to preserve. The local schoolmaster takes pride in showing the crypt with its Romanesque columns. After lingering awhile among graves of Nils and Per and Lars, Dalghrens and Anderssons, we lunched adequately at Dalby Gästgifvavegård—that is to say, guest-house or inn. It stands on the Place of the Tinghus, or town hall, with a sign on its brick wall announcing that refreshments are served in its garden: *Gästis Trädgårdsservering!*

The Agricultural College at Alnarp may be visited en route from Malmö to Lund. A long-suffering husband gets the same reaction to my protracted tarryings on farms and in gardens as I to his on docks and premises where fish is cured.

"Cows are such awkward critters," my Illustrator insists. "Why can't they use their front legs when they get up. Any horse could give them pointers. 'Sitting Bull' may sound ferocious for an Indian, but sitting cows...ugh!"

We had passed a row of tethered Holsteins rising laboriously for drinks on approach of the water-wagon. A dull life, we agreed, to be stabled except from mid-April to August.

"It's a wise sow can recognize its offspring in this day of standardization," I said to a student at Alnarp. We stood in the house of the sows— many were suckling litters of eleven. The smell, my Illustrator to the contrary, was not insupportable.

"Swedish Blombacka," said the student guide, "seven hundred of them. Our horses are Ardenner, powerful Belgian, you know.

"Thirty men are taking the dairy course. We own two hundred cows, giving 2,500 liters of milk.

Altogether we use 6,000 liters daily, two-thirds for cheese, 320 kilos daily.

"The boys, if high-school graduates, receive the title of manager in a year, otherwise it takes two years. Some will direct estates in Skåne, and others go north to Ultuna, near Uppsala, to the Government college that gives the degree of Agri - nom. Here at Alnarp there are two hundred students studying to be farmers, gardeners, dairymen. We work on the farm by day and attend lectures at night. Besides these two colleges there are twelve agricultural schools in Sweden.

Lund was our next stopping-place. Rooms at the Grand Hotel on the square of the fountain tempted us to tarry. The university was not in session, and, traveling as we were with a graduate of the University of Uppsala and admitting a northern bias, we yet felt the dignity of the place and regretted that the intellectuals were out of town. Even the house of Tegnér (not far from the statue of the poet author of *Frithjofs Saga*) was undergoing repairs, but the Kulturhistoriska Museum, in interest rivaling Skansen, delighted us with interiors illustrative of the development of local arts and crafts. Figures in native dress, with provocative artistry, have been stationed at accustomed tasks. Coaches conjured into being in our imagination the champing horses which once drew vehicles to castled estates... traversing the dusty unfenced fields of Skåne. What of the lords

and ladies who mounted the high steps? Like the
steeds they are dust, but our memories of their
deeds revive on reading the names of the donors
of the coaches—names still potent in the province
of Skåne.

I have said that the intellectuals were out of
town. Perhaps I should not have insisted upon
this point had we not visited the Cathedral at
time of mass. As compared with northern Swedes,
the people were slovenly, the women, according to
age, in black or white uniformity of hats. What
men there were showed naught but credulity. The
service, intoned interminably, came to us as waves
of sound, words indistinguishable.

At twelve o'clock, so read the sign, the me-
chanical clock would perform. Crowds assembled.
Anticipation ran high. The great clock struck. We
waited until it was borne in upon us that there
was no need to wait. Groups, mostly from Denmark or the provinces, stolidly questioned the
verger. On Sunday, it seems, the clock performs
at one. Patiently the crowd returned, was indeed
augmented. The miniature knights clashed swords
as the hour of one struck in the belfry, and after a
moment of suspense the tiny trumpeter lifted his
horn, the door clicked, and the procession of the
Magi encircled the Virgin. The most rewarding
part of Lund Cathedral is the crypt with its wealth
of horizontal tombs—kings and queens and potentates of the Middle Ages slumbering in time-

blackened effigy. The size and character of the arches recalled the famous Norman crypt of Worcester, England, once visited by us at time of a Three Choir Festival.

The castles that come to mind when my thoughts turn towards Skåne are those where the hosts gave us the most cordial welcome. The three are of unequal merit, Borgeby, Skarhult, and Bosjökloster. These we visited from Lund, not to mention in detail Ellinge (estate of Baron Wrangel, whose ancestors, like those of many other barons, were generals under Gustavus Adolphus), Örtofta, Viderup, or Knutstorp, birthplace of Tycho Brahe. We had seen Tosterup with its added tower built by Brahe as an observatory.

Ernst Norlind, the artist owner of Borgeby, studied in London with Brangwyn. He has also written many volumes which prove his skill as a literary artist—one of the latest, on Italian art and religion, has been translated into Danish. In appearance Mr. Norlind is an example of an American's idea of a foreign artist—sensitive, bearded, vivacious, though not Bohemian.

The approach to Borgeby, past clustered stables and through a tower marked 1400, is medieval. The glass of a skylight is the only innovation in the newer castle (where Christian IV was entertained) dating from 1600.

"Even good kings got drunk in those days," said Norlind. "The king told an aide to write a report of the banquet, because he could never remember on the cold gray morning after. Even the aide had to use a system of stars—from one to six—to describe the function, he being half-seas over. It is said that at Borgeby he began with all six, for, at the banquet, Christian toasted twenty-six kings. Each time the noblemen broke their glasses. The final toast was to the Devil—at which the windows of the castle were smashed.

"Bishops, too, conformed to the standards of the day. The Bishop of Lund, to whom this estate once belonged, took all the land he could see from the tower of our little fort yonder to enlarge the mantle of the Holy Lawrence. No better than a common robber!"

Norlind, in his own painting, has been influenced by the Italians, but he has developed a style individual, modern, and sincere. There is a subtle use of color, a spiritual content in these canvases that links them to the Chinese. His most prized possession was a cast of a head of Christ...the very one, by an unknown sculptor, that had excited our admiration at Trondheim.

"O to have time to do all that one wants to do!" he exclaimed. "When I was young I carved wood; I was a goldsmith. Why do we live under pressure? Now in the old days there was a countess who lived in this castle and she liked a game of an evening. One of her two companions was called away, and it is not possible to have two dummies. The countess sent her man to the highway with orders to stop the first well-dressed person and ask him if he played cards. The stranger was a young man. The trio played all day, they played all night, the next day and the day after. Weeks, months passed... all the young man's life. In those days one had time to play Preference!''

Baroness Schwerin, who, with her sister, is the present occupant of Skarhult, rejoices in the fact that her brother's son, the heritor of the castle, is not only a doctor of philosophy but an archæologist.

The Baroness was born in the castle. Every brick and stone is beloved by her. She cherishes, too, the branching ivy planted by her mother on the major tower, the astonishing hedges, the decorative cat—a lordly white Angora. It was her father who purchased the place from Karl XIV Johan (Bernadotte). The oldest portions are twelfth century. The hedges nearest the house are of box, but others are of beech too high for any but an athlete to vault, and these surround welltended grass plots. We were consumed with curiosity as to the gardeners' method of entrance.

In impeccable English the Baroness told us of the finding of a secret stair. With the aid of a torch held by the butler we were allowed to peer into a subterranean cell inhabited for two years by a witch. It must have been witchcraft that enabled her to survive.

Trolleholm

Trollenäs has been so modernized that it suggests the country-house of an American multimillionaire. My Illustrator refused to look at it, so, leaving him in the car, I explored the grounds. They have, in common with most Scanian castles, moats with swans, beds of pink spiræa, diversity of formal hedges, espaliered fruit-trees, one (always one) spreading copper beech, and more than the usual number of tortured-looking "up-sidedown trees," the Japanese weeping birch, popularly supposed to be planted with roots in air. The castle was built by Nils Trolle, whose monogram it bears as well as an immense relief of a troll, symbolically brainless but with trailing tail. Baron Trolle, I understand, is the nephew of Count Trolle Bonde, head of this illustrious family and owner of Trolleholm. The latter is a widower who spends much of his time in Stockholm or on the Riviera.

Trolleholm, most impressive of Skåne's castles, is a symphony in brick, the whole harmonious as a composition by Beethoven. A cloud-burst and our arrival were simultaneous. Roads were flooded. Semi-darkness reigned. Lightning caressed the emblematic iron trolls topping the towers and threatened to rock the open-boat crests of the Bondes. Marooned in our car, we waited, and as the storm subsided to a dripping from rain-drenched chestnuts, an intermittent patter in cross-flecked moat, we could distinguish with our mind's ear strains similar to Debussy's "Jardin sous la Pluie."

Trolle Ljungby, Trollenäs, Trolleholm are names not to be trifled with by any sorcerer's apprentice. Although Count Trolle Bonde was not in residence, we were indeed honored to be received at Bosjökloster by his younger brother, its owner, Count Bonde. In the person of this Swedish nobleman the Bonde family tree has borne rich fruit. His welcome was, we thought, all the more courteous because of the limitations of his English (and of our German). How much the easier part

to refuse to see us! How greatly to the benefit of
world amity and international fellowship to receive the stranger at the gate!

The white walls of Bosjökloster are those of a
former convent. The buildings, facing about a
court, include a parish church, beyond which a plot
contains tombs of long-forgotten nuns. The *kloster*
or convent was erected in 1110. An iron-studded
outer door to the main building bears the date
1564.

Our credentials having been presented, we
awaited in the courtyard. The door opened, and
on the threshold, unmistakably, stood the Count.
In his person he seemed to sum up the sterling
qualities of the Swedish nobility. Stocky, of medium age and stature, he was, more than most,
courtly. He welcomed us to his castle and apologized unnecessarily for his English. He was
dressed in the sport clothes of a country gentleman—gray, like those of most Scandinavians who
rarely wear the ruddy browns affected in England.
With pride the Count showed us a scroll with the
coats of arms in color of the owners of the house
since its foundation, beginning with a shield with
the figure of an abbess. Modestly he had not yet
added his own, although he had bought the estate
thirty years ago, presumably upon the death of his
father, having spent his childhood at his birthplace, Trolleholm. Most valuable of documents
shown us was one in Latin, dated 1354, sent to the

convent by the Pope. It is kept in an Italian cabinet whose secret drawers require a slender hand to open. A drawing-room on the second floor was furnished in a taste so resplendent as to be to Americans breath-taking. On the walls hung paintings by the teacher of Rembrandt; mirrors in ornate frames reflected a marble Mercury in size more appropriate to an art gallery. A crimson-and-gold salon held family portraits. The somber dining-hall seemed more in keeping with the spirit of the place, as did a corridor with stair and view over the lake. Here were mounted antlers of deer.

"Do you hunt?" my Illustrator inquired. To which our host replied:

"It is not hunting, that is done on horseback, but we still have good shooting."

The Count was pleased to hear of the excellent impression made by his youngest brother, attached some years ago to the Swedish legation in Washington. At parting the Count chose a felt hat and cane and stepped outside to see us off. After much bowing in the garden he stood beside the convent well. Around him fluttered pigeons, white as doves or pallid nuns, in keeping with the tradition of Bosjökloster where peace reigns, as it reigned in cloistral days.

"Bosjökloster," I said to Carl, as we returned to the car, "how does one pronounce it?"

With an inimitable twinkle in his eye Carl mimicked, "*Boo shö kloster,* if you are a woman, but it is more manly to say *Boo chö kloster—j* is funny in Swedish. I think, though, the Count said it the more refined way!''

Båstad may be reached by an inland route from Lund or by the longer coast drive by way of Landskrona with its view of Ven, Tycho Brahe's island; Hälsingborg, with its ferries plying to Helsingør, its dominating Kärnan or Keep; Sofiero (country-place of the Crown Prince), with gardens open to the public daily from one to two o'clock, its English borders, bear-cub fountain, and Princess Ingrid roses; Kullaberg, with its lighthouse and over-vaunted cliffs. We chose to go by the shorter road knowing that we should return along the coast on our way to Copenhagen.

The cloud-burst that had overtaken us at Trolleholm had caused floods at Båstad. The estimated loss was a million kronor in damage to market-gardens and dwellings, to be covered by a *Tipsmedel* or lottery of sorts.

Sheltering hills, hot sunshine, and air from the sea give to Båstad a climate unique in Sweden. There can be no more dramatic demonstration of the results of this combination than the phenomenal growth of trees (planted since 1900) in the period gardens at Norrviken. A student guide would willingly have given me the botanical names of the eighteen thousand specimens!

The beach at Båstad, having so recently been flooded, was still muddy and is, at all times, inferior to that at out-of-the-world Torekov. Visitors to Båstad bathe frequently at distant Torekov because, owing to its situation, the water is saltier than on the tideless Baltic.

Skånegården ("the Skåne House") is unparalleled in Scandinavia. Indeed, there is nothing quite like it anywhere else in the world. My Illustrator and I add it with enthusiasm to our list of romantic de luxe hotels: the Taj in Bombay, Shepheard's in Cairo, the Hôtel de la Cité at Carcassonne. The gratitude of travelers goes to Mr. Ludvig Nobel, nephew of the famous Alfred, who created this hotel and makes it his hobby. Gueltler, the architect, has wrought wonders in cloistral form. The building, of hand-pressed bricks, is constructed around an outer and an inner court. Every detail of wrought iron, woven stuffs, furniture and rugs, does credit to Swedish craftsmen, but the triumph of the whole, the three-crowned glory, is to be found in the gardens. It is small wonder that the unknowing translate the word "Skåne Gården."

"His Majesty!" exclaimed an Englishwoman. To habitués of the restaurant on the water where guests at Skånegården lunch and dine the sight was no novelty. The tall lean figure of Gustaf V, King of Sweden, central personage at a table in an alcove was easily distinguishable to diners. It is the King's habit to stay at Skånegården during the international tennis matches held annually in

July. Indeed, practically the entire hotel is given up to the royal party. We were amazed that we should have rooms so near to those of the King.

The service, our first night at the restaurant, was above reproach. At nine o'clock an operatic soprano, addressing herself especially to His Majesty, sang an aria from *La Bohème* and, as encore, "The Blue Danube." After the departure of the King the supper-dance began. The next evening was less successfully arranged. Cottagers had gathered for the annual tennis ball. Those who were not willing to pay an extra two kronor were required to depart before nine-thirty. The King, swathed in a military cloak, had come the mere step from the hotel in one of his five Cadillacs. The ladies of the dinner-party were in line to receive him, and he shook hands with each one —in full sight of diners and with villagers' noses pressed to the window-panes. The party took their places at table. It was then that the demoralization of service began. Most of us—but not all—were content with the rôle of the proverbial cat. Our neighbors on this occasion were from Chicago. The loud-voiced head of the family shouted to the distracted maître d'hôtel:

"We've been waiting an hour for raspberries. Is there any chance we'll get 'em?"

The waiter, in the awed voice appropriate to the occasion replied: "The *King* is dining here to-night and his party must be served."

"If I'd known the King was here, I wouldn't have come," yelled the rambunctious one.

Later in the evening the peace of our cloister was broken by the same irate voice, its owner probably raspberryless. A door stood ajar and, in the glow of light, we glimpsed outspread motor maps. "See," said the evidently unpacified, "see, we could get to Ystad to-night!"—with vicious accent he pronounced the word "Worsted."

Next morning, the King, in white flannels and dark coat, carrying a tennis racquet, left the hotel for the courts. A program of the tournament, posted in the hotel, gave the schedule of the matches. As usual, Gustaf V was entered as "Mr. G."...his incognito. He played daily during our stay, in doubles from twelve to one fifteen, and again at three. No blazing sun was hot enough to daunt his spirit, although he would, we noted, frequently lift his felt hat from thick gray hair to mop his brow—evidently depending upon its shade while in action. A valiant figure, we thought, for a gentleman whose eightieth birthday is to be celebrated in June. As we watched him play at the Casino, supported by the agile Matejka, we felt that we had beheld a similar scene before. Indeed we had, in many news reels. The right arm with thin gold bracelet, sleeve rolled to the elbow, possessed swift strength. Not only at net but especially in back stroke the Sovereign exerted his wizardry. His quaint good humor when out of luck, his readiness to applaud an opponent, was as kingly as kingly could be. An English girl was umpire, and the language used, even in scoring, was English.

A thoughtful Swedish friend had written to the Countess Lewenhaupt, hostess and director of the hotel, to arrange to have us presented to His Majesty. We were told that the matter would be brought to the King's attention at eight in the morning when he received his mail. Then came apologies that His Majesty had been too hurried to look at his mail. On the third day of our stay the Countess joined us when we were breakfasting. She had given the cards to the King's aide who would present them when opportunity arose ... she hoped, but could promise nothing.

Shall we spend this last morning dawdling here, we asked each other, waiting for a message that will probably not come? Yet we found ourselves lingering in the garden, watching for the now familiar car with its immense crown of Sweden. Enchanting at all hours of day and night was this garden, with its terraces of fragrant bush honeysuckle, its borders of regal phlox, its swallows dipping over the sunken pool where lilies, mammoth white or crimson, flaunted their beauty among ruffled pads. White butterflies fluttered over the lavender; outside the King's windows the blue-and-yellow flag of Sweden stirred in the breeze.

An hour passed. What fools—such ardent democrats as we are! How scathing we have been about friends who presented their daughters at the Court of Saint James. But Gustaf is such a democratic King...if there are to be kings...almost an old friend...we have seen him so often.

A messenger for Mr. and Mrs. Oakley! The King's aide-de-camp will arrange a meeting if they will be at the tennis courts at two-thirty. Never had I expected to be presented at court and certainly not at a tennis court!

How appropriate for a tennis-loving King to receive at tennis—a French inheritance perhaps. The match His Majesty had been watching ended promptly at two-thirty. Surrounded by ladies and gentlemen, whose faces and even costumes had become as familiar to us as those of Queen Mary, the King was seated in a wicker chair in the reserved section. The aide presented our cards to the chamberlain, the King's shadow (a gentleman resembling M. Picard who told us that he was Scotch) who gave them to the King. We were summoned. The King rose and advanced to meet us. The aisle in which the presentation took place gave me scant room for the appropriate curtsy and my Illustrator none at all for a courtly bow. The King spoke of our book and, when asked if he would be gracious enough to accept a copy, said it would give him pleasure to receive it. We spoke of mutual friends whom he had decorated—the editor of the *Amer-*

ican Scandinavian Review, and a translator from the Swedish, of the Wettergrens to whose names he warmed; of our pleasure that the Crown Prince would come to Philadelphia in June. "Oh, yes, I know about the celebrations in Delaware," he said.

We expressed admiration for his gardens at Solliden, shown us by Baron Rüdbeck the year before. "I could not have been there," he said, implying, in courtly fashion, that had he been he would have received us. Again, at parting, our hands were shaken cordially, and the spare figure, the patriarch of Scandinavian monarchs, made a kingly exit to a waiting Cadillac.

"His Majesty is so kind," the Countess had said, and Gertrud Wettergren had used the same expression. Kindliness is a characteristic not frequently associated with kings. We thought of the Monument to Bernadotte that marks the spot at Hälsingborg where Napoleon's Marshal landed in 1810—elected to be crown prince of the Swedish people—and we were convinced that in the troublous century that followed the peoples of Scandinavia must never have regretted the introduction of the house of Bernadotte.

Long live the King!

Part Three
DENMARK

Copenhagen ‡
Højbroplads and the Spire of St·Nicholas

In the City of Bicycles

CHAPTER XII

COPENHAGEN THE METROPOLITAN

KRONBORG on the right is, to a returning expatriated Dane, what the Statue of Liberty is to a home-coming American. The battlements of Hamlet's castle rise abruptly from the sea, blocking the vision of low-lying Elsinore. Less than two hours will bring the voyager to the copper spires of Copenhagen, and if he be of Danish birth, this is the sight for which he has long languished. To him the saddest sight on earth is Kronborg on the left.

Copenhagen is a yachtman's paradise, and, at heart, every Scandinavian has inherited a love of boats, both great and small, from Viking forebears. Our first arrival aboard a transatlantic liner was complete as to impressions of Skagerrak and Kattegat, of Kronborg on the right, but in Copenhagen stopped short at the free port, where we were deposited as though, like the bales about us, we were but pausing for reshipment, as indeed we were. Another year's approach was of more enduring worth, for this time we had come from Sweden by ferry from Malmö, past Åland barques riding at anchor, and were to dock amid the turmoil of lesser shipping—passing within hail of the King's Palace as well as of the fish restaurants of the Gammel Strand.

To me the life of Copenhagen's water-front, devoid of any sordid docks, in summer scintillating in sunlight or brilliantly lighted after dark, is the most alluring of her many attractions... with which the imported gaiety of her night-life does not compare. The dwellers in the capital boast not, as they should, of the harbor round trips to north and south, an hour each, or of the twenty-six-minute route from Christianborg beneath the bridges... although they have indeed named these local boats for Aladdin. (Ours was a drab *Aladdin VIII*.) In this respect the powers that be might take a leaf from Stockholm's book.

Among remembered yesterdays the morning of the arrival of the *Gripsholm* stands clear-cut as the dragon-tailed spire of Copenhagen's Bourse. Our impatience to greet relatives had brought us to Langelinie while yet the *Gripsholm* floated like a white swan on the horizon. With magical rapidity she swallowed space, transforming herself, before our astonished gaze, into a legendary queen of ships, proudly wearing for decoration the three crowns of Sweden. Curtailing her magic speed, in deference to mortal docks, she allowed herself to be drawn shoreward by four rollicking dolphin-

like tugs... recalling to our minds the mytho-
logical Gefion, whose fountain stands hard by,
ploughing the island of Zealand (on which Copenhagen stands) from the soil of Sweden (where
now Lake Vänern remains) with her four sons
turned to oxen.

Gently the giant liner nestled to the wharf.
Greetings had been waved to those recognized so
high and mightily removed upon the promenade
deck. What more fitting than that we, united with
our family, should celebrate but a stone's throw
away, at the Pavilion of the Royal Yacht Club,
whose restaurant, set amid flowers and flags of
visiting nationals, overlooked the white yacht of
the King and the innumerable smaller craft of his
devoted subjects!

Leaving the Yacht Club and the wooded promenade of Langelinie, where, near the *Gripsholm,*
were anchored steamers from Liverpool, Barrow,
and Bombay (the P. and O. liner *Viceroy of India*
luring us with familiar hull and high buff cabins,
the motor vessel *Canada,* outfitting for Orient at
dry-docks of Burmeister and Wain), we turned towards the heart of the city. To some travelers this
will mean the plaza of the Hotel Angleterre, while
to others, who stay at the Palace Hotel, it will
mean the square of the Town Hall. I remember
saying to a taxi driver, "The Palace," to which he
replied, pithily,

"Do you mean the Palace or the Palace Hotel?"

The Turisthotel had repelled us by its name—*tourist* in English having a less happy signification than *traveler*—but I have since heard that this is indeed one of the few modern houses where mine host occupies himself with the welfare of his guests according to the good old tradition.

My impressions of Denmark's capital are threefold—by boat, by motor, and at night. In any daytime excursion the city's copper spires are conspicuous, and our first consideration on arrival was to visit the numerous churches to which these appendages belong and the Bourse and Christianborg (seat of the Rigsdag), possessors of two of the more noteworthy. The three-crowned spire of Christianborg rises perhaps most delectably when seen from the peaceful enclosed garden of the Library—once, incongruously, a war harbor where ships were outfitted. To-day no water remains but in the lily-pool. While on paths between the rose-beds children feed pigeons, the philosopher Søren Kierkegaard looks benignly from his pedestal. In a near-by park we were to see the quaint seated figure of Hans Christian Andersen, such a speaking likeness that one can almost hear his voice telling the stories from the book he holds. On his birthday and indeed on high days and holidays Danish children still pile nosegays at his feet.

The handsomest churches, as well as the Bourse, and Christianborg and Rosenborg palaces, date from the reign of that enterprising builder King Christian IV. The style used has come to be known as Flemish Renaissance. Because of its numerous churches Copenhagen might well be deemed a very religious city. The Church of the Saviour is, perhaps, the most harmonious of the older buildings architecturally because erected at one period. The immense mass of carved oak that is the organ bears the date 1698. It is supported by two almost life-sized blanketed elephants. The effect was to me ludicrously incongruous.

"Why elephants?" I asked a Dane who had accompanied us.

His face was solemn. "Because," said he, "the elephant represents the highest wisdom. You will see stone elephants at the entrance to the Carlsberg Brewery. The highest order in Denmark is the Order of the Elephant—rarely given to any but royal personages."

"Oh, the Order of the Elephant," I said, still but half convinced of the seriousness of my friend. "I shall remember."

"Other lands, other ways," I thought, swallowing my surprise at the statuesque angels guarding the chancel, the cherubs hovering about the too-much-gilded font. I had in other Scandinavian countries become accustomed to the glare from white glass windows thrown upon portraits of former pastors, which to my lay mind would more appropriately have adorned a museum or parish-house. The spire of this Church of the Saviour on the island of Amager is one of the most alluring. An exterior helical stair mounts to its summit. The steeple of the Nikolaj Kirke is perhaps, in interest, its only rival. The King attends the marble church adjacent to the Amalienborg Palace. In the Cathedral, better known as the Church of Our Lady, are the Thorwaldsen Christ and Apostles. The Round Tower of Trinity Church is now used as an observatory for amateur astronomers. This tower overlooks the quiet court where honor students at the University are domiciled in quarters suggesting by their dignity the Temple in London. In the neighborhood is Landermærket with its wealth of quaint houses, a surviving bit of old Copenhagen.

Grundtvig's Church is in another category. It is still under construction upon an eminence on the outskirts of the town. As an example of modern Danish architecture it is unparalleled. Built entirely of the native brick, a Pompeian yellow, it is a brilliant adaptation of the typical Danish village church. The result of corbie-steps magnified to a Gargantuan scale is striking and not unpleasing. The uncompleted interior is perhaps a little less grateful to eyes accustomed to a Norman or Gothic arch and to a "dim religious light" conducive to meditation.

The chapel is already finished, as are the apartment houses forming units of the architectural whole. To my queries as to the need of such a structure the replies were all in the negative. It will never be filled except on an occasional holy day, was the consensus of opinion. The Danes are not church-goers, not even religious like the Norwegians and Swedes. As for Bishop Grundtvig, he was not a bishop in the ordinary acceptation of the word, but was given the honorary title of bishop for his good works in the field of education. More than any other, Grundtvig (born, at Udby in Zealand, in 1783 and died in 1872), by his reawakening of national pride, and by the establishment of schools for adult education and more especially the appropriate instruction of youthful farmers, aroused the Danes, lethargic from adversity, and inspired them to tread the path of progress.

A fashionable quarter of the town is the district known as Hellerup. Here, in a dignified mansion on the water-front, dwell the counselor of the American Legation, Mr. North Winship, and his charming wife. During the interim between the departure of Ruth Bryan Owen (now Kammerjunkerinde Rohde, who would have won the hearts of the Danish people by her gay little book *Denmark Caravan* had she not already done so as the American Minister from May, 1933, to August, 1936) and the arrival of Mr. Alvin Mansfield Owsley of Texas, her eloquent successor (who, despite his recent residence in Ireland, where many go only to kiss the Blarney Stone, still rel-

The Fish-Market

ishes calling a spade a spade), Mr. Winship held the office of chargé d'affaires. Fortunate possessors of a letter from this distinguished gentleman to Turistforeningen, we were showered, I might almost say pelted, with courtesies during our entire sojourn in Denmark.

The Director of the Tourist Bureau (like that in Finland partly under government patronage) was an executive American advertisers might envy. He was a typical Dane, blond, ruddy, robust,

of Copenhagen ✦

youthful for one in such a position, and, after the fashion of the land, smoking a strong cigar. He had given up an engineer's career, he told us, to study advertising. Conversation moved intermittently as telephone calls interrupted and astoundingly high piles of letters were brought to await his signature. His zeal was, we found, as indefatigable in play as in work. Under his tutelage we were to be participants in the night-life of Copenhagen.

"Danes can be happy because well off," remarked the Director. "We are honest, clean, and sober—the soberness the result of high taxes on liquor which have saved the workingman in spite of himself. If you ever see a drunken man, it will probably be a sailor or a Swede who has come to get a more generous share than is allowed under Swedish prohibitions. Men who drink to excess are not respected in Denmark. The Danes no longer say, 'Oh, he's a jolly good fellow,' as is still said in some countries.

"In Copenhagen we know how to enjoy an evening, spending no more than an American dollar. Families may go to certain restaurants for coffee, bringing food. There is a café for motor cyclists, and there is Tivoli. Come with me to-night!"

Thus it was that at nine that evening my Illustrator and I found ourselves on the open road with our new-found friend, wedged into a battered Citroën. Kerlövkro (*kro* being garden and Kërlöv the name of the suburb) was the first dance-hall visited. This is the motor cyclists'— not to mention cyclists' and motorists'—paradise. Throngs, many in leather togs, were dancing on a platform beneath the stars. On the stage a German band accompanied a warbling Gretchen. Tables were jammed. Fifteen øre was the charge for beer. Others lingered over an order of coffee or *snaps*. Any waiter hurrying the humblest guest in Denmark would be instantly dismissed.

Our next stop was at Tivoli, where we threaded
our way through the reproduction of a medieval
village—a lay-figure of an alchemist leered from
a latticed window opposite the apothecary shop
beside the lake, where stands the Ferry Inn.

"In old times," said our host, "boats were in-
adequate, and folks were delayed for days waiting
their turn to cross the water. This is a replica of
an old-time ferry inn, and the people who frequent it are habitués. They come to drink beer and
sing ... and if you don't sing, or don't know their
songs, they will throw you out or make you serve
them. The waitresses wear their names on plaques
so you can tell Ida from Sophie. There's no for-
mality at the Ferry."

The room shook with sound rising from lusty
young throats. The air was dense with smoke, and
it was with relief I noticed there were no empty
places, feeling sure that we would have been
thrown out; but as we pushed our way between
tables, our host joined in the songs with such
gusto as to cover our deficiency.

Leaving Tivoli we went to the Family Gardens,
so many that, like the fish restaurants, they are
known by numbers. These are situated in shaded
allées in a distinctive district known as Frederiksberg, once a suburb, now completely surrounded by
the metropolis but keeping its identity and not a
part of the municipality of Copenhagen. The
Family Gardens are a remnant of days when ex-

cursionists were permitted to picnic here. The humblest workers come to dance, and fiddle, and sing, bringing their own refreshments. At the entrance a stout dame presided over beer bottles, while a strident vendor shouted to the lads to buy flowers for their partners. At every table under the trees, oil-burning lamps, with petticoats of various colors, presented a contrast to the festoons of electric bulbs seen at Tivoli. A sign *Welcomen* hung over what we were told was a "closed" but hospitable party of dancers.

On to Lorry's! Not to know Lorry's is not to know Copenhagen, we had been told, yet Lorry's is in the "village" of Frederiksberg!

"The French," so our informant had said, "are stupid. They go first to the café, then home to bed." We demurred...then remembered that Parisian night clubs are run for foreigners.

"Now in Copenhagen we go home to dinner, then go out. There's Lorry's. You may stay all night but not in one section. You begin in the beer-garden; you go to Drachmann's Inn; to Lynby which closes at two; then you may dance in the night club."

At Lorry's, as elsewhere, our host met friends and fraternized with waiters and strangers—after the fashion of young Danes. He beamed with pride in the wholesome amusements shared by his country's humblest citizens, and his good-fellowship, as was evident, was not assumed but of the heart.

He led us first to the Drachmann Inn (in French taste at the time of Molière), dear to the Danish poet as was Bellman's tavern to the Swede.

Here, under ancient rafters, and in a congenial atmosphere, two mellow artists sang to us refrains beloved by Scandinavians, with plaintive undertone of harp-lute and mandolin.

Lorry's climax—the bar and jazz of the night club did not tempt us—came at Lynby, the Tyrolean indoor beer-garden where the sun sets nightly with Alpine glow and realistic stars glimmer overhead. Our party ensconced itself at a central table, ordering, according to taste, beer, grapetonic, or *snaps,* caviar and shrimps, and more and bigger cigars, and still more black coffee—seven spoonfuls to the cup is the rule in Denmark. Stage shows by members of the band amused the throng. Our own enjoyment was doubled when a huntsman after playing a horn curtsied like a maiden. Our host was surprised to hear that in the United States actors do not curtsy. Songs by the audience alternated with stage shows. The Danish melodies were followed by "The Merry Widow" in German, "Tipperary" in English, American college songs popular in Scandinavia since movies, schools, and radios have made English familiar ... and before we knew it, two o'clock was striking—closing time for the Tyrolean garden.

Tivoli is perhaps, since Vauxhall is no more, the most famous amusement park in the world.

In addition to display of electrically illuminated fountains, cascades, the fantastically lighted frigate, the usual switchbacks, it gives the visitor, in return for a trifling entrance fee, acrobats, a pantomime in the old tradition, a symphonic orchestra. Open-air restaurants within the grounds are not beyond the most modest purse, while Wivex, in letters of light, proclaims itself at the gateway—perhaps the most renowned restaurant in Copenhagen. The name Wivex brings back memories of an evening when, after duck with *mirabellen* and an *Is Bombe* (a candle-lighted ice dolphin in conjunction with a bowl of frozen custard) we entered Tivoli to attend the concert. It was the night when Ove Peters, Denmark's lately risen star, was soloist in César Franck's "Symphonic Variations for Piano and Orchestra." When an enormous wreath was presented to the player, the audience rose, clamorous in applause, and was rewarded by a magical performance of Chopin's "Minute Waltz."

Acrobats were swinging in midair. As we passed, a girl from the audience, in clinging henna gown, was persuaded to mount a trapeze. Roars of laughter greeted her awkwardness. Losing hat and handbag, she was in a fair way to lose her balance.

"Don't worry," commented a friendly youth. "She does this every night...she is one of the best gymnasts."

The Frigate of Tivoli ◆

To restaurants in Copenhagen, I should say, there is no end. Many gourmets would give the palm to Frascati (*"Paris on Raadhus pladsen"*) or to Oscar Davidsen—carrying on traditionally with leather-aproned servitors as it has since the days of H. C. Andersen. It was here we first noticed smartly clad women smoking cigars—a sight as commonplace in Copenhagen as cigarette smoking in New York. My preference is for the Søpavillon, to lunch beneath the shelter of a flamboyant parasol beside "the lakes" on which youthful scions of the Vikings watch their miniature boats dart uncontrolled before the wind.

Sleeping and waking hours are punctuated at the Palace Hotel by the persistent chime of the Town Hall clock.

"What does it say?" I inquired—for obviously it had a message to impart.

"Oh, that is the town-crier's tune," I was told, "waking the citizens at six and ringing the curfew at nine."

We had explored even the innermost recesses of the modern Town Hall, of which Copenhagen's natives are duly proud—even unduly, I was about to say, remembering Stockholm.

"Who are the prehistoric horn-blowers?" I asked, referring to figures on a pedestal outside our bedroom windows. For answer I was sent to the National Museum.

Mr. Broholm, curator of Danish Antiquities, not only transported us, as we hung on his words, to the section of Danish Antiquities, but vivified for us, as no human being had ever done before, the Ages of Stone and Bronze.

Room after room of treasures of fabulous value
was unlocked. Our ignorance was abysmal. No one
had troubled to tell us that this collection is
unique. Nor had we known the wealth of finds
within the realm of Denmark. Passing numerous
cases of arrows and flint hatchets, prehistoric
utensils, we reached the Age of Bronze and what
we had come to seek—the bronze *lurs*. There were
seven in perfect preservation. The central case
contained a pair of these immense S-shaped battle-
horns.

"The trumpeters went in pairs," Mr. Broholm
explained, "never singly. If you wish to hear the
sound of a *lur,* you have only to buy a record!
You are right in calling the horn-blowers prehistoric. They were not Vikings, as many suppose,
but of the Bronze Age, and we know how they
were clad." So saying he led us to a case in which
a man's brown woolen tunic and cloak shared
honors with a woman's upper garment, belt-
buckle, and short skirt.

"How do you know they wore such clothes?" I
incredulously inquired.

"Because these are the actual garments...
found in their oaken caskets in Denmark, where,
even to this day, treasures are unearthed."

Sun chariots have always allured me, for I am,
at heart, half sun-worshiper. The National Museum possesses a chariot fashioned to propitiate
a fickle sun-deity who had perhaps—if modern

times are a criterion—veiled his face too often
from tillers of the soil in dire need of favor at
seed- and harvest-time.

"One room more," Mr. Broholm commented,
and I remember thinking it would be an anticlimax. But no, the entire contents of the gallery
were rune stones. Some of these mysterious
masses of carved granite are attributed to the
Bronze Age while others are as late as the Viking
era. The runic characters can be read by archæologists, but there is one upright stone that defies
them. It dates from a later period than most, for,
in addition to the chiseled serpent, there is a cross.
Perhaps the symbols around its border are mere
decorations. In the courtyard of the museum we
lingered to admire a central rune stone and vine-
topped chambered cairn.

"Since our visit to the museum we know why
Denmark has chosen to put a dolmen on her five-
krone notes," I said.

"Yes," the curator replied, "on the five-krone
notes, not on the ten—because archæologists are
all poor!"

Let those who will delight in the New Glyptotek
and Thorwaldsen Museum; to me they must take
second and third places partly because of the in-
discriminate showing of replicas in stone or plaster in conjunction with original Greek, Roman, or
modern sculpture. The artistry of the whole is
thereby sacrificed.

The Thorwaldsen Museum is built in the form of an Etruscan tomb. The master lies buried in the central court. It seems fitting that this son of an Iceland carver of figureheads should, after a life spent mostly in Italy, rest among his long-famous works. Here is a model of the popular "Lion of Lucerne" commemorating the Swiss Guard of Louis XVI; here are familiar heads of Sir Walter Scott and Lord Byron, and the seated Byron to be found at Cambridge.

Georg Jensen, called by art critics "the greatest craftsman in silver for the last three hundred years," began life as a sculptor. He attained an international reputation early in life, and examples of his work are to be seen in the museums of the world. The shop that bears his name, at 40 Ostergade, is a Mecca of tourists. Indeed, when a cruise ship is in port, travelers flock to Jensen's in such numbers that the management is often obliged to close the doors. On our visit we were shown an oval fish platter with stylized dolphin curveting on the cover, a piece designed by Nielsen for H. R. H. Crown Prince Frederik of Denmark. An inkstand, to be used in signing papers of State, was presented to His Majesty on his Silver Jubilee. Examples of Jensen's own design are often embellished with motif of conventional flower or fruit. Jensen silver is, of course, always solid and is distinguished by its luster, being first oxidized and afterward polished. On the walls hung a portrait of the founder, who died in 1935 at the age of seventy, and a map of the world showing communities to which Jensen exports—including Greenland and Afghanistan.

"Only Russia," we were told, "does not buy from us."

At the factory we met Jørgen Jensen, one of the artists, recalled from Stockholm where, at the time of his father's death, he had his own establishment. Many of the craftsmen begin their training at fifteen, as did Harold Nielsen. Prince Sigvard, son of the Crown Prince of Sweden, is a noted designer. We were permitted to visit the establishment where a hundred and fifty craftsmen, including a few women, work in daylight and good air, under altogether perfect conditions, for eight hours a day with an eight-day holiday once a year. The most highly trained worker receives seven thousand kroner yearly, a high wage for Danish labor. This is the largest artistic silversmith manufactory in the world.

"Silver is a noble metal," said our guide. "It does not tarnish; it is the copper mixed with it that does. We buy silver in the raw—we call it 'pearls'—from England."

"From England!" I exclaimed.

"Well, it comes originally from Mexico, but it is too difficult for us to deal directly with the Mexicans." He held up a handful of brilliant silver nuggets.

Nyhavn

Huge ovens melt the "pearls" to bars. The heat
that emanated from the furnaces seemed to us
enough to melt human flesh, but the workers were
apparently unconcerned and unconscious of the
deafening noise of hammers. Handwork and the
name of Jensen are synonymous. Even the flat
silver pressed in molds is afterward hammered
and fashioned with fine saws. Sweepings of silver
sawdust are gathered. Fifty thousand kroner a
year is the value of the siftings from the sinks.

Royal Copenhagen porcelain is known the world
over. The factory was founded in 1771 under the
patronage of Queen Juliane Marie. Every Danish
home with any pretence to comfort has a set of
the traditional *Müssel mallet,* a meandering sweet-

pea design in blue copied from the Chinese. Much of this pattern is sold to England and some to the United States. Hordes visit the show-rooms of Royal Copenhagen at Amagertorv—in an ancient house which legend associates with the name of Dyveke, the Dutch girl-mistress of Christian II, who died from eating poisoned cherries.

Our first impression at the factory was astonishment at the number of parked bicycles. There are eight hundred workers, most of whom live in the suburbs, and seventy-five per cent commute on bicycles. As at Georg Jensen's, conditions for the workers seem ideal. Many of the decorators are women. Several, we noticed, wore radio earphones, while others had raised rare plants, and a profusion of flowers transformed their workshop into a bower.

Botanical subjects have been popular since 1800, when the Czarina ordered a set of dinner plates decorated with plants in color, each bearing its Latin name on the reverse. About fifty years ago a process was discovered by which three colors might be fired under the glaze—the popular blue-gray ware so familiar to us in vases with floral or fish design. Cobalt blue, chrome green, and gold are the only ones that will withstand such heat. Only two firings are needed, before and after the glaze, but in the elaborate pieces with additional color or gold to remain golden, a return to the oven is necessitated. A fantastic conceit and triumph over technical difficulties is "The Princess on the Pea," a figurine illustrative of the Andersen tale. The Princess, in elaborate court dress, is seated upon piled mattresses, but her high and mightiness is not deceived!

Figures by Georg Thylstrup are still popular, as are others in blanc de chine and copies of Chinese celadon. Despite the allure of some of the modern styles of pottery, each bearing a name, my preference is for the traditional blue-and-white cherished for a century by generations of Danish housewives. We watched all stages of its manufacture. When, after receiving its hand-painted pattern, it is dipped in glaze, it turns dull white with design obliterated, but after firing the readily absorbed glaze becomes transparent. The ingredients in the true porcelain—the easily recognizable Royal Copenhagen—are threefold: kaolin from England, felspar from Norway, and quartz. Look for the mark: a royal crown and three wavy lines in blue on white shield, each "wave" representing one of the famous "belts" of Denmark —the Great Belt, the Little Belt, and the Sound.

Little but Danish blood flows in Danish veins. From the American point of view, that is, perhaps, Denmark's chief source of weakness. One of America's leading conductors has just stated that the supremacy of her symphony orchestras is due to their international personnel. A player is chosen on merit and not because of the accident of birth. Initiative in art and invention seem to be dormant in Denmark. Indeed, inventiveness has hardly been in evidence since Viking times, nor does the creative spirit manifest itself outstandingly in literature, music, or the fine arts—in striking contrast to Norway, Sweden, and Finland. Of what avail are bigger and better breweries and cement plants, manufactories of Diesel engines (the inventor was a German!), coöperative farms and consumer coöperatives, adult education, and colony gardens save as a means to a more abundant life?

Copenhagen's past can best be visualized through her parks and palaces. Remnants recently unearthed of the original castle on the site of Christianborg date from the foundation of the city in the year 1167 by Bishop Absalon. Rivalry with the Hanseatic League caused the destruction of this castle in 1248 and of its successor in 1368. Fire has twice destroyed when war and the will of kings had spared. The present Christianborg Palace, with older portions incorporated, was erected in this century as a House of Parliament. It also contains audience chambers where the King receives twice monthly any of his subjects who have legitimate cause of complaint.

Frederiksberg Slot has become an academy for the training of army officers, and its park the setting of the Zoölogical Garden. In the Royal Deer Park is Dyrehavsbakken ("The Hill of the Deer Park"), a cruder Tivoli, but one that should be approached on a night when, among century-old beeches of the king's preserve, deer lurking in shadows, torches flare.

To reconstruct the lives of former sovereigns the visitor should repair to Rosenborg Slot with its secular trees, now known as Kongens Have or King's Garden, where H. C. Andersen reigns in bronze seated upon a pedestal throne. The *slot* or castle is one of the notable examples of Flemish Renaissance architecture, dating from the reign of Christian IV. It has become a chronological museum of the collections of the kings of Denmark, as well as housing the crown jewels. In its spacious cellars tradition requires that barrels of Rhine wine be stored for two hundred years before reaching the table of the king. A bottle used is, of course, immediately replaced.

The exterior of Rosenborg possesses a certain charm inherent in roseate brick and Renaissance towers, the whole surrounded by a moat with, in the foreground, wild rhubarb, dear to Danish landscape painters. The interior would probably be no less pleasing had one eyes for anything but the collections. The effect of these collections upon an impressionable soul is culminative and devastating. My sympathy perhaps wasted itself upon Christian IV for having had to live with such a wealth of ornate furniture, yet the portrayed sovereigns whose eyes were riveted upon me seemed not out of place in such surroundings.

The crown jewels vie in splendor with those to
be seen in the Tower of London. The king's crown
(never worn by the democratic gentleman who is
actually an uncrowned king) glitters with sap-
phires and is topped by a diamond cross set
upon a ball of turquoise. An historic crown (that
of Christian IV) ornamented with blue dragons
and cherubs set in pearls would have graced the
head of a story-book king. Had I been offered my
choice—a fairy godmother would have been in
keeping with the whole experience—I should have
gone off with the queen's second best, her diadem
of emeralds. My interest centered, primarily, in
seeing with my own eyes the chain of the king's
Order of the Elephant. The *Elephas Indicus* motif,
in gold and blue enamel, alternated with golden
towers, the pendant being a larger elephant with
cross of diamonds. To think that once I had been
unaware of the existence of the Order of the Elephant! Had I not actually scoffed and been incredulous? Yet in Denmark, as in Siam, nothing is
held in greater veneration than an elephant.

Perhaps the elephants should have prepared me
for the throne-room. We reached it after a journey through rooms groaning with the weight of
ormulu, bronze, china, and silver and cluttered
with the belongings of sovereigns rhythmically
alternating Christians and Frederiks. Before the
massive throne stand three silver lions of formidable proportions representing the three

"belts" of Denmark. In an alcove, still in keeping with an Oriental idea of the status of women, the queen's throne is ensconced. I glanced into a recess where *chinoiseries* are stored, then, weighed down by the burden of it all, I stepped into what I had supposed from the guidebook would be a refreshing display of sparkling glass —like a cup of cool water to my thirsting spirit.

The alcove was embellished with woodwork, in pseudo-Moorish taste, of fantastic design. A honeycomb of glass-topped shelves was edged with gilded fringe, cherub heads, and wooden tassels. From wires dusty glass bells hung in profusion. Immense glass plates and vases, many with opaque design in spiderous webs of china-white, were reflected endlessly in mirrors. As though the administration feared that thieves might break through and steal, bars had been placed between the collection and the beholder. Trapped! I caught sight of my startled, caged self reflected *ad infinitum*. Above my head, in lieu of the sword of Damocles about to fall upon me, was a hitherto unnoticed chandelier unstably poised, threatening to crush me with its atrocious weight. Enough! I fled—as though from an insane dream—from the alcove, from the throne-room, from Rosenborg.

In the street there was a joyous sound of music, the tread of marching men. Down the Gothersgade, headed by their band, marched the King's Life

Guards—cobalt uniforms contrasting with white accoutrements and bearskin busbies. Noon was about to strike. With my Illustrator hard at my heels I followed the eager crowd to Amalienborg to watch the ceremony of the Changing of the Guard.

Amalienborg Palace is an example of rococo at its best. Originally constructed by four noblemen, four similar but detached mansions around a central square, these structures preserve an eighteenth-century dignity. After the burning of Christianborg in 1884, Christian IX, father of Queen Alexandra of England, Dagmar, Czarina of Russia, and grandfather of the present King of Denmark, moved to Amalienborg. The northwest quarter is to-day the residence of King Christian X and Queen Alexandrine, while the Crown Prince Frederik and his young wife Ingrid, daughter of the Crown Prince of Sweden, occupy another quarter. Daily, when the King is in residence, the ceremony of the changing guard attracts a crowd, not alone of tourists afoot and in autocars, but of townspeople for whom it never seems to lose its novelty. Red-coated postmen pause on their bicycles with mouths agape, while Frederik V on horseback reviews the troops from his central pedestal.

The Changing of the Guard is an historic survival. The rosy faces of the youthful guardsmen carry no sinister message of belligerency. No mili-

tary illusions deceive these regenerate sons of
ancient Vikings. They are children of a new day.
Anyone who happens to be in the neighborhood of
the Palace at eight in the morning may see the
King, in the undress uniform of the Danish
Guard, mounted on a thoroughbred, ride forth
alone. It is said that many Danes set their watches
by His Majesty's appearance.

King Christian is not only the tallest monarch
in Europe (he measures six feet six), but he is
probably the most democratic. On the occasion of
his Silver Jubilee, on May 15, 1937, an event
which brought ten royal guests from Norway and
Sweden to Copenhagen, no troops, not even police,
were in evidence to keep in order the throngs that
lined the route to the Cathedral, nor were they
needed when the King received the congratula-
tions of the Rigsdag in the afternoon and of the
Danish students in torch-light procession in the
evening. It was a heart-stirring occasion, as those
of us who listened to the address of the Prime
Minister, the valiant Stauning, and the response
of the King can testify. The contrast was the more
apparent, even by radio, because of the very few
days that had elapsed between this anniversary
and the crowning of the King-Emperor in London.

"If we are to have kings," say some, "let us
have show of arms and medieval pomp of Church
and State." I demur. Perhaps kings are an

anachronism. All who believe in democracy will admit the day of the absolute ruler has passed. There are many Europeans, however, who still cherish the tradition of a sovereignty not incompatible with constitutional government. If, then, we are to have kings on earth, let us give thanks for the example set by Scandinavian monarchs.

A Carlsberg Elephant

Frederiksborg Castle:
The ancient Tower

CHAPTER XIII

FROM HAMLET TO ANDERSEN

RURAL ZEALAND possesses many attractions that
rival those of the capital. To balance Copenhagen's Rosenborg, for instance, rural Zealand
can muster Frederiksborg. As introduction to a
week-end excursion the splendor of Frederiksborg
stamps itself upon the memory as a never-to-be-
forgotten vision on the road to seaside Hornbæk,
while the return to Copenhagen of a Sunday or
Monday will, of course, be via Helsingør and
Hamlet's castle.

Frederik the Second's *borg* or castle was built
on three islets beside a lake. Here on April 12,
1577, an heir to Frederik was born—none other
than the future King Christian IV. Almost a century had elapsed since the birth of an heir to the
throne of Denmark. The records tell of the killing, not indeed of fatted calves, but of four hundred pigs, seven hundred lambs, and more than

a thousand chickens. Having reached man's estate, Christian IV—for he had been crowned at the age of eleven—proceeded to rebuild the castle and transform it into one of the most magnificent in all Denmark.

The story of Christian's birth was told to us as we sat over coffee-cups in a garden overshadowed by an ancient tower. Lunch had been spread for us within this round tower, and now our host, Otto Andrup, was saying:

"Do you know that Christian was born here?"

"Yes," I replied, "I have read that he was born at Frederiksborg."

"But not in the castle," our host explained. "Here—in the rose-garden. In those days this was a tiny isle. The lady-in-waiting in attendance had gone to get her needlework. When she returned, the queen, all alone beneath a gigantic rose-tree, had borne a son." Our eyes followed his glance, and, with surprise, we saw an infant sleeping peacefully beneath the shade of a spreading tree.

"Not the queen's babe but the sovereign of my family," chuckled the curator.

As director of the museum, for the castle now ranks as such, Mr. Andrup is permitted to live in one of the oldest portions, dating from the original foundation. The garden close is entered by way of low buildings known as the Royal Mews, as once they were, now housing negatives

of objects in contemporaneous and pertinent collections. On the brick wall of the mews, facing
the garden, our host had trained both pears and
apricots, now heavy with fruit, while the son of
the house had planted a row of maize which would,
in this climate, rarely ripen, but in autumn would
be valued for its foliage.

Frederiksborg is situated at the ancient town
of Hillerød, which it dominates with architectural
splendors of the Renaissance. In magnificence the
castle reminds me of certain châteaux on the
Loire, of Chambord, of Blois—if not, indeed, of
Versailles. Careful restorations, made by Government assisted by I. C. Jacobsen's Carlsberg
Foundation since the disastrous fire of 1859, have
recreated the reality of Christian's fantasy in
brick and stone and copper-sheathed cupolas and
spires. Over a period of fifty years our friend the
curator has labored, with consummate skill and
plenty of money supplied by the Foundation, to
install appropriate furnishings. Opportunities
have arisen owing to the impoverishment of many
of the noblemen living in Danish castles. Purchased portraits of historical characters, as at
Gripsholm, enrich the walls.

Approached by drawbridges spanning moats
(there is water aplenty at Frederiksborg), the
castle surrounds a central court at the entrance
to which stands the Neptune fountain, the work of
a Dutchman, Adrian de Vries. So carefully has

the fountain been restored the beholder has to be reminded that some of the original statues were carried to Drottningholm by victorious Swedes. It was neither high day nor holiday at the time of our visit, and yet, with prodigality, the fountain played.

"We had not hoped to see this!" I exclaimed.

"It plays in your honor," explained our host with a courtly bow—impersonation of the hospitality of the Danish people.

Such was our welcome, our initiation, into the splendors of Frederiksborg. Not only did the fountains play, but mammoth clocks performed with tuneful hymn or tinkling chimes suggestive of Antwerp. In the cobbled court of the fountain the sun was hot, but within the castle was coolness and tranquillity. Bowls of fresh roses brought a verisimilitude of other days. Had Leonora Christina, in the freshness of her youthful beauty, stepped from the frame of her portrait, it would hardly have caused us surprise—so immersed were we in the spirit of the time of this ill-fated daughter of Christian IV.

The handsome features of Christian the Builder looked upon us, the homely ones of Christian V. Mediocre portraits of the present King and Queen, of the King's parents, of Alexandra and Edward VII, of Dagmar and Czar Alexander III, call to mind the consanguinity of royal families. The Riddersal or Knights' Hall has been reconstructed in all its immensity with minstrels' gallery and ornate ceiling. Indeed, the ceilings, rococo and baroque, are crushingly apparent throughout the palace. Not an hour or two or even an afternoon can give other than a cursory impression of so vast an edifice and such a wealth of princely furnishings. To some the climax is the chapel—weighed down with ornament, enriched by a pulpit and reredos of ebony and silver inlay, a masterly example of German art. In this chapel the kings of Denmark were crowned until the year 1863, when coronation ceremonies were abolished as incompatible with the modern conception of monarchy.

The killing kindness of friends had induced us to spend a week-end swimming and sun-tanning at the fashionable beach resort Hornbæk, and, moreover, to linger over a banquet there when we should have been motoring in the direction of Hamlet's castle. By the time of our arrival at Helsingør (Elsinore) the route to Kronborg was already blocked with cars and autobuses. As we trudged beneath interlacing trees leading to the ramparts, we were confronted by a departing throng of green-starred Esperantists. Danish and Swedish trippers had scant courtesy for would-be lingerers. Caught in a human tide, we were swept, scarcely knowing why, into the bowels of earth. Casemates, subterranean passages, prisons, followed in quick succession, lighted by a lamp describing smoke circles in the encompassing hand of pompous guardian. His pronouncements began in stentorian tones but ended with wise-cracks at which the people tittered. Warned not to stray, we mustered our serried ranks and stumbled after the ray of light. A youth was cornered to represent a Protestant minister who had been more and closely walled in until, at last, standing-room only remained. Anticlimax came in the account of how this pastor—whose death and burial we had foreseen—had survived many years after release. Water dripping upon necks, as in the dark we stooped beneath low arches, touched like death-cold fingers our cheeks, sending shivers down spines. Goose-flesh rose as we came, in semi-blackness, upon a sleeping warrior, in stone.

"Holger Danske, Holger Danske!" cried the eager voice of a Danish lad.

"Ogier le Dane," murmured a French tourist.

To those of us who remember our Andersen the story is familiar. Holger the Dane will come should Denmark stand in need. The tale runs that centuries ago a condemned slave was sent to this subterranean chamber at Kronborg, none other daring to go whence the sound of clanking armor came. Their heads upon their arms, gigantic warriors sat around a block of stone. Holger arose, splitting the rock to which his beard had grown:

"Greetings to thy master," said he. "Tell him that when the time is ripe, we come."

Shakespeare had undoubtedly heard of Holger Danske—lover of Morgan le Fay—lurking, troll-like, beneath the soil of Denmark. To some it seems that it was the Holger legend that suggested to the playwright the rôle of the ghost in *Hamlet*. History is silent as to whether the bard actually visited Elsinore. It is within the realm of possibility, and tradition would have it so, for it is known that his friends, Thomas Bull and William Kemp, actors and morris-dancers, came there to perform. There were great doings at Kronberg in 1589, when Princess Anna, sister of Christian IV, was married by proxy to the son of Mary Stuart, James VI of Scotland; and again the following year during a remarriage and prolonged stay of the bridal pair. Shakespeare's intimate knowledge of Danish manners and customs has been given as proof of first-hand knowledge—for example, the reference to the Barbary horses, described as "the Danish stakes in the bet." The king's six white Barbary horses at Kronborg had dyed red tails, so bore the Danish colors.

Needless to state, the English-speaking traveler's primary interest in Kronborg is its Shakespearean associations. If he has seen the John Gielgud production, he feels himself no stranger at Kronborg, but whether his Hamlet be Leslie Howard, John Barrymore, Walter Hampden, Sothern, the lamented Forbes-Robertson (my own choice), or Sarah Bernhardt, he strides with pos-

 Kronborg ‡

Hamlet's Castle at Elsinore ⬩

sessive tread to the "platform." To him this Flag
Battery with its view of the sea belongs, far more
than to the little Danish sentinel pacing, as others
before have paced, in actuality and on the boards.

A platform by the sea! What liberating winds
blow upon us now, but lately escaped from suffo-
cating dungeons, as once upon immortal Hamlet!
What have living kings or kings of history to offer here comparable to his memory? There is indeed a maritime museum in the castle's north
wing, a chapel far more to my liking than that
where the kings were crowned at Frederiksborg, a
magnificently restored Knights' Hall, and a Hall
of the King's Councillors hung with historic
Gobelin tapestries woven at Elsinore by order of
Christian IV; but all these glories pale before the
memory of a haunted figure pacing a platform by
the sea.

"To be or not to be"...the words ring down
the centuries, challenging a troubled world. The
tongue in which they are spoken erects no barrier
to their inner poignancy. Bernhardt is said to
have spoken them as a youth whose trembling
mind had been wounded to insanity, Moissi as a
neurasthenic, Katschalov—the Russian—as a dis-
illusioned modern. The story, based on the life of
an actual Prince Hamlet who dwelt on the mainland of Jutland, had been used even before
Shakespeare's day. The Bard's play was first put
into Danish in 1778, first played in that tongue in

1813. In 1816 it was given in the casemates of Kronborg. Its latest interpreter at Kronborg was Laurence Olivier, who came with fellow-members of the "Old Vic" company from London to perform in the courtyard from June 2 to 6, 1937. Five performances were given—only one a matinée. It was said the ghost did not like to stalk in broiling sunshine. He need not have worried. It rained most of the week, and several times the production had to be transferred to the hotel (once a summer palace) at Marienlyst. Although three thousand seats were sold for each performance, although the actors gave their services, the receipts were not enough to pay for living expenses and transportation from London.

Other associations with Kronborg are that it was once the prison of Caroline Mathilde, wife of the debauched Christian VII of Denmark and sister of George III of England. Arrested on the night of a fancy-dress ball at Christianborg, confessing her guilt in an affair with the King's German physician Struensee, the Queen was brought in a golden coach to Kronborg where she languished behind bars from January to May, until three English men-of-war were sent by her brother to take her, not, as she had hoped, to England, but to Hanover. The guns of Kronborg fired a final mocking salute of twenty-seven rounds. At Hanover the unhappy lady died of smallpox at the age of twenty-four. On a window-pane at Kronborg the prisoner had scratched, "O keep me innocent, make others great."

"The Path of the Dane" is the name given in the Danish national anthem to the Øresund, the Sound that separates Sweden from Denmark. At the entrance to this gate to the Baltic stands Kronborg—"on the right" of the passenger coming from England. The Danish king Erik of Pomerania placed a fortress, Krogen, here in 1426 in order to collect a levy from passing ships. His monument stands on the market-place at Helsingør with the motto, "My trust is in the sea."

The earliest portions of the present castle date from the reign of Frederik II, who began the construction in 1574—and paid for it by the collection of Sound Dues. The Renaissance château dates from the reign of Christian IV, following the fire of 1629. In those days it was not Britannia but Denmark that ruled the waves. The king's fleet was constantly on the lookout for pirates, and lighthouses were erected. In return for this service each ship was taxed, but later, with the growth of tonnage, the tax was put on cargoes. England, in 1583 and subsequently, paid Denmark to obtain a permit to sail around the North Cape in order to trade with Russian Lapland. In 1625 Elsinore had become the second town in Denmark. In the year 1796 twelve thousand ships passed, striking their topsails and paying their toll in order to avoid the guns of Kronborg. The decline of Elsinore, decimated by war and plague, dates from the abolition of Sound Dues in 1857.

Although no tolls are exacted to-day, the Minister of Marine provides an observer to record boats, even sailboats, passing an imaginary line drawn from Kronborg to Sweden, an oblique line, in order to avoid the direct route of the ferry. As the crow flies, the distance between shores is less than three miles. To swim the Sound has become the ambition of strapping Danish wenches—not all as young or as successful as the idol of the moment, Jenny Kammersgaard.

Before leaving Helsingør we saw the Church of Saint Olai and the former Carmelite Monastery, whose hospital was built as a refuge for "poor foreign mariners"; the pharmacy, still in use, bears the date 1577 ... we wonder if it specializes in modern drugs or legs of frogs captured in the full of the moon.

A powerful example of modern interpretation of legendary theme is the fountain of Hercules and the Hydra. The sculptor, Rudolf Tegner, shows many of his monumental works, effectively silhouetted against the sky, on a heather-clad moorland at Kiltekrog, near Hornbæk.

Frederiksborg no longer resounds to the triumphant crowning of Danish kings, but Roskilde still awaits their ceremonious burial. Because of this it has been compared to Westminster, but comparison to an English rural cathedral is more

appropriate. Winchester, history tells, like Roskilde, was once a capital with Canute the Great
for master. The Cathedral is an immense edifice
of brick with twin spires, the whole reminiscent
of Germany.

Our visit to the tombs of the kings was well
timed. We were on our way from Copenhagen, via
Sorø and the ferry, to Odense on the island of
Funen. As we stepped into the aisle of the Cathedral of Roskilde, we were greeted by a gruesome
howl, and lifting our eyes to the heights, we discovered that the sound issued from a dragon that
Saint George was about to slaughter. The hour
was four, and we stood beneath an ancient me-
chanical clock. Another item, spirited amid sur-
rounding gloom, was the representation on a grill
of a troll (life-sized, shall I say?) guarding a
vault supposedly sacred to the Trolle family.

Anyone who has been depressed by monuments
in Westminster and Saint Paul's should avoid
Roskilde. Nothing has been spared in the way of
posthumous honors. Poor mortal remains are en-
cased, for the most part, in sarcophagi of ponderous stone, while others have been left, as though
awaiting burial, in copper or velvet-covered oak
coffins. The latter style has been used for Christian IV and his first wife, and there is also a
Thorwaldsen statue of the king. The chapel of
Christian IV was erected by the ruler (he also
added the spires to the Cathedral) and is en-

hanced by a metal grill wrought by one who has commemorated himself in this fashion: "Caspar Fincke is my name; by this work I am known."

Hastening past the monuments to the parents of the present King, that of the Empress Marie of Russia, glancing at the column where numerous tall sovereigns have been measured, we lingered at the tomb of Queen Margaret of Scandinavia. The effigy in alabaster of this beautiful woman and astute ruler was erected, ten years after her death in 1412, by her grandnephew and heir, Erik of Pomerania. With her is said to be buried the whetstone sent by her German brother-in-law, Albrecht of Sweden, with the message to sharpen her needles and leave swords to men. For answer the Queen sent her armies to Sweden, and Albrecht, who had grown unpopular with the Swedes, was taken prisoner. No more romantic figure graces the pages of Scandinavian history. Margaret, who was daughter to King Valdemar of Denmark, was wedded at the age of ten to Håkon VI, King of Norway. Her son Olaf was elected King of Denmark on his grandfather's death and inherited the throne of Norway. At a time when the crown of Sweden was within his grasp, Olaf died at the age of twenty-one. Margaret, who had reigned as regent of Denmark and Norway during her son's minority, in 1388 was chosen by the Swedes as "Sovereign Lady and Ruler." Gotland (sacked by her father Valdemar

Atterdag) and Schleswig she obtained by purchase. It was understood that she should provide a male heir to the throne of the United Kingdoms, and in 1389 her infant relative Erik of Pomerania was chosen—Margaret remaining virtual queen until the day of her death. Denmark cherishes the memory of Margaret as England that of Elizabeth. Both were, in all probability, hard and wily potentates, but sovereigns of bounteous ages in their countries' history.

The beauties of Roskilde Cathedral are best seen from beneath the horse-chestnuts in the courtyard, on which give offices of the commune housed in what was once, I understand, a palace. After lingering here we betook us to the Jernbanehotellet Café, and, pressing a button marked *Tjerner,* the word used by Danes in calling "waiter" we settled down to refreshments on the terrace.

Sorø could have detained us long. There was time to see only the exterior of the noted boys' academy, Denmark's nearest approach to the public school of England. Holberg the dramatist, whose fortune was left to the school, lived at Sorø and is buried in the Romanesque church, unique remnant of the former Cistercian Abbey. Olaf, son of Margaret, and his grandfather Valdemar Atterdag lie here, too—the Queen was moved to Roskilde; and back of the altar are interred the remains of Bishop Absalon, founder of Copenhagen. In the capital we had remarked the statue of the city's founder, the Bishop, battle-ax in hand, towering over the market-place. It had been explained that a blow from such a weapon could dispatch a man without loss of blood, and therefore, unlike the sword, it could, in those days, with all propriety be wielded by a bishop.

Fate smiles on Sorø. Its illustrious past, its scholastic present, have created an atmosphere rarely found in practical modern Denmark. The quiet street with its book-filled shop windows, its tempting display of navy-blue brass-buttoned uniforms and all that young gentlemen might require in the way of bedding leads to an ancient groined gate. Within the portals, beneath the shade of immense trees undoubtedly set out by the Cistercians, one meditates on past and future, lingering on the green, wandering along the yew-lined paths in the churchyard or lakeward to Holberg's Academy.

Charles X and his army crossed the Little Belt from Jutland to Funen on the ice and even traversed the Great Belt to Langeland en route to Copenhagen. Our own crossing from Zealand to Funen was by ferry. The most hazardous feature of our adventure was not at sea but ashore. We had negotiated for a comfortable car with English-speaking driver. Imagine our astonishment when, at the hour of departure from the capital, the car that we had been told would really hold seven proved to be none other than a Copenhagen taxi! The chauffeur might once have been an English scholar (he dwelt on a sojourn in America), but with the days of his youth the memory and understanding of our language had vanished. He was a gentle soul, like all our Danish chauffeurs Hans by name, touchingly anxious to give satisfaction. Careening in darkness to Odense, the car barely avoided other vehicles. My Illustrator ventured to suggest to the one at the wheel that he turn on the lights. This the Gentle Soul seemed reluctant to do. Perhaps the glare was injurious to aged eyes. We compromised on parking lights. It was with relief that we eventually drew up before the Grand Hotel at Odense, chief town and capital of the island of Funen.

The Grand Hotel is in every respect, save one, worthy of its name. The food is superlative. The rooms are spacious, the decorations modern—we reveled in a Van Gogh sunflower. The bathroom of our suite was palatial in appointments—nowhere are fittings more lavish than in Denmark; but can tiles and shower curtains or even chromium fixtures atone for lack of water, or gasometers for lack of air? They can not, nor for tubs designed to drain in geysers on the floor.

Odense, birthplace of Hans Christian Andersen —the two are synonymous. Highly-colored imaginings transported Andersen beyond the reach of sordid circumstance. Few great men have been more humbly born. His father was a cobbler; his

Hans Christian Andersen.

mother, illiterate and none too temperate, was wont to kneel on the river-bank with the washing that eked out the meager existence of herself and

Hans after her husband's death. The cottage that housed the trio consisted of one room; the bed had shreds of black material still adhering at the time the child reached the questioning age. It had been constructed from a catafalque for the coffin of a nobleman. Behind the cottage, however, was an overhanging gooseberry bush, and beneath this bush, as upon the river's brink, the future poet dreamt his dreams.

In 1819, at the age of fourteen, Andersen, who would not follow his mother's advice and learn to be a tailor, set out, with the equivalent of five dollars in his pockets, for Copenhagen. He lived there in dire poverty in a windowless room, becoming an unpaid choir pupil at the Royal Theater. When he was dismissed, because of loss of voice, he won the attention of Jonas Collin, one of the managers, by a play he had written. Collin secured royal assistance for the overgrown youth, who was sent to grammar school with boys much younger than himself. It was not until he entered the university that Andersen met those with whom he could at last mingle on a footing of equality.

Despite the poverty early in his career, Andersen was able, during his life, to make twenty-nine trips abroad, where he is said to have fraternized with "poets, scientists, noblemen, and royalty." In Italy he met Thorwaldsen. In Sweden he took the Göta Canal trip and formed an abiding friendship with Fredrika Bremer. Leaving Leipzig for

Dresden, Andersen experienced a true adventure —a ride in the new-born train. This was in 1841. In England he spent several weeks with Dickens at Gadshill. A cartoon appeared in *Punch* at the time of Andersen's second visit to Dickens, in 1857. It showed the lank creator of the *Fairy-Tales for Children* encircled by youthful British admirers.

"My life is a beautiful fairy-tale," said H. C. A., "happy and full of incident"; to which he added, "Every man's life is a fairy-tale written by God's finger."

A happy conception of this life may be gained at Odense. The Childhood Home may be seen at Number 3 Munkemøllestræde. It has preserved the atmosphere of other days although the city has encroached between it and the river. The street lies near the Cathedral of Saint Canute. Another house, where Andersen was probably born, though the event may have taken place at an aunt's near-by, was, in any event, the home of his infancy. The original low-ceilinged cottage contains seven rooms. It has belonged to the city since 1905, the centenary, and since the one hundred and twenty-fifth anniversary of the birth a museum has been added in which to house the rich collection of books, manuscripts, pictures, and mementos.

Accompanied by the erudite daughter of our friend the director of the Frederiksborg Museum (after her marriage to a teacher in the high school at Odense English interpreter and one-time acting director at the Hans Andersen House), we hung over the cases of souvenirs. It was an age of sentiment, of scrap-books and pressed flowers, yet even such slight remnants are pregnant with romance when the sender is H. C. Andersen, the recipient Jenny Lind. Successful in love Andersen could not be called. Three times his love assumed the proportions of a "grand passion," and each time the lady of his choice preferred another. The first love, the sister of a school friend, was the youthful Riborg Voigt, whom he met at Faaborg. Riborg was secretly pledged to another. The second was Louise Collin, daughter of his patron. With the Collin family his friendship endured throughout life; he was to become "uncle" to Louise's children. The third, as is well known, was Jenny Lind, the "Swedish Nightingale" who inspired the stories "The Nightingale" and "The Angel." The spectator is tempted to groan, not with heaviness, as do the cases, but with sympathy for the early woes and blighted loves of the hero whose story lies for all the world to read like these open books. A faded purse bears a label in the hand of Jonas Collin, Jr.; translated it reads: "This leather purse was found on the breast of Hans Andersen, after his death. It contained a long letter from Riborg Voigt, the beloved of his youth. I burned the letter unopened."

Andersen eases his heart on paper when Riborg rejects his suit, when Jenny Lind, well met in Dresden, does not ask him, as he hoped, to Christmas dinner.

The first furniture ever owned by Andersen is displayed—as once it was at the Chicago World's Fair. A silver leaf of wild rhubarb with snail is shown, gift of the principal of a girls' school on the occasion of the thirtieth anniversary of Hans' arrival in Copenhagen. You remember, of course, "The Happy Family" and the snails' paradise of being served on a silver dish on the table of a nobleman. The flower of the collection, however, is the books and manuscripts displayed in the North Room. There is the manuscript of the *Story of My Life* (*Mit Livs Eventyr*), the only one of this prolific writer's works that in any way approaches the popularity of the *Fairy-Tales for Children*. (A Danish publisher living in Leipzig issued the first edition of the collected works in 1848-1851, thirty-seven volumes in German.) On these crowded shelves we may see the fairy-tales in over thirty languages, including Arabian, Hebrew, Chinese, Japanese, and Greenlandish. Especially amusing, we thought, were the pictures in the Chinese version, but our Danish friend assured us that these are hardly more exotic in conception than, for example, those of Rackham. Most Danes consider the ingenuous Pedersen drawings, whose child-like simplicity corresponds with the text, as much

Odense: H·C·Andersen's House

a part of the whole as Tenniel's are acknowledged to be with *Alice's Adventures in Wonderland.* Vilhelm Pedersen was a Danish naval officer who died before the completion of his task. The pencil originals, given to Andersen on his seventieth birthday, adorn the walls of the museum, as well as sketches by Andersen and imaginative paper-cuttings—an art at which Andersen was adept.

If there were a Book-of-All-Time Club, publicity would be given to the fact that the fairy-tales are world best-sellers second only to the Bible.

The natives of Odense like to remember that Denmark's most renowned inhabitant was made an honorary citizen of the town of his birth in 1867, while all Danes rejoice in the memory that, in 1875, Andersen was told on his seventieth birthday that a statue was to be erected in Copenhagen. He did not live to see another birthday. Shortly before his death, I learn from the foreword to my own thumbed complete and unabridged copy of the fairy-tales masquerading in America under the title of *Stories for the Household,* the poet was touched by the love of American children who wished him to cross the Atlantic.

"Tell them," he said to the writer of the preface, Hjalmar Hjorth Boyesen, "if you could telegraph me across to the American children, I should start to-morrow."

Hans Andersen was a born raconteur. The beauty of his words was matched by the beauty of his voice. To-day, by means of the spoken word, Paul Leyssac interprets the tales, not alone for the present generation of children, but for adults. Like Peter Pan Andersen never grew up. Children were his chosen companions. Remembering the period of his own studies there, he wrote into the first clause of his will a legacy to the most diligent boy in the workhouse school at Odense.

In Denmark Hans is an everyday name, so is Christian, and no less so is Andersen; the three occur in well-nigh endless repetition.

"Don't call him Hans Christian Andersen," a Danish friend exclaimed. "The children won't understand you."

"By what name do they know him?" I inquired.

"Try H. C. Andersen," he said, summoning his flaxen-haired Lone and an apple-cheeked toddler.

"Do you know the stories of Ho Say"—for so it sounds—"Andersen?" I asked. The radiant smiles evoked by the name are the unwithering laurels of Andersen's immortality.

A singing language is spoken on the island of Funen. No one, or so it seems to me, could be ungrateful enough to live on such an enchanted isle without uttering his thoughts in song. If you will not let a word of it reach to Zealand or to Jutland, I shall confess that, to my mind, Funen has, of the three, greatest cause to chant the Magnificat. Larks sing on the wing above the clover-fields, the pastures, the nodding grain, above the shaggy thatch of cottage roofs, the tiles of white-walled churches. Indeed, the lark would be a fitting symbol of bucolic Funen.

"Doesn't it remind you of Devon?" my Illustrator asked, and I replied:

"Yes, of Devon without the char-à-bancs."

We were on the first stage of a day's tour of the island and were motoring between hawthorn hedges. Director Andrup's daughter Merete was our companion. She remarked the incongruity of careening through the lanes of Funen in a Copenhagen taxi, a taxi that was obviously not free, but which, owing to some trick of mechanism, bore a conspicuous *"Fri"* for all to read.

"It reminds me," I said, "of the Danish habit of hanging a sign *'Welcomen'* on dance platforms already taxed to capacity."

The *Fru* high-school-teacher's-wife soon made another discovery. "You said," she remarked, "that your chauffeur did not understand English, but I find that he does not, even in Danish, know left from right. I'll do my best to keep him to roads on the map."

"Have you noticed," I queried, "that whenever I speak to him, he says, very politely, 'Yes, sir!' ... my husband wouldn't believe it until he heard it with his own ears."

Viby, village of thatched cottages clustered around a white gabled church, typically Danish in form, within easy bicycling distance of Odense, was pointed out as an Ultima Thule of newly-weds. Love in a cottage demands just such dwellings. As to cottage gardens, their gay profuson of flowers, seen in August, rivaled those of the Cotswolds in June. There is, though, a fly in the ointment of perfection. Hills worthy of the name are absent. To bicyclists—and are not all Danes bicyclists?— this may be an asset.

Our first stop was at Moreskig near Snave. We had come to see the burial-mounds—grass-grown, with stone markers showing them to be under the care of the National Museum at Copenhagen. Four thousand years is the age attributed to these tombs. We clambered over the slippery hillocks and entered the one left open for the delectation of the public. Blackness prevailed. Bent double we entered a cavernous corridor leading to the dramatic climax of the cairn. Matches threw merely enough light to accentuate the prehistoric monstrous stones that loomed above us like threatening menhirs in a fairy-tale.

Only about a thousand years old are the imbedded relics of a Viking ship recently discovered and preserved in its burial-mound at Kertinge near Ladby. Although the wood has rotted away, the myriad nails remain, an elaborate leash where dogs were tied, the skeletons of dogs and horse— for, it seems, the beasts accompanied their chief to oblivion.

Anne Hathaway's cottage had embodied my idea of the rural picturesque—that is to say in Northern Europe, a necessary proviso because of a Pyrenean standard. English thatch, however, must give place to Danish. Nowhere but in Funen have I seen such prodigality. Half-timbered buildings, squat, white-plastered, are erected around three if not four sides of courts. In each case the dwelling faces the quarters for cattle, while between are stored grain, tools, and machinery. Seamless roofs lure the artist to depict their undulations.

We now sped southward. Cows punctuated the lush fields with red ... many tethered in neat rows after the old fashion while those belonging to young farmers had regained more liberty. Lombardy poplars abounded, chunky stumps, pollarded after the manner of willows. We wished that Danes were not so undeviatingly practical. To admire butterflies in Funen brings the inevitable reply: "Pretty, but bad for the cabbage!"

We did find one rift in this cherished garment of utilitarianism. The Dane has not yet discovered the need of country inns if he would attract tourists to rural districts. Seashore and Copenhagen seem sufficient for Danish holiday-makers—town dwellers on vacation. The rural population lives unmolested on the land, rarely eating except at home, a fact that accounts for the present type of inn, such as the *kro* at ... let it be nameless.

The Danish word *gaard,* encountered first in Norway, is in Denmark often used for a handsome manor or even castle, as at Hesselager Gaard, dating from the sixteenth century. This imposing mansion is still in the family of Baron Blixen-Finecke who married Augusta, sister of Frederik VIII, therefore aunt of the present King.

Funen corresponds in Denmark to the province of Skåne in Sweden as a last stand of aristocracy.

Counts and barons are plentiful, living in castles of varying magnificence. Peasants likewise abound and, as a class, are astoundingly slow-witted and empty-pated. The contrast to boastfully modern Copenhagen is the more apparent—the pages of history seem to have been turned back at least a century. To lovers of the picturesque this is no drawback.

Brahetrolleborg, aloof upon a lake, did not detain us, nor Bernsdorffsminde, residence of the Reventlow family, still much respected because of veneration for the memory of the Count who in 1780 obtained freedom for his countrymen. Of the numerous castles visited in Skåne and in Denmark, none pleased me more than Egeskov, situated a mile or so from Svenborg, the easternmost of Funen's two southern ports, the other being, of course, that artist's haven Faaborg.

Egeskov, dating from 1554, is, architecturally, early Flemish Renaissance. Its three and a half stories of time-mellowed rose-red brick pricked out with tiny windows, its typical roof-end, as of two adjoined step-gabled houses, its ample coiffed towers, reflect in a moat of exceptional clarity. Our approach was by an *allée* of prim lindens. A solitary swan craned its neck as though accustomed to being fed...the family, we had been told at the gardener's cottage, were away. A clear bell rang the hour of six. Egeskov, for the nonce, was ours, with all its mirrored beauty, its hos-

pitable drawbridge, its stables with high pitched
roofs, its clipped yew hedges, its beechwood maze.
We hoped that Grev Ahlefeld-Laurvig's eyes, accustomed to so much princely splendor, had not
let familiarity dim the Old World enchantment so
potent to comers from a New World. No char-à-
bancs to mar the peace, we had said in Funen...
not even bicycles to-day. To what kind fate could
we attribute our good fortune? Perhaps to the
lateness of the hour. The sun was low in the heavens. Stillness reigned in the land, stillness, peace.

Not Svenborg, where Christian X may be seen
steering his yacht between Funen and its adjacent
island; not Svenborg with its steep streets, its
church of Saint Nicholas; nor yet Faaborg with
medieval gates and quaint dwellings, at the same
time the delight and the despair of artists, its
museum displaying the works of the Funen school
of painters and sculptures by Kai Nielsen, creator
of the Ymer Well; not Egeskov itself, proved to be
the highlight of this luminous tour. Past a school
of gymnastics we had sped, past coöperative
dairies and a school of agriculture, past meadows
where hay was stacked in formidable tents, past
wheat-fields and marshes where bulrushes waited
to be harvested for thatch, past water-side rhubarb,
food for snails; yet none of these held us like the
coquettish whitewashed farmhouses, capped with
shaggy thatch casting faint shadows, as do lashes
on the white cheek of a maiden—farmhouses cross-

hatched with red or green or tar-black timber, farmhouses, where barn-doors opened to cows herded by tow-headed urchins, farms superlative in the region of Aastrup. A comfortable sound, this *-up!* We rolled it on the tongue, Aastrup, Snarup, especially Gummerup.

A land of barons and a sturdy peasantry, a land where time delays, a land refreshed by the breath of the sea—in sum, Funen: Land of H. C. Andersen.

Roskilde

The Praises of Fanø
have been too little sung.

Fanø Beach.

CHAPTER XIV

JUTLAND, DENMARK'S MAINLAND

DENMARK boasts of being the oldest kingdom of the world. Herself unconquered, she remembers when a Danish sovereign, Queen Margaret, ruled over all Scandinavia—including Greenland and Iceland. Her conquest of England under Canute is unforgotten, although trade has, in our century, replaced military conquest. Like England an island kingdom, Denmark's prosperity depends in large part upon her ships. As a ship-building country tiny Denmark ranks fourth, giving precedence only to Great Britain, Germany, and Japan. Unlike England despite being so largely an insular kingdom, Denmark has foothold on the continent of Europe. Jutland, Denmark's mainland, is by many considered the very heart of the nation. The rugged Jutlanders, proud even of their dialect, will no more tolerate condescension from Copenhagen than Provençals patronage from Paris.

Northern Jutland is separated from the peninsula by the Limfjord, running from the North Sea to the Kattegat, while the continental soil is severed farther southward by the Kiel Canal ... but this is quibbling: Jutland is—and, proud in the return of North Schleswig under the new title of South Jutland, I trust will remain—Denmark's mainland.

Coming from Funen my Illustrator and I crossed the Little Belt by the bridge opened in 1935. Even the largest ships may pass beneath its immense span. Our wonder grew at how Charles X of Sweden had dared to march with his troops from ice-bound shore to shore, confounding the Danes. The previous year, when we had gone by rail from Copenhagen to Hamburg, it had been necessary to make the stage from Zealand to Falster, like that from Gedser to Warnemünde, by train aboard luxurious ferry, although we had had a glimpse of the incompleted wonder span across the "Great Stream" later opened by King Christian on his sixty-seventh birthday, September 25, 1937. The erection of the Zealand-Falster bridge was financed partly by the State and partly by a tax on gasoline. Jutlanders are somewhat disgruntled that, although the new bridge does not concern them, they, too, have to pay the tax. Still more keenly do they regret the passing of interest from their own bridge, one of the longest in Europe, to its rival, measuring

10,432 feet across open water, acclaimed as Europe's longest bridge.

As a prelude to our motor tour of the province, we crossed Jutland to the North Sea and thence, via a short ferry from Esbjerg, to the island of Fanø. The Central Hotel at Esbjerg, catering to the English tourists stopping en route from Harwich to Copenhagen, provides its guests with superlative sole, plaice, and lobster. The Hotel Kongen av Danmark at Fanø is under the same management, and, weather permitting, the island is the place to spend a rewarding week-end. The women of Fanø, unique among their Danish sisters, save for wearers of caps among Amager fishwives, still may be seen in traditional costume. Authorities state that this bit of local color derives from Dutch sources. No lover of the picturesque should leave Fanø unvisited.

"The lands from which the Northmen came make a special appeal to English wayfarers," writes the author of *Denmark and the Danes.* Says Clive Holland, "Danes have much in common with ourselves [the English], and many characteristics which are a joint heritage." It is natural that the Englishman should feel at home in a countryside so suggestive of his own. The Danish climate is, on the whole, preferable to that of Denmark's neighbor across the North Sea. It is warmer in summer and colder in winter; half the rainfall is from July to November, and, paradoxically, April is, of all months, the driest. The practicality, placidity, not to say stolidity, of the average citizen force the comparison with Britons or with certain Swedes and Germans—whom the Danes seem to resemble in temperament far more than they do the Norwegians or Finns who, like ourselves, possess a Celtic or other leaven. One Dane confided in me that he knew for a certainty that naught but Danish blood had flowed in the veins of his family for the past three hundred years. Perhaps this undoubtedly typical circumstance accounts for modern Danish limitations. The Vikings were more venturesome.

Danish artists have long known Fanø, as have naturalists on the lookout for bittern and green heron, but its praises have been too little sung in the world outside the confines of Denmark. Fanø, until recent years a fisherman's island, now harbors a popular bathing resort in high favor with the English. The island can be reached in twenty-two hours from Harwich. The village of Nordby, a mere twenty minutes from the mainland, has made few concessions to these summer guests—a sprinkling of villas, a shop or two displaying North Sea amber, dolls garbed like the mariners' wives who sell them. The summer season is short. Nordby men, conservative as their sires, still turn to the sea for livelihood, still prefer to see their women garbed in the costume hallowed by centuries of use—intricate turban head-dress, long-sleeved bodice, and five superimposed skirts of various hues. One of the four surviving schools of navigation in Denmark is at Nordby. Sønderho at the island's southern tip leads its own life to all intents and purposes unmolested.

Our first glimpse of a Fanø costume was of one worn by a veritable seeress on the market-square at Esbjerg. Arrived at Nordby we found our interest was divided by the novel characteristics of the thatched brick cottages, on which pear-trees were trained in espalier, and which were further embellished by green gable-ends, checked window-curtains, and riotous dahlias. All of these features are accentuated at Sønderho, and, in at least one case, with the arresting addition of a wooden image of a gentleman in a black stock peering over the gate of a fenced house-yard. After the first shock we remembered having been warned of this strange use for old figureheads in favor at Fanø.

Even in the graveyard is felt the presence of the sea. Kaptein Hans Møller Harbye, Skipper Jens Peder Knudsen, Skibsreder Niels Jepsen Outzen, are among the inscriptions on tombstones at Sønderho. Does this imply that even after death the Dane is a stickler for titles? Carved doves of peace, symbol dear to mariners who know the power of waters, have seemingly alighted on tombs, bearing olive-leaves of hope. Only the exterior of the church shows marks of restoration. Within the building blue box pews brought from

Ribe Cathedral, ancient font and pulpit, form an appropriate setting for the many ship-models hanging, spiderwise, above the aisles.

A wearer of the costume was busied in the churchyard, for gardening is woman's work when man must go to sea. Greetings were exchanged with the buxom dame, who admitted that her own daughter would not wear the heavy native dress. Among the married it is still the rule. Seen against the background of their cottages, hoe over shoulder or child by the hand, the matrons of Fanø form pictures of somewhat the same genre as those still seen at Plougastel.

Remembering how the Bretons wade out to rake in seaweed, we were not surprised to hear that the natives of Fanø also wade into the cold North Sea to garner its fruits—in this case amber. At one time, we were told by the leading dealer, a meticulous soul whose winters are spent in cutting, polishing, and setting, amber was so abundant on these shores that it was used by the natives as fuel.

"You see this lump," said the dealer, lifting a spongy example. "It should have lain under the sea another couple of hundred years. It's not yet hard enough for jewelry—the women will pick it up—but good amber is still brought in after the winter storms. I have specimens with flies, as you see. These are for schools and collectors...the ladies don't like insects in their necklaces.

"The amber for sale on the mainland probably comes from the Baltic... you'll note the tag '*Naturbernstein*' "—I interjected that I had already when purchasing at Zoppot—"but when you buy from me you can be confident that you have a genuine souvenir of Fanø."

Mussels and oysters and clams, scallops and crabs and conch-shells, cork floats attached to shreds of fish-nets, driftwood, skate and shark eggs, foam of the sea—all else we gathered in both hands on Fanø beaches, but never the amber we sought.

Not at the hour when bathing-machines drawn by docile horses were in demand—tide being a circumstance on the North Sea—did we find our favorite phase of Fanø, but on wild days of wind, when waves lashed to the dunes. Sea and dunes and heather... heather and dunes and sea! These spell Fanø, these, too, evoke neighboring Jutland.

A day in Ribe is a day spent in a picture-book town. One longs for a sip from Alice's bottle to become in scale with the minuscule brick buildings whose red-tiled roofs and gables are often within arm's reach.

The inhabitants of Ribe are no more carefully counted than are the storks. "We had only about twenty nests this year," said the teacher, whose guests we were, as she conducted us to a point outside the Cathedral, where we might, at one glance, watch two stork families—one on Bishop Hans

Tausens Hus. Cartwheels are put enticingly on house ridges. To kill a stork, harbinger of peace, is a serious offense in Denmark.

"Hard to tell parents from offspring," I remarked.

"Yes," the lady answered, "they are well grown now. If you had come one week later, not a stork would you have seen. They are already discussing the trip to Africa," she continued, as one proud parent with clapping of bill, incisive as a shoemaker's hammer, flapped on mammoth wings close overhead.

"There," she went on, "is the house where Jacob Riis was born. He left Ribe when many from Slesvig-Holstein (taken from Denmark by the Germans) were emigrating to try their fortune in America. Let me translate the tablet:

JACOB A. RIIS
1849 JOURNALIST AND PHILANTHROPIST
DIED MASSACHUSETTS 1914
FAITHFUL TO HIS TOWN
CALLED BY PRESIDENT ROOSEVELT
["Theodore," my Illustrator interposed]
AMERICA'S MOST USEFUL CITIZEN."

"His name is revered in New York," I said, "for his civic righteousness. So this is *The Old Town* of which he wrote."

Ribe is the antithesis of everything modern or American. Perhaps for this reason it is one of the

Ribe.

sights in Denmark most appreciated by the traveler from overseas. In the Middle Ages and even
as late as the sixteenth and seventeenth centuries
Ribe was the most prosperous town of the region.
The approach of the German frontier in 1864 was
the cause of the town's stagnation, inundation another (hundreds were drowned in the neighborhood in 1634), another the lessening navigability
of the River Nibs. The removal of the German
frontier farther south, in 1920, came too late
to be of commercial importance to the town.
Esbjerg, the upstart, has replaced Ribe as a port.
"Preserve, O Lord, the dikes and dams in the
King's Marsh Lands," reads a Danish prayer,
and trusting not alone in the efficacy of prayer,
but in the new dike constructed in 1911, the citizens no longer fear a further catastrophe by flood
like those recorded by the marker on the river-
bank.

To the tourist the stagnation of Ribe comes as a boon. The Old Town at Aarhus is bereft of inhabitants, but Ribe, actually vying with it in quaintness, still pursues its interests in a way entirely compatible with its decorous old age. When a new building is to be erected, it must, of necessity, be in keeping—indeed, hardly distinguishable from the originals. There seems no danger that tranquil and historically minded Ribe will dislodge its storks or do aught to trifle with its local color—the goose that lays the golden eggs.

The Cathedral, with Gothic watch-tower dating from the thirteenth century (rebuilt 1594), although less harmonious than Saint Catherine's (founded the same century, with restored cloisters perhaps the finest in Denmark), is an effective mass around which the little town, bereft since 1644 of its castle, nestles. Likewise on the market-square stands the chief hotel and the Wies' Stue, a Danish tavern in continuous use since 1700... one meal will amply suffice, but the atmosphere of the past is impeccable.

An American child lunching beside us asked repeatedly, "Mother, why is it called Reba? Mother, is its real name Rebecca?" "Rebecca," we thought, would be a not inappropriate appellation for the birthplace of Jacob Riis.

"To visit the Town Hall"—where antiquities are shown—"apply to the jailer," we read. It had a dangerous sound... it seemed safer to confine ourselves to the Post Office (an ancient bishop's palace on Puggaardsgade) and to the Library. The librarian said that she occasionally had visits from English students from the International People's College at Elsinore and showed us a copy of the college's popular quarterly published in English, *The Observer*. We admired a picture of Henrik Pontoppidan, who had celebrated his eightieth birthday on July twenty-fourth, and read the impressive list of his works. We spoke of Johannes Jensen, perhaps the most distinguished of present-day Danish writers, himself of Jutland origin; of Jacobsen's masterpiece, *Marie Grubbe*, poignant life story of the degeneration of one nurtured in a Jutland homestead; and of our fondness for any links connecting with H. C. Andersen—in Ribe it was the storks.

"And the children!" added the librarian. "On this same street is the Cathedral School, founded in 1145, in a building dating from the sixteenth century. You will know it because a stork—the children put out sugar for it—has built its nest there."

"At 212 Puggaardsgade," I exclaimed, "is a delectable house, completely as it should be even to the stork's nest, and what did I find on looking a second time? A sign *Damefrisørsalon*—hairdressing and beauty specialist! When beautified where does one go?"

"Well," it was admitted, "there is no night life in Ribe. The housewives who sit at their 'busy-bodies' [mirrors in which the quiet streets reflect] don't find even an abdication to gossip about in these days."

At noon we had listened to "Dagmar's Tune" played by the bells of the Cathedral. Danes have long memories. The story is still told of Queen Dagmar, daughter of the King of Bohemia. The castle of her husband, Valdemar II, whose reign began in 1202, stood upon the river-bank at Ribe, and from here, nine years after her marriage, Dagmar dispatched her page to advise the King of her mortal illness. Valdemar leaped upon his horse and galloped all the sixty miles from Skandeborg. He arrived too late; yet so powerful was his love and the prayers of her ladies that, it is said, the Queen returned a moment from beyond death's portal to bid her spouse farewell. A statue of Dagmar marks the site of the castle—destroyed, in 1644, in a battle between Danes and Swedes.

The marshes around Ribe are as flat as the Netherlands and, especially when ablaze with tulips grown on a grand scale, suggest Holland, that other land of windmills and dikes. These lowlands have a character of their own, shared only with those around Tønder to southward, eight miles from the sea. Tønder, like Ribe, has somewhat over six thousand inhabitants nowadays.

The ornate façades of its mansions recall the heyday of its prosperity, as do the capacious brick homesteads in the environs. A forgotten area lies between Tønder, Møgeltønder, and the sea. Storks frequent its frog-ridden pools, the road to the border village of Rudbøl has become a rutted way. Not much intercourse is held to-day with the land that flies the Swastika, though a martial sentry paces at the German end of the bridge that spans the waterway.

This territory to south of Ribe—with four towns, Tønder, Sønderborg, Aabenraa, and Hadersle—constitutes what was formerly North Schleswig, but since its return to Denmark in 1920, by plebiscite following the Treaty of Versailles, it is now known as South Jutland. It was once a portion of Schleswig-Holstein, the latter united to Germany since the duchies were wrested from Denmark in 1864. The territory had become Danish at the time when Christian of Oldenburg, its count, became King of Denmark. When he died without issue, Germany would not recognize the right of his successor, Christian IX, to the duchies. Denmark went to war to defend her own, but the Danish forces met defeat near Sønderborg. It was at this time that many thousands of Denmark's sons emigrated. Denmark's loss was America's gain.

On our return from the frontier we motored through Løgumkloster, where, with carrousels, the populace made merry...and where, when we asked directions, the answers were given in German by a burly fellow born in Texas but returned, since 1920, to his father's boyhood home. Although Danish flags were riotously in evidence, we noted, both here and at Aabenraa, a conspicuous German survival in long-stemmed pipes and dachshunds.

Leaving the south, we motored by way of Jelling to Jutland's capital, Aarhus. In order to feast our eyes on rune stones we careened in our Copenhagen taxicab—still announcing to all who might read the auspicious one word *Fri*—through a copse of beeches. Our car, apparently not attempting to follow the road's brusque curves, lurched periously.

"What's wrong? Have you a puncture?" I inquired.

"No, sir," replied the Gentle Soul, addressing me, not my husband, "no, indeed, sir."

Minutes passed—minutes in which we reviewed our past lives. "Stop!" my Illustrator shouted. "You have a flat."

The moment was opportune. With tipsy deliberation the car drew up beside a gasoline station ...a rear tire down to the rim.

"Now what do you know about that!" murmured the Gentle One in his purring Danish.

The spare tire was examined and its threadbare condition pointed out. A group of curious Danes had gathered about us. News spread that a dusty old taxi had come all the way from Copenhagen.

"Let's send the old girl back at once," I said. "But no, think of the hurt feelings...the Travel Bureau, the powers behind it...a diplomatic scandal...an international breach. No, doubly no! Long live the King! Better to risk our necks and carry on as planned to Aalborg."

Perhaps one reason Jelling was so enjoyable was that at Jelling we were on terra firma. Not only did we tread our way on the level, but we mounted the fifty-odd steps to the top of the mound that forms so impressive a burial-chamber for that old pagan Gorm—the first king who emerges from the dim past, with his wife Thyra, the first Christian queen. The son of the pair, Harold Bluetooth, was to attain historic importance as grandfather of Canute, the conqueror of England. In about 980 "Harold, the king, caused this memorial to be erected," so read the runic characters upon the monument, "to Gorm his father and Thyra his mother. He was the Harold who united under him the whole of Denmark and Norway and ordained Christianity for the Danes."

The stone stands, incongruously, at the door of the village church, a building dwarfed by its position between the two formidable mounds. The massive boulder sacred to the memory of Gorm has been called by an authority "the most impressive of all existing runic monuments in Denmark." A crude figure of Christ decorates one side while another surface depicts the struggle of a serpent and a dragon, both intricately woven and intertwined, root and branch, with a Tree of Life.

In the tenth century the royal pair apparently dwelt at Jelling. In our time King Christian X and Queen Alexandrine come yearly to sojourn at Marselisborg on the outskirts of Aarhus. This Royal Summer Residence was given to them at the time of their marriage, in 1898, by the Danish people. It is not the King and Queen's only house in Jutland, for they are fond of a simple villa by the sea, Klitgaarden ("The Dune Farm") near Skagen. Marselisborg Woods are visited not only to see the Residence with its king's guardsman pacing at the gate, its cluster of whitewashed gardener's cottages, its expanse of vivid lawn polka-dotted with gulls, but because of the singularly poignant memorial to Danes killed in the World War. This monument in Mindeparken takes the form of a walled enclosure. Its chalk surfaces are embellished with bas-reliefs and covered by names of Denmark's sons engulfed on both sides of the world cataclysm.

Aarhus, with about a tenth the population of Copenhagen, is the second city as well as the second port of Denmark. Since 1933 it has been the seat of a university. The traveler will wish to

Aarhus ‡ ✠
Den Gamle By ⋅ ♛

visit the Cathedral of Saint Clement, if not, as well, the Church of Our Lady. Saint Clement's, begun in 1201 but restored in the fourteenth and fifteenth centuries, boasts of being the longest religious edifice in Denmark. It possesses an elaborate reredos and archaic frescoes—Saint George despatching a prostrate dragon, King Christian II sword in hand.

Like other Danish churches on the mainland, the Cathedral's exterior is of brick while the interior is of a demure Protestant whiteness. Perhaps one must be born a Dane or a Quaker to enjoy worship in such stark surroundings. Cleanliness, in Denmark, has gained an upper hand—almost to the exclusion of godliness.

The same overtidiness and fresh-painted appearance mar most of the antiquities in the land. Den Gamle By or Old Town at Aarhus suffers from oversolicitude. These fully equipped houses, dating from the reign of Christian IV, have been reassembled in order to preserve them, but the spirit of an actual village has not been recreated —as, for example, at Lillehammer. Perhaps we had too lately come from Ribe to do full justice to the extraordinary collection assembled at Aarhus. Perhaps, having recently visited Oslo and Lillehammer, Stockholm, Lund, and Copenhagen, we were satiated with what is, after all, an admirable and unique Scandinavian institution—the open-air museum.

The Great Cairn of Knebel

The Vikings were partial to wild peninsulas. They frequented the haunts of the prehistoric peoples who had already erected, in such wind-swept regions near the sea as the Mols Hills, their innumerable monuments. A short drive from Aar-hus brings the motorist within sight of the ruined castle of Kalø, where Gustavus Vasa, taken as a hostage by Christian II, was imprisoned. On a heather-clad moorland we at last came upon the Great Cairn of Knebel, so much master of the sur-rounding scene that it actually may be compared to Stonehenge.

An enticing sign induced us to follow the arrow pointing to Tinghulen. That we had not the slight-est idea of what Tinghulen might be added zest to the enterprise. To Tinghulen we would go. Hans encouraged the idea. Indeed, the words—he

rarely attempted English—"all same ice" caught
our fancy. Clearly Tinghulen had to do with the
glacial epoch. We trudged along a sandy path
around the shoulder of a hill and up a distant
slope. Here we met returning Danes. "This,"
they said, in German, for they were South Jutland Danes, "is Tinghulen."

"And what then," we asked, "is Tinghulen?"

"This bowl or hollow in the hills," they answered, pointing, "glacial formation."

"Oh," we exclaimed, " 'all same ice!' "

Here too, we liked to think, Vikings may have
met, with outposts silhouetted against the sky to
guard against disturbance of their *ting* or court.
The desire to linger in so mysterious and hidden
a retreat conflicted with our longing to visit the
Noah's Ark town of Abeltoft and the market-
place of Grenaa, renowned for half-timbered
houses. Curiosity conquered.

"Visit Aalborg and its environments!" reads a
local leaflet. According to some authorities, Aalborg is the most ancient town in Denmark. There
is no question that it has preserved pleasing remnants of its past despite the modernity of its main
thoroughfare, Vesterbro, which would do credit
to a larger city. The same might be said of the
Hotel Phønix, situated on this street, from the
windows of which the Cathedral may be seen.
This outlook pleased us especially on days when
cattle were driven to indoor markets, where, after

much inspection by prospective buyers, they changed hands. Push-carts with flowers would also pass, and milk-wagons in combination with immense tanks to be filled at the distillery with dregs for swine.

Scandinavians, being of a sturdiness rarely met elsewhere, are uncomprehending of physical limitations of the average traveler. It was impossible to accept all the invitations received to visit cement factories (we were told that twenty-five per cent of the world's supply is Danish), manufactories of cigars and the *cigarillos* fancied by the women of Denmark, the Danske Spritfabrikker— the spirit most esteemed being *snaps*. To this latter plant, however, situated near the bridge across the Limfjord connecting Aalborg with Nørre Sundby, we gave a thorough inspection. Containers, mammoth though they be, are all of polished copper, contrasting with sea-green walls and other pipes whose colors, to the knowing, proclaim their contents. The immense barley crops find justification in the malt room, where vats of sprouting grain are kept to temperature with aid of thermometers stuck like seed-markers in a garden.

De Danske Spritfabrikker, Ltd., was founded in 1881 by Chr. H. Olesen. The son of the founder is its present manager. Since 1923 the company has monopolized the production of yeast and alcohol in Denmark, and since 1934 the Government has granted it a ten-year concession, limiting its action by certain stipulations. The company's two distilleries are in Northern Jutland, at Aalborg and at Hobro, both central to the potato-fields whence comes one raw-material source. The smell of dregs saved for pigs and cattle warns of the approach to the D. D. S. F. almost before its silos come in sight. Although *snaps* or *akvavit* is the pride of Aalborg's plant, it comprises only from ten to thirteen per cent of the total output. Other products are liqueur, perfume, and alcohol for scientific purposes.

At the end of our two-hour trek, Mr. Sørensen, who accompanied us, remarked: "If you had come to Denmark a century ago you could have visited twenty-five hundred lawful distilleries! Now there are but two. You will agree, though, that this distillery and the Carlsberg brewery in Copenhagen are among Denmark's principal sights."

Wearily we agreed. "But where," I asked, satiated with explanations of gadgets, "are the workmen?"

"You've hit the nail on the head," replied our companion. "There are only the few you have seen, chiefly polishers of copper. The saying goes that Mr. Olesen could sit in his office and push a button to keep the whole plant running."

In the cellar of Jens Bangs Stenhus, a Renaissance mansion of 1624, is to be found a tap-room worth the seeing, even though you may not share the Danish enthusiasm for beer. Jens Bangs, it appears, was a merchant who wanted to become a nobleman, but in his time such a transition was frowned upon. To spite the peers who would borrow his kroner but would have none of him, Jens, all in a year, built this palatial edifice which put the dwellings of the nobility to shame. Near-by stands the house of the hapless Ellen Marsin who was burned as a witch.

My favorite of the points of interest that Aalborg offers is the seventeenth-century castle—unlike, I venture to state, any other castle on earth. Approached from the street it has a somewhat formidable appearance, but once within the courtyard you find yourself surrounded by half-timbered structures on which paint and whitewash vie for ascendancy. Here dwells the Chief Magistrate of the province. My Illustrator expressed the hope that the gentleman's wardrobe is in keeping with the Gilbert and Sullivan setting.

The name Aalborg indeed suggests *opéra comique*—"the castle of the eel."

"Do you know this one?" Mr. Sørensen had asked us, "*Raa aa aal*—the Danish way of saying Raa [a Zealand town], river eel."

Rebild National Park lies a few miles to the south of Aalborg. It is of interest as an unusual gesture in brotherliness between Danes and Americans and, moreover, because of the intrinsic beauty of the site. The idea of a park where Danish-born and other Americans might celebrate the Fourth of July arose in the mind of Dr. Max Henius of Chicago at such a celebration at the Aarhus Exposition in 1909. The project grew rapidly, and in 1912 a tract of moorland (now extended to four hundred acres) in the Rebild Hills was presented to the Danish Government. Flags, given by different states of the Union, annually line the path to a Lincoln Log Cabin Museum—the logs sent from different states by resident Danes. The cabin, symbolic of the mode of life often led by the Danish pioneer in America, was dedicated on July 4, 1934, in the presence of the King and Queen. Ruth Bryan Owen, then Minister to Denmark, spoke eloquently on Lincoln. There were forty thousand spectators on this occasion, and a hundred thousand visit the park annually for recreation and to picnic in the heather-clad hills. The museum contains a collection of Indian costumes and utensils, made by the Senecas and presented on behalf of the Iroquois by the Rochester Museum of Arts and Sciences, and a prairie-schooner, gift of the State of Utah.

Our own explorations in Northern Jutland were not made in the prairie-schooner taxi that had borne us lurchingly from its Copenhagen base. No, as by previous arrangement, it had been, with its willing driver, safely shipped aboard a ferry for Zealand. We had been provided instead with a spick-and-span Nash and chauffeur, wearing the three stars of the Royal Automobile Club, who drove, nevertheless, at such a pace the landscape blurred. Not for this had we come to Denmark, the author and illustrator ungratefully protested, not to be taken here, there, and everywhere, an unwilling cargo, but to see, to absorb, to record. To be bucolic under such circumstances was a feat, but, in retrospect, bucolic is the word that best sums up our first day.

At Løgstor, where we lunched at the Hotel du Nord (the place for plaice), we were intrigued by the to us arresting sign of *"Bad W.C."* By way of Bjørnsholm, where unemployed youths are given agricultural training ("Concentration camp!" mumbles the communistic minority), we pursued the road to Aertbolle. To our surprise the immaculate Nash showed the mettle of a spirited Ford. Undaunted by meandering tracks across sweeps of sand, it nosed its way to the very beach where were the kitchen-middens we had come to seek. Four groups bear the marker of the National Museum, but, truth to tell, the section preserved in Copenhagen is actually more rewarding. The surroundings are appropriate setting for these refuse-heaps of prehistoric man—lean pastures, bouquets of pines, peat-bogs.

Cliffs, otherwise unknown on Denmark's mainland or indeed on Funen or Zealand, form the distinguishing feature of Buljerg. We crossed the

Windmills of

Løgstor Bredning by ferry to attain this dramatic climax of cliffs facing the North, or, as the Danes know it, Vesterhavet, the West Sea. The approach is through miles of stunted pines, a fifty-year-old plantation, part of the Government's effort to anchor the refractory sands. As we made our way across dunes to the headland lashed by the open sea, our mood completely changed. Bucolic Denmark was, for the nonce, put out of mind while our thoughts flew swiftly to Cornwall and to Brittany, to Penzance, to Camaret, to the Pointe du Raz with its Bay of the Dead—scene of the legendary *Cathédrale Engloutie.*

A guest from the hotel had joined us at our wind-blown post. "That," said he, pointing to where the waters lashed, "is called Jammerbug—

northern Jutland

the Bay of Horror." An international language is spoken by the sea.

Although I have called Buljerg the climax of our day, yet there was no anticlimax in the route that led us to far Feggesund to observe the bird life on the marshy shores of Løgstor Bredning or in the homeward drive, after sunset, to where, at Aalborg, this sheet of water joins the Limfjord.

The historic Hamlet (Amleth, grandson of Rorik, King of Denmark) on whose tragic story many plays have been based is said to have dwelt, a thousand years before the building of Kronborg, in the neighborhood of Feggesund. Eerie as the voice of the Ghost in Shakespeare's *Hamlet* were the cries of the sea-fowl. "Swear!" one seemed to reiterate to our intently listening ears.

Battalions of lapwings formed and reformed and reconnoitered along the expanse of marshland. I was drawn irresistibly from the cushioned automobile to assist at their deliberations, deaf to warnings of bogs, aware only of the *"peewit"* of the birds—friendly to an extent hitherto unknown, strutting in pride of white fronts, dark ties, and perky crests like grandees in dinner-coats and coronets.

Later our attention was to be turned to the farmhouses with their turf-like thatch from which grew windmills casting graceful shadows. Mills north of Limfjord possess an exquisite delicacy unknown in the more Teutonic south of Jutland.

"Pinwheels!" exclaimed my Illustrator.

Pinwheels indeed they were, feathered like prehistoric birds, twirling or arrested, lithesome as birches against white plaster walls. Low barns, tethered Holstein cattle, a man on a bicycle leading seven chained cows in straggling formation, houses pink as Danish heather, marsh grass rustling at dusk, and geese—geese strutting, geese craning, geese hissing—thoughts of golden eggs, of Chanticler, of H. C. A. (that Ugly Duckling of Ugly Ducklings), thoughts of Mother Goose and of the faithfulness of ganders ... so ended, drowsily, our day.

One more excursion was to be made from Aalborg—the friendly Aalborg. This was to the thumb-shaped peninsula that forms the northern-

most tip of Jutland and therefore of Denmark.
Here king and commoner alike find summer recreation among the dunes at Skagen—the Skaw. The
beach from Blokhus to Løkken is, dangerously,
open to motorists. For ten miles the pedestrian
would find himself in surroundings as remote from
man as the setting of Stevenson's "Pavilion on
the Links" were it not for the coming of ubiquitous motors. My query, "Have they not all the
roads of Denmark that they must come here to
spoil the beach and threaten the lives of bathers?"
fell on deaf ears.

It was at Løkken that the Prime Minister, the
valiant Stauning, idolized by Danes of every
party, had fallen and broken his leg. "The old
bear is mending," we heard on all sides. "He
smokes his cigar as usual"—a reference to the
popular fact that Stauning began life as a cigar-
roller and has always circumvented a high tax on
cigars.

The Kandehus Hotel at Kandestederne has a
local reputation among painters as it is run by a
member of the brotherhood. It is a base for visit
to one of the strangest manifestations of Nature
to be found in Denmark. This is the Raabjerg Mile
or Desert of Kandehus. The desert consists of a
vast expanse of dunes marching, so our host informed us, from Skagerrak to Kattegat (that is,
from west to east), until one day, so old folks say,
it will swallow the town of Frederikshavn. Its

present pace is fifty yards per annum. Constantly
modulated dunes are transfigured by sunlight and
shadow until they assume the proportions of
glacial snow-fields. Instinct warns the birds, even
in flight, to avoid the Sahara of Kandehus.

Any visitor to the west coast of Jutland must
be impressed by the insidious power of sand.
Borne on the wind that so often rages over the
North Sea, sand has inundated western Jutland
to such an extent that in some portions, such as
the Raabjerg Mile, not even marram will grow,
while elsewhere nothing more profitable than
heather. When, however, Slesvig-Holstein was
lost to Denmark and the country faced an agricultural crisis, Colonel Dalgas was inspired with
the idea of creating new cultivated land by means
of heather-burning, ploughing, and irrigation.
The Danish Heath Society is the outgrowth of
a movement which has planted many thousand
acres of forest and actually redeemed so much
moorland that some day the heather-clad slopes of
Ribild National Park may be a unique survival.

A few kilometers from Kandehus, beyond the
church like the Sphinx half-buried in sand, lies
Skagen. The fame of Skagen consists in the fact
that here, dramatically, the West and East Seas
meet. At times the battle rages high between indomitable Skagerrak and no less invulnerable
Kattegat. A mountainous wall of water surges
off Denmark's final tongue of sand. Here, where

spray flies and ocean-going gulls hover, where dunes are paramount, the Danish poet Holger Drachmann came to meditate on man's transitory lot. Here, by his own wish, he rests, a dolmen for his tomb.

Although summer visitors disport on Skagen's beach, yet they leave little imprint on the fishermen's village.

There are graves aplenty at Skagen—of those who manned life-boats in gales no boat could weather, of English marines lost, in May, 1916, in the Battle of Jutland. Nightly the piercing ray from the lighthouse, incisive as a radio announcement, blazes forth its message: "This is Denmark."

Denmark! On arrival we had had to cope with a certain undercurrent of acquired Swedish prejudice against the Danes. "A Teutonic race of middle stature," we had read, "with habits more like North Germans than like Swedes." Now, faced with reality, we were audibly moaning at the bar of departure. Our last day in North Jutland had overtaken us too cruelly soon. We were lashed with desire to remain. Remembered voices of new-found Danish friends whispered in our ears. Bound by our schedule as inexorably as martyr to stake, we embarked dutifully at Frederikshavn ... headed once more for the unknown.

Part Four
FINLAND

Helsinki ✦ The Railroad Station.
Masterpiece of Saarinen.

Porvoo.

CHAPTER XV

HELSINKI, WHITE CITY OF THE NORTH

HELSINKI has been called "the White City of the North," perhaps because this northernmost capital of Europe lies for so long a period beneath a blanket of snow, perhaps because of the paleness of its native granite (although there are few white buildings in Finland's capital), perhaps because its natives befriended the White Russians and expelled the Red.

At midsummer there is magic in the white nights of the North. Even in late July, time of our arrival on Baltic shores, dim twilight merged blithely into dawn. White nights were never meant for sleep. Plant life, seemingly aware, pushes miraculously from bud to fruition. The emphasis, as it was in the birth of our own Republic, is on the rising and not upon the setting sun. Finland, old in wisdom, was reborn with the birth of the

Republic. Centuries of foreign rule were as unable to quench the light of the Finnish spirit as the pall of winter has been to darken the electrically illuminated boulevards of Finland's capital. Like a superbeacon in a fog-ridden world the white ray of Finnish integrity flashes its steadfast message—an augury of hope to distressed ships of state.

"Helsinki! Do you mean Helsingfors, the capital of Finland?" I am asked. "Are they the same?"

Yes, and no. Who can fail to hear the clink of ice in the cool, crisp vowels of the first, the clear-cut modernity of the Finnish designation—come into its own since the War of Liberation? The second smacks of the old régime and the more smugly rounded language of the Swede. With the intolerance of youth the young republic, admitted to the family of nations in 1918, makes short shrift of those who would have its affairs transacted in any but the vernacular—a mere ten per cent of the inhabitants of the country claim Swedish as mother-tongue. The duality of place names and, along the coast, street names, however, plainly reflects the enduring strength of the Swedish racial strain, for the Swedes, be it remembered, possessed Finland for over six hundred years.

A Finnish-speaking Finn—popularly known as a Finn Finn—must study Swedish at school, while the Finlanders—natives of Swedish descent—are compelled nowadays to study Finnish. Wrested from the Swedes by Alexander I, in 1809, the country was at first an autonomous duchy with the Czar its paradoxically tolerant grand-duke (Russian animosity was originally against Sweden and not against the Finns). Alexander II restored the Finnish Diet and recognized the Finnish language, but in days of Panslavism and later of Bolshevism Russia became anathema to the Finns.

"Welcome to Finland, Mr. and Mrs. Oakley!" The words rang reassuringly above the babel of tongues as our Scantic liner lowered its gangplank.

Who could she be, this vital female, who had braved the elements at 7 A.M. to greet us on the dock at Helsinki? Beneath dripping umbrellas it was hastily explained that she had received word of our coming from the Finnish consul in New York (himself unknown to us) and that she was to arrange meetings with officials in the Foreign Office—officials who, as it proved, would strew our path with roses.

"Magic," we exclaimed. "It's in the air. The Magic North...the Land of the Magic Word."

Our friend-to-be beamed approvingly: "So you know the *Kalevala*. Then you will understand the Finns."

"Everywhere you will hear English," we had been told. A traveler's tale! Fortunately we had never believed it. It was not too long before we learned, however, that one of the outstanding characteristics of the Finn is his ability to perform the seemingly impossible. (Not by accident has the nation survived more than seven hundred years of alien rule.) The powers that be at the Foreign Office, realizing that we should enjoy hearing English, arranged that in every town visited during our stay in their country at least one cultured English-speaking individual would put himself or herself out to be agreeable to us. The "magic word" when put on paper and presented by us in the form of an introduction invariably proved to be open-sesame.

Despairing of conquering the native idiom (our knowledge barely extended beyond numerals and greetings) and finding ourselves faltering in Swedish; misunderstood in German half-forgotten since school-days; uncomprehended in French or English, save in certain restaurants and shops, we gasped in amazement at our Lady of the Dock who was fluent in all these tongues as well as in Russian!

Symbolic perhaps of the rather dour and not especially prepossessing exterior of the average Finn was the first impression of Helsinki in rain. On closer acquaintance with the Finn the veil was lifted, and, too, on the day after our arrival the curtain of rain rolled up to present a radiant Helsinki. Not again during the entire month of August did we have less than bountiful sunshine.

There is glamour
at Kappeli's

Imperishable is the glamour of those prolonged
evenings spent in the open at the restaurant Kappeli, where we lingered amid subtropical verdure
while the son-in-law of Sibelius conducted operatic airs, Viennese waltzes, or, by request, the
Master's "Valse Triste."

At lunch-time the roof-garden restaurant of the Hotel Torni is one of the world's gayest. Placed in a tower overlooking the spacious city and with view of the harbor and shipping, it is justly popular for its position as well as for its cuisine. The élite gather ravenously around the traditional central table where smörgåsbord must be chosen —the Finns have painted the lily by adding innumerable local fishes and dishes to the Swedish superabundance. (Should the caviar be red or black? Should we take Baltic herring or a slice of the salmon so temptingly displayed?—these were indeed perplexing problems.) One day there were scientists—physicists, geologists, zoölogists —fresh from a convention at the University, chatting in the tongues of the four Nordic countries. Another day the crowd was English-speaking with preponderant element of boisterous sun-tanned youth from the U. S. A. The Torni tower is a conspicuous feature of central Helsinki, doubly so because of the courteous Finnish habit of hotels to fly the flags of resident guests.

The national flag of Finland is symbol to the Finn not alone of glory but of hearth and home. Finns after a sojourn in America inevitably long for the high and intensely blue skies of their native land, for the white clouds which sail so incredibly far from earth. They feel oppressed by the low arch of our heavens which shuts them in. Sky-blue on white is the cross of their flag—simi-

lar in form to that of the other Scandinavian
nations. No other flag seems so harmonious a bit
of the heavens when unfurled in sunshine or mirrored in seas and lakes.

Wind-torn skies against which flags float high
in open spaces, and especially the vast cobbled
square dominated by the monumental station,
gateway to Russia and the East (on this our windows at the Hotel Karelia gave); glints of blue
sea at farthest street-ends—such are my salient
impressions of Helsinki. Busy thoroughfares are
lined with modern structures, for Helsinki is more
modern than New York—less of the old remaining. Banks, hotels, bewildering shops culminating
in the marvel of Stockman's (a Bon Marché,
Wanamaker's, and Harrod's in one, incorporating
what is perhaps the world's largest bookshop);
unrivaled florists' windows, open-air markets;
pâtisseries such as Fazer's unsurpassed in Paris;
palatial government buildings—none of these
forms my Helsinki. Strange how intangible it is ...
yet, no, not strange, for my Helsinki is itself a symbol—a symbol of Finnish rebirth. And Finland,
what is it—this land of the Finns, this free, high-
minded people, unfettered by tradition? Finland
is a land of open spaces, of far horizons, of interminable forests, of not a thousand, as has so
often been said, but of seventy thousand lakes.
Wide shaded boulevards, ample parks and plazas,
these the Finn demands in his Capital, and, no

less, avenues of exit innumerable by sea, by air, by
rail or motor. Every summer week-end finds the
city deserted—as it is indeed for the entire month
of August, when most habitable; but the well-to-do
native has responded to the call of lake and
forest and wooded skerries in the bay where he
may commune with Nature and Nature's God. The
Finn is not gregarious. He calls his soul his own.

Having abolished both poverty and riches, having built hospitals in numbers sufficient to cope
on modern terms with disease, having pushed co-
operative economics to furthest limits, having
built his city of Helsinki according to a plan
(Saarinen has drawn up blue-prints for vast future developments), the Finn rests not on his
laurels but is doing his utmost to encourage the
arts. Perhaps the far-looking Finn will be the first
to realize Frank Lloyd Wright's ideal city of the
future, endowed with vast wooded spaces, devoid
of congested areas.

Excursions to be taken from Helsinki are one
reason for the convenient and to me congenial
base. Shall I name a few that under no conditions
should be forgotten? First and foremost, that to
Fölisön, if we use its Swedish title, as the idea of
open-air folk-museum is borrowed from the Swedish Skansen at Stockholm. First, then, we shall
go to Fölisön or, as the Finns say, Seurasaari,
on its island. A slightly longer trip, necessarily
by boat, is that to the fortress of Suomenlinna, on

an island farther in the bay; and a still longer
excursion (a whole day this) would be by boat
to Porvoo, returning by autocar. These may be
shared by all. To some is added the privilege of
visiting the homes, hallowed shrines, of two outstanding citizens, Saarinen and Sibelius.

If there were time for but one impression of
Helsinki, I should insist that the one be Fölisön.
I must admit, however, that on the occasion of our
visit everything conspired towards enchantment.
To begin with, we were accompanied by our Lady
of the Dock, in whose company there are no drab
moments. We drove by taxi to the causeway,
where pampas-like sea-grasses, rising from brackish water, formed the foreground to distant
Helsinki, lighted by the setting sun.

The island of Fölisön was mysterious in shadow
—no sign of the deserted village which we were
later to come upon in fading light, dim, overshadowed by fir and pine. That the houses were
closed to us, for it was long past five, gave the
still stronger illusion that this (instead of being
an assembled exhibition of ancient log cabins) was
in reality a village... that the natives had already
retired, to rest from strenuous labors. It happened that the shed that sheltered the tar-boat
was open. Here, then, was a Viking boat, a boat
of the type used for shooting the rapids at Oulu.
We examined the oar, incredulous that a giant
could be found powerful enough to wield it, and

were told that from childhood the oarsmen are trained. From father to son are passed down the skill and the knowledge of how to negotiate rapids ... till now that tar-barrels come in more modern fashion, tourists with an eye to adventure have taken their places.

Was not one of these dwellings the house of a Volsung? That the former owners had called themselves Karelians was, to me, immaterial. This was the forest setting, this was the lair of Hunding. No doubt that the sleeping master lay within— while Siegmund and Sieglinda found rapture in awakened love. (Hereafter, when I attend *Die Walküre,* I shall be transported to the forests of Finland.)

A bear-trap formed of two prone trees, which roll together when the bait is released; a pit with top strewn deceptively with fresh-cut fir branches, recalled the hunts of wolf and bear in Aleksis Kivi's *Seven Brothers,* the first masterpiece to be written in Finnish. Later we were to come upon the two-roomed cottage where this Tolstoy of Finland lived and labored. We passed a village church unique in beauty, but all these had not brought us to Fölisön. We had come to assist at the last folk-dance of the season.

Antti-Gården was our destination—a group of old log-built houses surrounding a court in which a platform had been erected near the well with sweep suggesting an Egyptian shaduf. This part

Helsinki :
Barns in the open-air museum.

of the sleeping village had come to life. Few seats were left on the benches, natives overflowed onto the stoops of houses and even on an upper wooden gallery, reached by outside steps now utilized as seats.

Our companion exclaimed, "Look at the Americans!" Yes, brazenly American they were, bronzed by a cruise, conducted by a clerk from the shipping office. Except for this inevitable group the perhaps two hundred assembled were friends of the dancers and others indistinguishable.

A hunch-backed violinist appeared on a doorstep. Couples emerged in provincial costumes, some grouping themselves beside the fiddler (never more than six couples danced at a time). Polkas were announced in Swedish, and the name of the province of origin. Six girls wore blue skirts striped with yellow (how like the Swedish flag!), blue bodices, embroidered blouses, plaid shawls, and snug caps. The others were in red with fluttering ribbons.

To much stamping of feet and whirling of full skirts the Paul Jones changed to a Swedish version of the *"Tempête."* Then came a figure in which the girls twisted bits of material into reins to drive their partners, another called "The Big Shawl"—first the weaving, in and out, and then the close knots with boys and girls massed in the center. Perhaps the most amusing was when the men took the floor, clad in buff breeches and red or green waistcoats, glowering, wrestling, knocking each other's heads, manhandling those with long hair, and with exuberant good humor sticking out tongues and thumbing noses.

"Both minds and bodies active," remarked our companion. "No time to flirt!"

"Perhaps afterwards!" we added, noting the flushed faces.

Return to Helsinki was made by boat from the foot of the restaurant garden. We passed the powerful government ice-breaker *Jääkarhu,* idle at its pier for most of the year. A watchman aboard displayed a solitary light. Ahead the city twinkled.

On the second Sunday in August we again boarded a boat—this time the tiny *Borgå*. We had planned to make the trip, four hours by boat, to Porvoo, better known by its Swedish name of Borgå. Accustomed as we were to the voluble departures of even the smallest boats in Latin countries or to the few gestures and more restrained language of English-speaking leave-takings, we thought this embarkation was unprecedented. Holiday crowds poured aboard till every seat was taken. Cabins overflowed, every inch of space was utilized by those who stood or found themselves camp-stools. No notice announced our destination; no officer or member of the crew was visible. At the appointed hour the boat put out to sea, passing at the adjacent dock the steamer *Runeberg*.

Had we chosen aright? Were we in fact headed
for Borgå? Uncertainty lent spice to the voyage.
Immersed in the pleasure of the moment, we did
not indeed much care. Helsinki, with its imposing
Great Church (a Lutheran adaptation of Saint
Paul's), its Byzantine Greek Orthodox Cathedral,
its highly modern shafts and spires, its well-
groomed water-front, receded rapidly. Now we
threaded our way in and out between wooded
islets. Buoyant-sailed racing boats from the yacht
club's island scudded past. For a while we felt
ground-swells from the open sea. Gulls swooped
and soared and circled, crying in a language we
could understand.

Not so the tongue of those about us. We observed that the chic toque with half-veil had
reached Finland. Instead of animated Parisian
countenances were incongruously broad bland Finnish faces, some with the pronounced retroussé
nose so often caricatured. Steady blue eyes gazed
unflinchingly ahead.

No bustle, no loud conversation, calm and peace
... then, surprisingly, a voice was raised, in solemn
strain. Other voices from the stern joined in, a
rich chorus of men and women. All sang with
fervor. One young man gazed towards the heavens,
as though he saw a vision there. Mournful are the
folk-songs of the Finns, to us almost undistin-
guishable from their religious chants. The most
haunting of all, and this we recognized, was the

"Song of the Karelians," sung with the fervor of a national hymn, the song of a long-oppressed people. Very mysterious it was to us. We fondly imagined, in our ignorance, that this was a spontaneous outburst. Later we were told that we traveled with a congress of school-teachers from a convention in Helsinki who were taking this opportunity to visit Borgå—home of the Swedish-speaking poet-author of *"Vårtland,"* Finland's National Anthem.

At Borgå our English-speaking "contact" was with Mrs. Elmgren, landlady of the family hotel Unter den Linden. As the name implies, the house stands on a shaded street sloping abruptly to the river. Across the way, also on a corner, is the former home of Runeberg—kept as at the time of his death. The ochre-and-white frame building with portico and elaborate painted fence, the quiet linden-shaded street, suggested, to my mind, Portsmouth, New Hampshire, doubly so because I had once visited the house there of Thomas Bailey Aldrich whose centenary we had recently celebrated in New York.

We confided to our hostess that we felt as though we had been to Church, so devout was the spirit of the singing of the young people on the boat.

"Yes," said she, "the Finns are a quiet and well-behaved people—not given to drinking, lipstick, and rouge."

"There was hardly a cigarette on the boat," we added.

"If you want to see the Finns at their worst," a fellow-traveler from Helsinki commented, "go to the Diet; that is where they wrangle. When a member tries to speak in Swedish (the mother tongue of many), the Finn Finns go to the restaurant. You can't blame them. To many Swedish is a foreign language. But it's politics...to be heard one must speak in Finnish. But they carry the feud rather far in Helsinki, where twenty per cent still speak Swedish. My landlord will not allow his wife to deal with Finnish-speaking tradesmen. He plays a losing game."

The old-fashioned garden of Runeberg's home is in an apple-orchard. The house-plants (or their descendants), the tasteless furniture of the period (Victorian of foreign flavor), were poignantly suggestive of Runeberg's declining years. His cushioned wheel-chair (with needle-point made at the girls' school) confronts one on entering. I seemed closer to the spirit of the poet, not here, nor at his monumental grave, but in the lake country, at the site at Punkaharju where he wrote "The Fifth of July."

A modern poet dwells at Borgå, Jarl Hemmer, the present occupant of Diktarhemmet. This cottage, of much the same type as Runeberg's and like it of one story (to avoid fire hazard), is government-owned and always at the disposal of a poet. Unfortunately Hemmer was on vacation and had left Borgå, which to us seemed an excellent summer resort.

Opposite this Poet's House rises majestically the only Lutheran Cathedral in the country for Swedish-speaking congregations. (The archbishop for all Finland dwells at Turku.) In accordance with the Swedish custom the belfry stands apart and is used as a mortuary chapel—in the old days funerals took place after Sunday service, when the congregation was already assembled. The lift of newly tarred shingle roof towered over one-story houses in the neighborhood. The church is of white plaster with a red-brick design, in Swedish style, at the end opposite the chancel. At a distance this is seen to be an immense cross. Surrounding the edifice is a grassy enclosure entered by lich-gates and shaded by lindens. Here the people come to rest and meditate beside the monument to the war dead, at the foot of which red tuberous begonias glow—red being unmistakably the favorite color of both Finn and Swede.

Services are held on Sundays at nine for townpeople, at eleven for country-folk, and at one in Finnish, we were told by the verger, who conducted us across the way to the gymnasium or school where Runeberg taught. The assembly hall is now used as a museum of his son's sculpture, the next room lined with portraits of Lutheran bishops, the building now being the chapter-house.

It was unlocked for us with much ceremony, and the curved stone stair, worn by the feet of Runeberg's pupils, must have remained unchanged since his death in 1877.

A gibbous moon bathed the country in weird light as we sped along the highway to Helsinki. Oats rippled in light, gleaming like water, mists encroached upon the lowlands. Muffled in our coats we rejoiced at the flash of lighthouses—announcing the approach to the capital. Our bus, with others trailing it, whirled at last into its parking-space on the vast Square of Buses, upon which the station tower looks down, the face of its clock lost in darkness but the hands and numerals gleaming.

Russian rule in Finland began with the Treaty of Fredrikshamn, September 17, 1809. As Åbo (now Turku) was at that time entirely Swedish in sympathy, the seat of government was moved to the village of Helsinki—founded in 1550 by Gustavus Vasa. To a German architect, Engel, trained in Saint Petersburg, was entrusted the development of the new capital. The Senate Square—dominated by the domed Great Church (formerly Saint Nicholai); with its monument to Alexander II, the popular Czar who permitted the use of the Finnish language and reconvened the Finnish Diet; its State Council Buildings; its University—is typical of this era. The birth of modern architecture coincides with the founding of the Republic, which has only lately counted a score of anniversaries. Three men are outstanding: Sonck, designer of the Kallio Church (and, incidentally, of the Cathedral at Tampere); Sirén, who has given the Diet building to the world—a frigid monument reminiscent of ancient Egypt, cold and rigid in line as the glacial North, with its mirrory marble corridors, its crystal windows and ice-clear chandeliers; and Saarinen, a Joseph to whom his brother architects bow.

The architect Saarinen has lived for many years in Michigan, where he and his wife employ their talents at the Cranbrook School in Bloomfield Hills. Ever since Saarinen received honorable mention in the Chicago Tribune Building competition, he has wielded a profound influence on architecture in America. Despite the fact that he has felt compelled to leave his native land in order to achieve a wider success, Saarinen remains a loyal Finn. Every year he returns for six or seven weeks to his country-place at Vittrask, about forty kilometers from Helsinki.

Accompanied by the devoted Miss S., we had taken train to Luoma, where her cousin's open car met us. From the train window we had observed red barns such as may be seen in Sweden, or, for that matter, in Delaware or Pennsylvania; fields of clover, hay drying in characteristic fashion. Two children on the platform giggled as we alighted and addressed a question to our friend.

"What is it they talk?" she translated, and then, as they choked with laughter, "It is very amusing to hear a foreign tongue!"

As we approached Saarinen's retreat, the country became more typically northern—New Hampshire, Maine, Canada, we thought. Fireweed, in flower or blowing seed, bordered the encroaching forest, as the road became a mere trail through dense stands of pine, spruce, and birch.

Saarinen was no longer in residence, but much of his spirit hovers within the confines of this cherished house, built about 1901—after his first great success at the Paris Exposition of 1900. We passed under a low arch hung with scarlet woodbine. Far below to the right lay the lake, not seen as we approached. Instead, we found ourselves shut in between two buildings, the one to our left a Finnish farm of the old style, stone below, weathered logs above. This a professor shares, in summer, with cattle and farm implements. To the right the lower house is lived in the year round while the main dwelling adjoining is kept in immaculate readiness by a sonsy caretaker. The same, in blue checked gown, a well-groomed Finnish Gretchen, greeted us with curtsies...the more welcome because of the onslaught of a wolfish dog. Indoors and out the rustic style of the building is in harmony with its setting.

Huge charcoal drawings of Saarinen's design for the current bank-notes confronted us on entering. The realistic nudes, here on such colossal scale, would have startled us somewhat had we not lately traveled in Sweden, where the realistic nude is an obsession...Tampere was yet to come.

Windows gave upon the lake, sketches of the railroad station betrayed the master's hand, as did the design of the furniture—his work-table under a panel of cubby-holes of intricate design; a cushioned recess enriched with Karelian linen embroidered in blue and red. We walked through the immaculate kitchen to a hall with throne-like divan, Finnish rugs on the walls, a Moorish lamp swung at the foot of stairs, a vista of formal garden.

From the second floor the views of the lake are superior, views between towering pines and rough-barked birches, steep shelving steps leading endlessly down to the water. We were to wander along an inviting path which led us to a fantastic forest setting—ponderous granite boulders fern-clustered, overshadowed by spruce from which dangled shreds of pallid moss. Far away from human life, we seemed, back in the setting of Norse mythology. The silence made us receptive to the inner voices...the "magic words," to hear which the Finn seeks solitude.

What Paderèwski is to Poland, Sibelius is to Finland—the people's ideal personified. To us,

The House
of SIBELIUS

before leaving America, Finland had meant the land of Sibelius, and still more vividly was this true since we had trodden Finnish soil. Familiarity with the First, Second, and Fourth Symphonies, the "Swan of Tuonela," "En Saga," "Finlandia" (the tone-poem of which performance was forbidden in Finland during the years of unrest preceding the end of the Russian régime and now "in the repertory of every orchestra and brass band," says Cecil Gray, Sibelius' biographer), not to mention the "Valse Triste" (written for Arvid Järnefelt's *Kuolema* and the copyright sold for five pounds), had left us with a keen desire for knowledge of the other compositions of this most prolific of modern composers. Above all other introductions did we value the letter given us by one of America's foremost conductors to his friend Sibelius.

Knowing that the master had, the previous December, celebrated his seventieth birthday at Helsinki, amid plaudits of the world, that visitors were not always welcome to this ardent worker, we sought a tactful way of approach and found it through Mr. Y. A. Paloheimo, whose brother is married to the eldest daughter of Sibelius.

Thus it was that on a certain August afternoon my Illustrator and I descended from an autocar on the outskirts of the village of Järvenpää where Mr. Paloheimo and his Ford car—in which he had crossed the United States from his orange-grove in the Ohai the previous winter—were in waiting. In having with us this charming young man, who after years spent in America had returned awhile to put his agricultural knowledge into practice on the farm of his ancestors within sight of the windows of Sibelius' house, we should avoid the dilemma of a certain outrageous compatriot who went, we were told, to call upon Sibelius unaccompanied and unfortified by sufficient knowledge of a common tongue. The Master was all too tardily rescued from her bombardment of questions which he was attempting to answer by means of a Finnish-English dictionary!

It was a fertile, rural scene, stretching with fields of conspicuously drying grain to the, in Finland, inevitable lakeside. Above us, a mere stone's throw away, rose a wooded hill.

"The estate of Sibelius," our friend remarked. "He now owns the entire hillside which he calls his 'island.' He built the villa in 1904; it has been his home ever since he took possession, though he does go to the Hotel Karelia from time to time in winter, to see his daughters—all married and living in Helsinki."

A curtsying maid, white kerchief bound about her hair, ushered us into the music-room, where we sat upon painted chairs, in the style of Louis XVI, until we caught sight of a case filled with medals and, hanging beside the piano, an immense laurel-wreath with blue and white streamers on which was stamped in gold: *"Jean Sibelius... Suomi Kansalta, 1935"*—that is, "from Finland's people" on the occasion of the seventieth birthday. A bowl of fragrant violas spoke to us of Madame Sibelius—the ardent gardener, aunt of the present Finnish minister to Washington— who, as we knew, had been called unexpectedly to Helsinki.

The Master entered. Garlanded as he was in my mind's eye with laurels, I was not prepared to have him literally wreathed in smiles, radiating welcome. He spoke graciously in careful English and seemed throughout our conversation to understand us. That we, beside our distant hearth in Pennsylvania, had listened to his voice and the concert of his works given at Helsinki on the occasion of the seventieth birthday seemed to give him genuine pleasure, emphasizing, as it did, the oneness of art and the wonder of science in our modern world.

We were led through a cosy dining-room—with porcelain stove, green with copper trimmings, a divan with Karelian cushions, over which hung an antique Finnish wall rug—to a third room, the library. My most cherished memories of Sibelius are in this room, as he stood before a solid wall of books in sumptuous bindings and all European languages. We drew low arm-chairs covered with hand-woven linen to the squat table upon which the little maid was to place a tray with silver pot of coffee and a profusion of cakes, jumbles, and four-petaled gingersnaps.

"Yesterday," said our host, "I had a call from a Hindu professor sent to me by Tagore, with whom I correspond and who has promised to visit me but has not done so. Tagore paints now. Art is different from music which one cannot do without technique."

"Can one really paint without any teaching or knowledge of technique?" my Illustrator queried.

Sibelius, with a quizzical smile, cited Van Gogh...which brought the subject naturally to Provence, and the time seemed opportune to present a copy of our book *The Heart of Provence*. The Master spoke at once of Mistral and what he had done for his people, comparing his work to that of those who have labored in Finland— to express Finland by means of music, art, and language. By now we were talking in French, in which language Sibelius is more fluent than in English (he has a veritable passion for the Greek and Latin classics), but it was not long before the forceful flow of his conversation burst over the artificial dams of convention in which he had confined it. Hereafter he conversed in Finnish, with Yrjö Paloheimo as able go-between.

Stokowski's interest in India and mysticism was mentioned, and also how by means of records he was reaching a wide public all over the world.

"America," said Sibelius, "has the finest orchestras to-day...none to compare with them." He spoke of Stokowski, Koussevitsky, Iturbi, cannily avoiding comparisons and summing up with, "You have many conductors of the first rank. Helsinki has a good orchestra in winter, but music doesn't exist in Finland in summer."

Talk turned to the piano. He had disclosed the fact that he has two Steinways. We spoke of the difficulty of finding his piano compositions in America and our admiration for his series of

Jean SIBELIUS

p *Cantabile* **Sempre Allegro**

trees. Knowing his reluctance to admit a preference for any one of his symphonies, we were
amazed to have him, after some hesitation, tell us
that the trees are his favorites among his own
works for piano.

"But I love all my compositions," he added,
quickly. "They are all my children."

"The wind in the pines," he continued, "often sounds like an organ. There are overtones, and, at other times, it is lower or higher—like a harp. I do not much care about surroundings, but I value quiet and stillness."

That we should have a complete list of his piano compositions he left us to go to his studio, over the dining-room, to prepare one in his own meticulous hand. During his absence Mr. Paloheimo mentioned how, a short time before, he had come into the house when Sibelius was improvising at the piano—which he rarely does except at night. He also told us that during an eclipse of the sun he was watching it with the Sibelius family when, suddenly, Sibelius said, "That has given me an idea," and hurried to the house to put down one of his finest symphonic themes. His inspiration often comes, as is well known, directly from Nature.

Erect, courtly in manner, noble as to appearance, Sibelius reminded us of another artist, Zuloaga, the Basque. Both belong to the true aristocracy of art and learning.

The World War prevented the Master's paying a second visit to the United States. He was returning to Europe after his triumphant tour with its climax of a degree from Yale when he heard aboard ship of the murder at Sarajevo. In December, 1917, the year of Finland's independence, the land was overrun with Red Finns and Red

Russians. Civil war followed in January, 1918, and Sibelius was in such danger, marooned upon his estate, that he was finally persuaded to take refuge with his brother in Helsinki. He described, impersonally, "the crescendo" of the German guns that saved the city for the forces of law and order.

Truly "above the battle" not only of guns but of the petty feuds of our time, Sibelius stands in relation to our modern world a giant of rounded personality. Our outstanding impression was of the unfathomable depths, of the inexhaustible reserves of the man who, having triumphed heroically over obstacles, has attained oneness with divinity. A master among men, a fountainhead of pure music, a giant to place beside Beethoven, of whom Karl Ekman, in his fine biography of Sibelius, quotes Sibelius as saying:

"He was a Titan. Everything was against him and yet he triumphed."

"God opens his door for a moment and his orchestra plays the Fifth Symphony," Sibelius wrote while engaged upon this opus; and while working at the Fourth, "The Symphony is breaking forth in sunshine and strength."

In Scandinavian mythology the wizards were of Finnish origin. The mystic magic of his race flows freely through the music of this Wizard of the Western World.

The Round Tower :
Solitary Survivor of Viipuri's Ramparts

VIIPURI : The Castle

CHAPTER XVI

FROM VIIPURI TO IMATRA

AT HELSINKI no cathedral, Greek Orthodox or Lutheran, no Parliament House, President's Palace, Court of Justice, or University, impressive as these may be, compares in dignity with the majestic railway station. Saarinen has undoubtedly created it as a symbolic gateway dividing the Western World from Russia and the East. As we crossed the vast cobbled plaza upon which the clock-tower of the terminus looks down, we felt ourselves inevitably drawn away from the civilization of which we were a part. Not since we entered the Suez Canal, India-bound, had we had such a sensation of having cut free from our former way of life, with its petty barriers and limitations, to essay a voyage on an unknown sea.

Bound for Viipuri, a night's journey from the capital, we were thenceforth to find ourselves

dependent upon Finnish phrase-books or an
occasional English-speaking individual. Swedish,
German, French were decreasingly understood.
Had my Illustrator and I each had a separate
compartment, we should have been first-class passengers, but preferring to share a stateroom, we
were rated as second. The train was of Continental model. What made it outstandingly dissimilar to other European trains or even to those of
the United States was its immaculate cleanliness.
Not even the Swedes can rival the almost clinical
absence of dirt among the Finns. No speck of dust
was to be seen on toilet bowls or draperies. The
hangings at doors and beds were of velvety black-
and-gray native weave, the ample sheets and
pillow-cases of finest linen, the woolen blankets
soft enough for a queen. Double window-sash kept
out the cold night air—moisture was to form on
the outer panes at dawn, when I forced my sleepy
eyes to look upon the passing scene. It was my
first glimpse of rural Finland. I could not, must
not sleep as we entered the province of Karelia,
so close to the Russian border. A pioneer country it was—scattered huts of roughly hewn
boards, painted the inevitable red; grain or hay
drying on poles or on fences; forests of spruce,
birch, again spruce, encroaching forests ... a look
of Canada. The roughness of the road-bed tended
to keep me from becoming too drowsy, yet the monotony of the scene was such that sleep conquered.

Mid-August though it was, a frosty air swept our faces as we emerged from the granite railway station at Viipuri—suggesting that at Helsinki, a later work from the brain of the same architect. Droskies were assembled on the square. It fitted our mood to try one, rather than a taxi, in this next-to-the-largest town of modern Finland, once capital of "Old Finland."

The address we gave was Hotel Andrea. Our way led along tree-bordered Karjalankatu, past the Torkkeli Gardens into the heart of the old town. We found ourselves on a narrow street, stopping at a substantial commercial house which might have been in France, Italy, or Spain. The concierge welcomed us with halting English words. Buttons was despatched to summon the manager. The latter appeared. The dignity of his mien suggested an English bishop. Our wants were immediately translated to the staff. Our gratitude was deprecated by hand upraised—as though about to give the benediction.

"Pray don't mention it!" our host insisted—he spoke with resonance. "We welcome guests from America. In these days of uncertainty the sympathy of your Republic is essential."

Rooms giving on the street of the Hotel Andrea are dominated by the belfry of the Agricola Church. This fifteenth-century edifice, named for the prelate who introduced the Reformation into Finland and who is said to be buried in the crypt, was formerly the cathedral. It was used as a store-house during the century of Russian rule and was not reconsecrated until the founding of the Republic in 1918.

Even in pagan times a trading-station stood at Viipuri. Raw materials from Savo, in central Finland, have for centuries come by way of the lakes to the sea, the trade route crossing that from Russia to Finland. It is only since the founding of the Republic that trade with Russia has ceased, while products from central Finland have increased beyond all expectation.

Viipuri, as we know it, grew from the building of the castle by the Swede, Marshal Torkel Knutsson, who in 1293, at the point of the sword, imposed so-called Christianity on the Karelians. Down the centuries this stronghold has served, with the castle (or *linna*) at Savonlinna to the north, as headquarters for defense against Russian attack. Birger Jarl, that almost legendary Swede, having subdued the province of Häme in 1249 and introduced Christianity to the Finns, it remained for Regent Knutsson, ruling for the Earl's son, to complete the crusade by appropriating Karelia. In 1323 the River Rajajoki was recognized as the border between Russia and Finland (then an integral part of Sweden), a frontier which remains unchanged to-day.

Viipuri is a hive which swarms with soldiers. Pitifully young they look, small, poorly clad in rumpled drab uniforms, yet busy in the line of duty as the proverbial bee and, on provocation, equally vitriolic in attack. We remarked their numbers drilling as we crossed the square, where a statue to the crusader Torkel Knutsson stands, facing the rocky island from which the castle rises.

A solitary sentry stood on guard. We were tolerated sufficiently to be allowed tickets of admission, purchased in semidarkness at arched entrance to the ramparts. We stumbled up a cobbled way, pausing at the stables where conscripts groomed sleek horses, pausing to express admiration which the taciturn Finns are quick to catch without words. The main tower, with slits of windows, has guarded its look of antiquity, the only addition being a stair which clings to the walls, by which we mounted. Viipuri, quivering in sunlight, lay at our feet. Hardly inferior is the view from benches overlooking the harbor. This is a place to linger, before encircling the fort, and meditate upon the vicissitudes of the city's past.

Granted a charter in 1403, Viipuri was attacked by the Russians in 1495. The castle was defended by Knut Posse, at whose command barrels of burning pitch were thrown from the ramparts— an episode flippantly known to posterity as the "Viipuri Bang." In the following century the now hoary building was the theater on which was staged a brilliant life in keeping with that of the Swedish Court. In 1710, during the Great

Northern War, the place was captured by the Russians, and by the treaty of 1721 it passed from Sweden to Russia. In 1788-90 the Swedish fleet, under command of Gustavus III, failed to enter the outer harbor and was forced, with heavy losses, to fight its way back to the sea. In 1812 "Old Finland" and Viipuri were once more united to the Duchy of Finland. Most vivid of all, however, is the remembrance that here in 1918, after five days of siege, the Red Russians surrendered to the White Finns, one of the final factors in the War of Liberation.

"Fat Katerina" is the disrespectful name by which the natives designate the round tower, solitary survivor of Viipuri's sixteenth-century ramparts. "Katerina" stands in what is now the heart of the city, overlooking the market-place. It must be recorded that she is broad and squat, with eyes of windows leering from beneath her frivolous peaked hat. Yet, for all that, she is dear to the hearts of the people. Since 1923 a restaurant has filled her comfortable interior. The hospitable alcoves, whose windows no longer suggest the sly glances they bestow upon the square, form an ideal setting for a tête-à-tête. The medieval character has been preserved, and the waitresses in puff-sleeved velvet gowns wear Elizabethan ruffs. Ensconced behind the smörgåsbord table in the room's center, a trio of violin, cello, and piano greeted us with the "Valse Triste" of Sibelius.

"You know the piece?" our waitress commented upon our prolonged applause. "Oh, you have met Sibelius, what good fortune!

"Did you ever hear of the man who met Sibelius for the first time at Kappeli's restaurant? The band was playing Strauss waltzes. The man said, 'I don't know much about music, but I do like Strauss' "Valse Triste" '!"

Aladdin's lamp was not more powerful than the magic that transforms Finnish market-places. Stalls blossom into being with bewildering rapidity. Here at Viipuri, as at Helsinki, flowers and fruits are brought by water, reserve boat-loads float temptingly at docks. For a few hours all is animation, then boats and carts alike disappear instantaneously. At noon not a vestige of merchandise remains. One must make an early start to see "Katerina," as we did, surrounded by her subjects: peasants in kerchiefs, men and women alike wearing Russian-looking boots, long-haired gypsies in regalia of flounced skirts and flowered shawls, drosky carts piled with tier on tier of becaged fowls, vendors of canary-colored mushrooms—precious as gold to the Finns.

Not gold or silver tempted me at Viipuri's antique shops, but I was vulnerable when confronted with Russian brass. White Russians, refugees of the old régime, fleeing across the border had brought with them household treasures. Icons and a samovar or two may be found still at Helsinki, and there is an even better choice at Viipuri. On Torkkelinkatu opposite the park and a stone's throw from where "Katerina" (wreathed not in vine-leaves but in red woodbine) leered and beckoned, I found my desired samovar. Like "Katerina" the type I had in mind must be ample of form and wear her years with aplomb.

My Illustrator and I had descended to the basement shop whose window had tempted us. Its occupants were a salesgirl whose American accent bore out her statement that she was lately from New York, a tousled Russian, and a drunken sot. The flaxen-haired girl showed us icons with obvious reluctance—"What do they see in them?" her manner implied. Our conversation had awakened the drunkard. He muttered that our purchase of Saint Peter and Saint Paul would surely bring us luck—this was relayed to us by means of the Russian youth who put it into Finnish for the girl scornfully to translate. By means of the same supercilious go-between we asked the Russian's advice as to the row of battered samovars, only one of which had the rotund proportions I had seen in my mind's eye.

"The straight ones," said he of the tousled hair, "bear the stamps of their makers, commercial marks of early in the century, before the Revolution—none like these has been made since; but that," pointing to the one with bulging figure, "must be a hundred. You won't make the mistake of burning charcoal in the house and risk asphyxiation, will you?" he questioned, seeing my enthusiasm for my purchase.

"We Russians start the fire outdoors—bits of paper, lumps of charcoal, matches; not till all the smoke has poured out and the coals have fallen do we carry it indoors. Foreigners complain, 'My samovar smokes'!"

Our talk disturbed the tippler. Sleep was all he demanded. That denied, he waxed belligerent, toppling over a table, smashing china and glass. An officer of the peace was summoned. As we left the merry scene, the drunkard, extricated from the mêlée and forcefully evicted from the shop, hurled back at us his belief in the efficacy of Saints Peter and Paul.

The seemingly inevitable ending to a Viipuri first day is to dine at the Pavilion, summer restaurant inviting comparison with Kappeli's in Helsinki. I remember that, in Finnish fashion, we lingered for two hours over our meal, leaving before dessert because of reluctance to spend another hour. Circles and squares of blue, green, and red lights gave a magical appearance to the flower-beds—the effect produced, to Siebel's despair, by Mephistopheles in *Faust*. A brass band playing "Valse Triste" delayed our departure.

The trip to Imatra by bus via Lappeenranta should by all means be taken, rather than the less rural direct route from Viipuri. On the day of our journey, farm-women, with kerchiefed heads or wearing knitted caps, crowded aboard our bus. Their sturdy physiques and placid faces were in keeping with their melodious voices. Men with rakes climbed in to descend at barns or farm-houses. We swung by fields surrounded by the typical fence of Finland—a primitive affair of slim logs mysteriously held together, looking as though erected by ingenious beavers. Hay had been garnered. Poles were stacked in form of wigwams. Harebells and ferns bordered the road-side. Magpies and gulls darted and soared.

A roar of waters greeted our approach to Imatra. The fall is famous as Europe's greatest cataract. Its lack of height and the harnessing of its power at first disappoint the searcher after the grandiose, but few remain unimpressed. All the waters of the Saimaan Lake system (estimated at 37,000 square miles) breaking through the watershed (a glacial eskar) churn tempestuously down a granite gorge on their way to Ladoga, Europe's largest lake.

Our stay at Imatra, in the admirable govern-ment-owned Valtion Hotel, was colored by the happy circumstance that we had in our possession a letter to the station-master there in domicile.

"A letter to the station-master!" my Illustrator exclaimed. "Now doesn't that take you back to India, land of station-masters omnipotent?"

"Yes," I was to observe, after meeting our railway official, "Indian station-masters know their jobs, but where, save in Finland, would a man of such culture be in charge—even at so important a junction as Imatra?"

The station-master regarded our coming, so he hastened to tell us, as a treat. Rarely did he have a chance to exercise his English. He would take a holiday. His first act was to entertain us at luncheon. How should we have known, but for our companion, that a certain dish on the *smör* table contained salt-cured reindeer with power to transport the mind to Lapland. Have you ever entered a shop, as we did at Helsinki, filled with moccasins, boots, and other articles fabricated by the Lapps? If not, the overpowering odor is a sensation that the future has in store, and if you magnify this odor to the nth degree, the result is the taste of reindeer.

To account for his unfaltering use of the American tongue our host explained that he had spent six years in New York when his wife's uncle was chief engineer of the Grand Central Station. He told us of his amateur musicianship and his friendship with Kreisler, of the parties at the maestro's to meet Metropolitan Opera stars, of his admiration for the late Gabrilowitsch and his brilliant wife, "the daughter of your Mark Twain."

At this point I threw a look at my Illustrator which meant, "Are you sure that this distinguished and so-enlightened gentleman is the station-master?''

He reminisced of a trip to France. As he and his friend were low in funds, they hired bicycles. He remembered that around Rheims the country-men had never heard of Finland. ''We said, 'It is near Sweden,' but they had never heard of Sweden ...don't tell that to a Swede!

'' 'Well,' I said, 'it is far away to the north.' So impressed were the peasants with the distance we had come that they refused money for our food and lodging.''

He showed pleasure when we told him of our admiration for the Finns.

''When you write your book, at least you won't make the mistake of one of your compatriots,'' he said to me. ''The gentleman thought every pretty girl or elegant woman he saw in Finland a Swede!''

If we had felt shortcomings at Imatra, not so at Vallinkoski. The river, widened, is forest-bordered. Perhaps Alaska might look like this, we ventured, and were told that salmon, famous as Alaskan, were to be found leaping above the rapids where the ubiquitous Englishman has his fishing club. From the brink we watched the roaring waters. Waves, in headlong breakers, thundered, shower-ing us with spray. Dizzy with sound and motion, we steadied ourselves against impacts which strove to tear away the rock-ribbed bank. Pine

The raging Falls of Vallinkoski

logs plunged from pool to pool flung to heights, striking hidden granite, catapulted into lower cauldrons to be carried headlong at length to drift down-current. We remarked upon the olive-green color of the churning waters, the chemical odor. This, we were told, was true—we must blame the pulp-works.

It had been arranged for us to visit Kaukopää pulp-mill that afternoon. Our friend beguiled the way, from the rapids to the car, with tales of winter sports. We passed an artist who had set up his easel near the brink.

"They come to paint Vallinkoski," said our companion. "The suicides prefer Imatra."

The station-master's eyes gleamed as he indicated a forest path where "everyone" skis. At the foot of the swift descent the way skirts the cliff that overhangs the river. Here the skiers must stop or be precipitated into space.

"Last year," said our guide, "there were two daredevils who deliberately went over the top. No fools like young fools! Well, they knew they could make it by clutching the trees."

Stopping at the Valtion, we were joined by Mr. Schauman (relative of the Finnish hero), sales-manager of Kaukopää, equipped with creditable English, and an engineer who spoke a garbled French, unintelligible, we were to discover, when accompanied by the roar of machines.

First sight of Kaukopää is breath-taking. Finished in September, 1935, the mill combines with its soaring height and plane surfaces, its more than Colonial simplicity and pleasantly pointed brick, the best attributes of modern industrial architecture. An immense clock-dial forms the walls' only decoration. The smoke-stack, tallest in Finland, stands apart, as do belfries of these Northern Lands. A ladder of metal rungs, leading to the top, is three times punctuated, at night, by lights to safeguard airplanes. The beauty of the site remains unmarred by such a mill as this ... despite insidious sulphuric fumes. Where were the drab shabbiness, the unkempt environs, the grime, so often associated with mills in other lands?

Where indeed! Not to be found in the interior. We were lifted to the roof with its idyllic lake view. The French-speaking engineer pointed out the spire of a church made famous, long before the building of the mill, by Edelfelt's painting *"Les vieilles femmes autour de l'église de Ruokolahti."*

Next we were conducted to a model café with furniture as modern and appointments as immaculate as those of the Diet Building in Helsinki. Girls in uniform dispensed food from the diet-kitchen at one and a half marks (five cents) a portion.

The pride of the mill was shown us, a Minton vacuum dryer, built in Helsinki under the supervision of its inventor, who came from Florida to superintend. Through peep-holes we gazed into the maw of this leviathan. A homely touch was where bottles of milk had been left to cool beneath the water dripping from the vast length of the machine. The mighty monster, having gulped raw mash, at the far end disgorges its digested product. This, looking for all the world like mere rough paper, is received and stacked by brawny women. This product, we were told, was brown pulp, known in America, for which forty per cent of it was destined, as natural pulp; it was perforated with holes, as we had remarked, to lower the rate of duty. It would, after reaching its destination, be chopped again before being converted into boxes and containers.

More than content with what we had seen, we were not to be released without a visit to mixing and mashing machines. Here the raw stuff (the

The Pulp Mill of Kaukopää

wood having been comminuted in chipper) is manipulated amid deafening roar and sickening heat; but this was mere purgatory to the final hell, assuredly as hot and sulphuric as accorded with tradition. Half-cooked, we had dreaded having to retrace our steps, but, as by miracle, we emerged into the open air. Our debonair companions, being factory-minded, assured us that it had not been hot or noisy either, as such things go. (The only solace in parting from the stationmaster, next day, was the knowledge that the longer we stayed at Imatra, the more factories we should unavoidably have visited!)

Our return to the hotel was enlivened by a discussion of things American. The engineer, who had cousins in the U.S.A., assured us that he, for one, would never go there.

"No! No!" he announced with conviction. "I hate your ways. My cousins come back to brag of how you do things. I know... I read the *Saturday Evening Post*. Everything in America is bigger and better. No, I shall never go there. You Americans are too boastful!"

I assured him that the views of the *Post* were not those of all Americans, that many of us wish to learn from other nations. Had not President Roosevelt sent a commission to the Scandinavian countries to study the coöperatives?

His friends reproved the gentleman for being rude. He apologized at parting but, with emphasis, repeated his vituperations.

The train that bore us to Sortavala was typically Finnish. The engine was of quaint model— its funnel-shaped stack reverberated, the fuel was chunks of white birch. As we pulled out of Imatra, we admired the modern bungalows, each with its garden-plot, houses of the mill-workers. Every station we passed had its red-capped official—often a woman. Horses, with high Russian collars, were harnessed three abreast to plows. Our only companions were a Finn who slept discreetly behind the shelter of his hanging overcoat, a French-speaking couple, and a Finnish woman. We were attracted to the latter, a well-groomed young person with glowing blond hair, a college-bred type. When we entered she was unconcernedly nursing a baby. Amusing ourselves with a copy of the popular magazine *Seura,* we were astonished to come across old friends under the title of *"Kolme Pikku Porsasta."* The wolf had modeled the three little *porsasta* of clay, and they were in the act of coming to life and crying—in Disney's vivid drawings.

"Sortavala," our guidebook told us, "a plain town, but well situated on the north shore of Lake Ladoga, is a busy commercial center and the focus of Karelian culture." Founded in 1632, Sortavala is the administrative center of the Greek Orthodox Church in Finland. All this is true, but how much more it was to mean to us!

Imagine our surprise to be greeted in fluent English by a middle-aged lady in the costume of the place. Her skirt was of striped red and green, an apple-green bodice worn over white blouse was belted, and from the belt hung a gay pouch.

"You are the Oakleys?" she queried. Explanations flew to and fro. Her sister, Madame Hainari, whom we had met that spring in America (at a time when Finland had seemed as far as the Pole), had received our letter. Their island was near Sortavala, therefore they had come to ask us to lunch at the hotel where Madame Hainari awaited.

To appreciate our emotion the reader must realize that Madame Hainari is Finland's foremost woman citizen—four times delegate to the League of Nations, President of the Council of Women's Clubs, whose recommendations rarely go unheeded by the Diet because they truly represent the opinions of the women of Finland. The "Jane Addams of Finland" she has been called. We had met Madame Hainari on the occasion of her visit to America to attend an Adult Education Conference in Washington. For the first time we were to see her dressed in the costume of her province. Years had rolled away with this transformation to the Karelian. Her strong and radiant face, with its classic features, should, we thought, be perpetuated in marble. On her head was a studded circlet with red streamers. She wore the traditional bodice and short pleated skirt of navy blue edged with scarlet, an embroidered blouse, and silver brooch.

We were led to the terrace of the hotel overlooking the lake, and Madame Hainari pointed to a distant woodland where she had attended school. Her education was given in Swedish. She explained how her husband had had a Swedish name —as at one time was required in school—but he was among the thousands who (not being of Swedish descent) changed when Stockman made his plea for Finnish names for Finns.

The mayor of Sortavala, their nearest neighbor, had brought the ladies to town by motor. If we should care to have supper on their island, an hour by motor-boat, it could be arranged. Thus it was that the launch *Ulappa* bore us swiftly to Vasikka Saari ("Calf Island"), on which the only habitation is the house built by Dr. Hainari for his bride. It was an ideal marriage, the widow told us. After her husband's death, over twenty years ago, she had gone on with the work for which he cared. He was a teacher—she, too, had taught Swedish and English. Dr. Hainari had striven to raise the intellectual standard of the people. He had felt the Finns, whether Greek Orthodox or Lutheran, should have their own teachers. When the Russians tried to Russianize the Karelian schools, Madame Hainari had undertaken to raise money and to watch over ten schools near the border— one was within two hundred meters, a perilous position for its teacher.

"When we built a school," said Madame Hainari, "then the Russians built one, and when they did, we put up a Finnish school. In consequence the young people trained in our schools were Finnish-minded and rallied to the Finnish side in 1918.

"Fortunately, after the 'February Manifesto' of 1899 there was no army in Finland. The national troops were disbanded by the Russians. Fortunately, indeed, for otherwise Finland would have been in the World War and on the side of Russia. Owing to passive resistance among the Finns, enforcement of the measure to compel service in Russian regiments failed. In 1918, when Red Russia and Reds in Finland tried to seize the government, the Civic Guards were formed to save us from a menace worse than the Czar."

The Karelians, like the Basques, are a people of one race and tradition divided by an arbitrary national boundary. The *Kalevala* was mostly collected in Karelia, and much of it on the Russian shore of Lake Ladoga—in the region known as Laatokka Karelia. These people, blood-brothers of the Finns, had been promised self-government by the Russians, but instead they were sent to Siberia and replaced by Red Russians. Gone are the former Finnish-speaking settlers of Uhtua and around Tuulijärvi ... banished, dead from privations, despair, disease—dead, but unforgotten by their brother Karelians.

"Finns have long memories," said their champion. "We remember the famine relief sent by Americans in 1892 and again through Hoover. We remember that the Germans, though themselves at war, sent arms and men to aid us in our dire need. We were taught as children that we must make any sacrifice for our country—not by force but only by intellectual superiority could freedom come to Finland.''

As we neared her dock, Madame Hainari explained that she was forced to economize because of the deflation managed by the head of the Bank of Finland, which had, however, been an invaluable help to Finland's foreign trade. Two sisters were sharing her summer home.

''One likes to cook,'' she told us, ''the other to garden. There is much work to be done—even to bringing birch wood from the forest!''

We commented on the ancient look of the weathered *sauna* (bath-house) beside the dock. It was explained that the bath-house is always built before the house—this one had reached years of discretion. Its age was over forty. We were shown the room with wooden wash-tubs for laundry work, the inner sanctum, akin to the one we had seen in Sibelius' garden.

The younger sister remarked, with a sniff: ''That smell of tar in a country *sauna* tells a Finn returned from foreign lands more plainly than words that he is home.''

A roughly constructed fireplace was topped with smoke-blackened stones on which water is poured until the room fills with steam. Bathers, liking to

SARIOLA
The House of Tilma Hainari.

be parboiled, we were told, move in turn from lowest to middle and topmost ledge—there is much rivalry as to who can stand the most heat—before plunging into the waters of a lake. There is playful switching among friends, in lieu of bath-maids with birch twigs, to stimulate circulation.

Reindeer antlers above the door of the cottage, red and green hand-woven hangings, Lapp baskets and slippers, though suggesting the American Indian, made us realize that this roughly constructed cottage with its rude board interior was not one standing among pines upon a New Hampshire lake. Except in summer, Madame Hainari explained, the house is closed with all it contains, while she goes to her apartment in Helsinki. We were shown a portrait of Snellman, "to whom we owe the rebirth of Finland." Pointing to a map our hostess exclaimed:

"We must not forget our country!"...no danger that she would do so, we thought.

In accordance with Finnish custom, supper was served long before seven. The sun still shone over the lake when we sat down to tomatoes and cucumbers, various breads and butter (it was the hard bread that our hostess missed most in America), hot smoked whitefish, choice of a warm currant soup or *viili* (bonny clabber) eaten with ginger or *talkuna* (a powder of barley and peas), hot vegetables, milk, and deliciously sweet gooseberries. Fading light made us leave this house where, despite the strangeness of new things seen and tasted, we had been made to feel at home.

Darkness threatened, but there was still time, not indeed to pass around the granite cliffs as we had come, but for our boat to push its way, with narrow margin, through a canal cutting an island. Rushes swayed in surging water. Stars appeared. It was after nine as our craft, and other late-comers, converged like participants in a carnival towards the miniature lighthouse of Sortavala.

In the summer of 1935 Sortavala had celebrated the hundredth anniversary of the publication of *Kalevala*—freely translated *The Land of Heroes*. Steinthal placed *Kalevala* second among the world's epics, while Grimm thought none but the epics of India in any way comparable. Although the origin of the *Kalevala* is forgotten, lost like some of the "magic words" of Finnish magicians, yet many believe that these legends long antedate the Christian era. The English translator of the poem, John Marion Crawford, points out "a profound philosophical trait in the poem indicative of a deep insight into the workings of the human mind and into the forces of Nature." When the heroes wish to overcome the power of an evil force, he points out, they chant the origin of this force. "The thought underlying the idea evidently is that all evil could be obviated had we but the knowledge of whence and how it came." "The atmosphere of action in Kalevala is super-real,

accentuating the power of spirit over matter,''
writes Emil Tolonen. ''Here, as in the legends
of no other people, heroes accomplish nearly
everything by magic, with word or song.''

Although Porthan and later Topelius had begun to collect the songs of the Finnish bards, it
was not until Elias Lönnrot, a humble country doctor, dedicated his life to the task that success was
assured. Lönnrot, having graduated from the
Academy of Åbo, chose the post of doctor at
Kajaani in North Savo, knowing that it was in
Karelia that he would find the treasured *runos*
(cantos) he was inspired to collect. In the garb of
a peasant—he was indeed of humble origin, his
father having been a tailor in West Nyland—
Lönnrot wandered among the people, equipped
with flute, knapsack, and shotgun. The cold of
Lapland, the privations encountered in Russian
Karelia, were powerless to deter this invincible
soul. After his first three slim volumes, *Kantele,*
appeared, his friends (members of the Saturday
Society, foremost among whom were the poet
Runeberg and Snellman, father of the Finnish
national movement, who with Lönnrot had moved
from Åbo to Helsinki after the fire of 1827)
founded the Finnish Literary Society, which
enabled Lönnrot to continue his work. This, it
must be remembered, was at a time when Finland
was under the rule of Nicholas I, Czar of Russia,
and when these young poets and philosophers felt

that the professors at the University were dominated by Russian influence. They sensed that it
was, primarily, the humble folk in the rural districts that possessed power to create a new nation.
As Arvidson had said, "We are not Swedes, we
do not wish to be Russians. Let us be Finns!"
There were in Lönnrot's youth only about a dozen
books printed in Finnish. His family possessed
the ABC book, the Catechism, Book of Psalms,
and a book of "edifying general knowledge." The
last eighteen years of his life were given to the
completion of a monumental Finnish-Swedish dictionary in which the Karelian (East Finnish) and
Tavastian (West Finnish) dialects were standardized into one language.

We had come to Sortavala with echoes from the
1935 festival singing in our ears. Mr. Seppala of
the Bureau of Foreign Affairs at Helsinki had
told us of the passing of the heroic bards of old—
of Shemeikka, him whom no storm could daunt,
skier in the forest by light of the aurora, who, unarmed, would tackle the mighty bear of the North;
of the majestic Onoila, who, dying in 1924, did
not long outlive his friend.

"But there are two survivors," Mr. Seppala
had said, "who took part in the festival. You
should be able to find them in the villages beyond
Sortavala." He had, moreover, given us a photograph, taken on that occasion, of the bards Konoi
Kyöttinen and Timo Lipitsä.

Our English-speaking "contact" at the Hotel Seurahuone (one of the most perfect of Finnish hotels, where, of an evening, a string quartet attracts summer cottagers from distant islands) explained that Lipitsä was actually the sole survivor known to him of the old school—the younger men not having learned the lays by word of mouth. A motor could be procured to take us to Lipitsä's distant home at Suistamo Koitto. First we should see the monument to Shemeikka on the hotel square. We told him that we had already admired the statue of the mighty bard, seated on a bearskin, with right hand resting upon a *kantele,* the Finnish harp. We had thought it represented Väinämöinen, heroic music-maker, legendary creator of the *kantele.* We had also visited Vakkosalmi, where two thousand voices had celebrated the centenary of the recording of the *Kalevala.*

Orders were given, since we could not communicate with our chauffeur (a type not unlike a Celtic coachman), that our first stop would be at the former home of Shemeikka, then to Suistamo where inquiries should be made, and return by the deep forest where we could perhaps find a "weeping woman." Our quest, it was explained, was an unusual one. No one we met at Sortavala knew the exact whereabouts of Timo Lipitsä... but it was believed that he was still alive.

Sleep, being of little concern to a Finn, never interferes with an early start, as it often does in

Latin lands. Finns are noted, moreover, for punctuality. We were off betimes, with lunch in car pockets and the long Finnish daylight in our favor. Mist hung low on the meadows, veiling mysteriously the birch forests bordering fields, distorting the grotesque hay-mounds into fantastic forms of runo-singers—seated, like Shemeikka, upon bearskins. Sheaves of grain tied to posts were mist-crowned with billowy bridal tulle, while scraggy bunched stacks assumed the dire shape of witches—only, as miraculously, to be eclipsed.

The log house at Karrjalan Sivistysseuran, home of Shemeikka earlier in the century, has been kept with its ancient furnishings as religiously as any at Fölisön. We were led in silence (alas! that silence should reign here, that Shemeikka the Great is dead!) to three graves. In a grove of pines, beside the cabin, stand two shafts of granite, each with the word *Runolaulaja,* and bearing the names Matjoi Plattonen 1843-1928, Iivana Onoila 1842-1924; and with the runo-singers lies Teppo Jänis, *Kanteleensoittaja*—kantele-player.

Ten miles beyond the village of Suistamo we found ourselves in a country of pioneer farms and encroaching forests. Black-and-gray crows, black-and-white magpies flashed, for good or ill, across our path and mocked our uncertainty from rustic fences. We came at last to a rutted lane leading to a hamlet.

"Suistamo Koitto," our ruddy-faced chauffeur announced with the legitimate pride of a sportsman who has run down his quarry.

Our car came to a stop before a yellow frame house having only one distinguishing mark. Over the door hung a bunch of rowan, the sacred mountain-ash. This, then, was the home of the bard. It was not till we had left the car that we could see that beside the modern addition stood an older Karelian cottage, almost a replica of the house of Shemeikka. A woman with pleasant face, head bound in spotless kerchief, gave us welcoming handshakes and disappeared down the lane. We stood, hopeful but irresolute. Our chauffeur made us understand this was the wife. Encouraged by the smile she had given us, we waited until, at last, we saw her again, emerging from a neighbor's ... and who beside her but the bard! Not as monumental in stature as his predecessors, but no less erect, the slender figure advanced towards us. A watery sunlight touched his silken hair and faded beard, accentuated the whiteness of his Russian blouse and the warm brown of his homespun. He offered us each in turn a wrinkled hand and ushered us, with welcoming gesture, to his hearthside. From an inner room he brought his ten-stringed *kantele* which he placed upon the table. A son and tow-headed grandchildren gathered near. We were to hear cantos from the *Kalevala* alternate with plucking of the instru-

Timo Lipitsä: Last of the
Runo-Singers

ment. Sunlight fell upon the leonine head of the
bard with its tossed mane. He gazed before him
into space—seeing, it seemed, visions hidden to
mortal eyes, yet, we only now realized, blind to
earthly sight. We knew from the repetition of a
familiar phrase that the song was of Väinämöinen
"the serious old one," of Väinämöinen "old and
steadfast," of Väinämöinen born old before his
time and therefore unable to win the maiden Aino,
who, rather than wed him, threw herself into the
lake, transforming herself at will into the semblance of a fish.

One deep-toned wailing note emerged at intervals above the twang of the high and wiry ones, as
the horny fingers plucked the strings. Canto after
canto of song was produced with gusto. Never faltering, the voice of the frail minstrel grew in
volume. We feared for him—so near the end of
life, so aloof from the world, so at one with the
heroes and heroic of all time; but he had forgotten, now, that he was singing for our sakes.
For himself he sang, for invisible hearers, mortal
or immortal, sitting among us thus, where the sunlight played, where the hearth-fire burned—
friendly, benign, yet infinitely far removed...
already one with the divine, caring not at all, it
seemed, whether he should ever return from "the
Land of Heroes."

In a witch's cottage in the deep forest (no car
could penetrate so far) we found the "weeping

woman"—she who is called to keen for the dead, she who has taken upon herself the woes of the world. To her, too, *Kalevala* supplies the words of her crooning, emotion the ready-flowing tears, to which her body sways with ecstasy of moaning, whose face, distorted with vicarious grief, is at last dramatically hidden. O pagan daughter of sorrow forever deprived of consolation, death alone will bring release!

Viipuri

Valamo : The Igumen
Prior of the Monastery

Valamo: The old Cemetery

CHAPTER XVII

MONASTIC VALAMO

OLD RUSSIA, for better or for worse, has gone beyond recall. To those of us who can never see it
with our eyes, yet delight to visualize it with all
its glamour and sensuous and romantic beauty
when listening to the music of Tchaikovsky and
his compatriots, the road to Valamo still lies open.

The group of islands, about forty in number,
known as Valamo is situated in the northern half
of Lake Ladoga (in Finnish Laatokka), Europe's
largest lake. This brings Valamo within the juris-
diction of Finland. Had the islands been below the
boundary, in the southern or Russian portion of
the lake, their inhabitants would not have been
permitted in this year of our Lord to pursue the
quiet order of their way. For the dwellers at
Valamo are monks of the Greek Orthodox Church

431

who, with brief intermissions, for seven hundred, if not a thousand, years have led the contemplative life on these islands and maintained a self-sustaining community.

"No, we have no photographs of Valamo," we had been told at the Foreign Office at Helsinki. "It is hardly Finland."

Hardly Finland, indeed, Finnish possession though it be, we thought, as we stepped aboard the *Valamon Luostari II* at Sortavala. Yesterday we had journeyed into the deep forest, to the ancient Finland of runo-singers and weeping women; to-day we were to be no less magically transported to non-existent ancient Russia. The steamer, like the islands themselves, is owned and maintained by the monks. Our baggage was carried aboard by one of the Order. Mounting to the upper deck, we noted that our pilot, in brimless hat and flowing black habit, had the finely chiseled features by which one could formerly distinguish members of the Russian aristocracy.

Pure and cold are the waters of Lake Ladoga— pure as the faith of Sergei and Herman, founders of the monastery. In spring and summer the temperature of the surface varies from 36 to 53 degrees Fahrenheit while from December to March the lake is ice-bound. Ladoga has been called an inland sea—a name, in consideration of its frequent tempests, perhaps more appropriate than lake. In size over thirty times that of the Lake of

Geneva, Ladoga receives its waters from seventy rivers, fed, in turn, by numberless lakes, including the Saimaa system above Imatra.

MacCallum Scott in his book *Suomi* forces the comparison between Finland and Canada. Shamanism, the faith of the prehistoric Finns, he compares to the religion of the American Indians; Lapps in North Finland correspond to Eskimos; while the White Sea, not far to the northeast of Valamo, balances Hudson's Bay.

Otaere the Norseman, it is recorded, voyaged in the ninth century through the White Sea to the site where Archangel now stands. Even at that time the land was cultivated by industrious inhabitants, the Karelians. The Swedish Viking Rurik established his capital at Novgorod. The Muscovite race, with its Asiatic strain, was thus to be infused with Slavonic, Scandinavian, and Finnish blood to form the Russian. Long after the Christianization of the Northmen, the Finnish tribes, both Karelians in the East and Tavasts in the West, knew none but pagan gods. In 1157, you remember, the Pope at Rome authorized a crusade to convert the Finns. We know of the campaign of King Erik of Sweden in western Finland. Probably it was not until the fourteenth century that missionaries of the Greek Orthodox Church penetrated northward to Valamo and, in the following century, to Solovetsk on the White Sea. Without show of military power they con-

quered, but by the power of the word—the word
no less magical than that extolled by the Finnish
magicians who had unquestionably prepared the
way for the mysticism of the Eastern Church. "In
the beginning was the Word..."

Legend has it that Sergei, a Greek monk from
Athos, the first to bring Christianity to the coasts
of Ladoga, was told that the "wise men" of the
pagans dwelt upon the islands, therefore Sergei
went thither and overcame them "by the power of
his words."

> *There is great power in words.*
> *All the things that ever get*
> *done in the world, good or bad,*
> *are done by words.*

On the largest island of the group Sergei built
his hermitage and took up his abode. Opinions
differ as to the year of his coming. Tradition puts
it in 992. Russian records insist that Christianity
was introduced into Karelia no later than 1227.
Historians seem satisfied to give the date of the
founding of a hermitage at Valamo as 1329. By
1500 the monastery was an acknowledged force in
the region with vast outlying possessions—one
hundred and fifty estates in Karelia, fisheries west
to the River Kymi, a salt refinery on the shore of
the White Sea. In the sixteenth century the Eastern Church had established twenty-six chapels
and ten monasteries in Karelia. Such a state of

affairs became intolerable to the aroused Swedes. Valamo was attacked by Swedish troops in 1581; the monastery was burned, the monks were murdered, save a few who made their escape to Novgorod. This remnant was destined to return and rebuild the convent, which was again destroyed in 1611. In 1617 a desolate and uninhabited Valamo was ceded to Sweden.

For a thousand years Russia had coveted an outlet to a western sea. For a thousand years Sweden had combated her rival's desire. For all these centuries Finland had been a territorial pawn on the international chess-board. Not until Charles XII of Sweden finally met more than his match in Peter the Great was Valamo retaken. In 1715 the Russians determined to rebuild the monastery. The church was completed in 1719, and since that period—despite devastating wars and revolutions (with a narrow margin separating its island from Bolshevik Russia), despite its territory becoming an integral part of overwhelmingly Lutheran Finland—peace has reigned at Valamo. The tolerance shown by the Republic for these monks of alien race and creed demonstrates a reassuring liberality on the part of modern Finland.

Christianity came to Russia in the year 992, when it was officially accepted by Prince Vladimir. It was not until 1054 that, following an excommunication by Pope Leo IX, the Eastern Orthodox Church (the Holy Orthodox Catholic Apostolic

Eastern Church, better known in America as
the Greek Church) was finally separated from the
Roman Catholic. The one had followed the Greek
philosophy while the other adhered more closely
to Roman law. The Eastern Church admitted no
supremacy of unique pope. Each of its patriarchs
was, at the outset, supreme in his own district.
The patriarch of Constantinople (who dwelt, paradoxically, at Kiev) became the virtual head of the
Church. In the reign of Peter the Great the
patriarchal system was supplanted by the Holy
Governing Synod. So powerful did the Established Church become under the Czars that there
were in Russia alone, at the time of the revolution, two hundred and forty-nine convents and
four hundred and eighty-one monasteries.

Since the Russian upheaval the Archbishop of
Estonia has become the head of the Orthodox
Eastern Church in Finland. We had remarked a
photograph of him, in sumptuous regalia, on the
wall of Timo Lipitsä's remote dwelling. Runo-
singers have belonged by tradition to the Orthodox
faith, for, to a man, they have come from the
Karelian district bordering upon Russia. We remembered the pride with which the picture had
been shown, no less than the enthusiasm about
Valamo (not shared in Helsinki) among numerous individuals at Sortavala.

Valamo, although since 1918 a separate parish
in Finland, uses the parish of Sortavala as an ad-

ministrative liaison with the mainland. We read that navigation on the lake is possible during only one hundred and eighty days (the time is very exact!), that snow-storms occur even in April and October. The monks, with perspicuity characteristic of their Catholic brethren, have chosen as the festivals most worthy of celebration ten which occur between the dates of June first and September fourteenth. The festival of Saint Peter and Saint Paul on June twenty-ninth is the most popular with pilgrims—Russians living within the Finnish borders or Karelians of Orthodox faith. We were fortunate in being able to arrange our visit for August fifteenth, perhaps the most esteemed festival of the year, known in Catholic lands as the Assumption of the Virgin but throughout the Orthodox world as the Feast of the Sleep of the Theotokos (*Theotokos* signifying the Mother of God, who is venerated but whose Immaculate Conception is not conceded and of whom there are icons but no images).

Of all the impressions that crowd to mind when my thoughts return to Valamo, none is more vivid than my remembrance of the voyage, a matter of a scant three hours but one which impregnated us with the feeling that we had embarked on high seas to a New World, a world beyond Time and Space. The intellectual face of our monastic pilot stamped itself upon my mind, his profile, fine as a cameo, with grizzled sparse beard suggesting that of a Chinese sage. I remarked the gilded icon above the wheel, the gleaming silver cross atop the foremast. In midvoyage our pilot, relieved from duty, strode to the lower deck, and I, from my perch on the upper deck, had glimpses of a head, the head of a Russian saint, silhouetted against the white welter of an uproarious sea.

"Do you know the reputation of this Lake Ladoga?" a woman's caressing voice murmured in my ear...the words blown faint on the wind.

The voice came from the undoubtedly high-born wife whom we had noticed with her excessively French husband on the train from Imatra. Her nationality had puzzled us, but when she spoke, it was instantly revealed—a Russian of the Old Régime.

No, it was our first experience, we admitted.

"You may be glad that you are good sailors," she exclaimed, with the spontaneous laughter of a happy woman—what resiliency these Russians possess! "Down in the cabin there are many in purgatory.

"My brother is a novice at Valamo," she went on, "my husband and I have come from Paris for the festival. I know the reputation of this lake. Soft water, they tell me, forms choppier seas than salt. We used to hear tales of Ladoga in Saint Petersburg—in the days when these boats carried pilgrims between Valamo and the capital. The gales are notorious...in winter the ice floes drift and freeze again, sometimes forming barriers ten times the height of a man. You know this was once part of the Arctic Ocean!''

Sortavala had faded away, shores were nowhere visible, when I heard an exclamation from my Illustrator:

"Valamo!" he cried, as our boat churned its way against an ever-breaking wave.

Dim on the horizon the isles emerged, made visible against the firmament by a dome which seemed to float like a moored balloon. Would it not, a pricked bubble, vanish upon approach? A thing intangible it might have been, fashioned of dreams, of wind and sky and sea...assuredly of sky and sea the blue dome of the mammoth church with its attendant cupolas, north, east, south, and west, while the solitary golden dome of an outpost chapel shone like a sun just risen.

Silently our boat, its ascetic helmsman once more at the wheel, glided past the gilded cupola of the Chapel of Saint Nicholai into still waters between the lesser isles. A sister ship, as crowded as our own with pilgrims, returned our whistled salute in heading to the open sea. The island of the blest loomed to port. Astoundingly majestic, blue cupolas against blue of sky, audaciously Oriental, the Church of the Transfiguration confronted us with the glory of storied Byzantium. In the terraced orchards that led to its height, future novices, in gray gowns and Russian boots, were assembled to watch the steamer's approach. In coves bearded friars busied with line and rod waved genially. Droskies driven by members of the Order clattered to the landing-stage. Outlandish pilgrims had come to watch our steamer dock.

Our acquaintance—who had conversed with us in English, in French with her husband (who was, we learned, a *sous-préfet* of the Department of the Seine)—was the first to go ashore. Her brother, a striking figure in the black habit, awaited with the face of a caliph purged of human emotion. Bearded monks greeted the lady with respect. Her cosmopolitan veneer had vanished as she stepped ashore—stepped on what seemed to her to be once more her native soil. From her lips poured a cataract of Russian. She became the personification of the aristocracy of the Empire of the Czars. How could we ever have hesitated as to her nationality? we asked each other, and decided that at first she had shown but a portion of herself and now had cast aside her veils. How can modern Russia afford to do without such dynamic sources of vitality?

A steep road and a still steeper flight of stone steps lead from the landing-stage to the hotel run by the monks for pilgrims and other visitors. Beyond lies the entrance to the monastery—the Sacred Gate. In line with others from the steamer we made our way to the vast caravanserai. Two brothers, one on each side the doorway, stood mo-

tionless as telamones. Novices were stationed
within the whitewashed hall to direct us silently
up the bare steep stair. At the top, seated at a
table on which were spread mammoth keys, was
an octogenarian monk with spreading beard.
Could this be Merlin come to life? Possessed, we
were convinced, of the knowledge of the lore of
stars, of alchemy, and of magic, this wizard-like
being deigned to interrogate us, by means of a
novice interpreter, as to the length of our stay.
When he learned that it was for both nights of
the festive week-end, he gave us a room of rooms.
It was but a few steps down the corridor where
a solitary oil lamp hung from the ceiling, its hood
suggesting the cardinal's hat so often suspended,
spider-like, in Spanish cathedrals. (How mysteriously, at night, was its shadow thrown on
high!)

Stories had reached our ears of "blocks of wood
serving for pillows," of dearth of mattresses, of
scarcity of sheets. Imagine our surprise to find
our whitewashed chamber, Number 72, graced
with twin beds immaculate as those in Finnish
hotels, and, moreover, a wash-stand—how had information erred! Pilgrims, perhaps, may sleep on
wooden pillows and wash or fail to wash at a common pump. Not so did we! A mirror that distorted our countenances, expressly to discourage
vanity we felt sure, was, by the same token, hung
inconveniently high. Color prints of monastery

✠ Valamo ⁘ Domes and Cupolas

of the Church of the Transfiguration

and patron saints, a porcelain stove reaching to the ceiling, chairs, and tables with fringed covers completed the furnishings. Deep window-sills glistened with fresh paint. Indeed, the brush of monkish painters, dipped in white or cobalt, must shortly before our approach have included all Valamo. Local color was not lacking in this domicile for two hundred guests. In the bare office a monk seated at a typewriter made us regret the passing of the illuminated manuscript. In the restaurant a friar, ensconced behind a counter piled with buns, was cashier. At meal-times both first- and second-class menus offered the same wealth of suggestions, but despite the good offices of French-speaking Russian waitresses, nothing more elaborate was served than *borsch,* ragout of veal, and stewed plums. Omelet soufflé was not to be procured, but omelet browned over an open fire, as omelets should be, was welcome fare when washed down with coffee from bubbling samovars.

The one English-speaking novice, a Russian graduate of the University of Helsinki, undertook to show us the library of twenty-nine thousand books and manuscripts, the refectory to which, later, we were to watch a hundred monks and novices march solemnly, the orchard, stables where stallions are bred, workshops. The refectory, with vaulted ceiling, is the oldest building extant at Valamo—it has stood for two hundred and fifty years. The two Greek monks, founders of

Valamo, look down from frescoes. Here, during meal-time, the Bible is read. We saw the tables set with pewter tureens of small beer, in which monks would soon ply ladles, while four brothers would dip with wooden spoons into each communal bowl. Meat is not permitted at any time, nor fish on fast-days.

We owed much knowledge to our youthful guide, who looked in black habit and biretta like a candidate for Catholic priesthood. (So aloof was he, however, that we hesitated, when meeting him again, on the day of our departure, to say "Good morning"—a greeting he returned without show of recognition.)

Facts flowed trippingly from our novice's tongue. There had been a thousand monks at Valamo until 1924, when there was a secession, the majority leaving to go to monasteries in Bulgaria and Greece.

"Because of a dissension?" we asked, and were told:

"The calendar, a difference of two weeks in changing from the ancient to the modern. The monks who departed were unwilling to change. They preferred to leave Valamo...."

"We have now about two hundred monks—one must be thirty to become a monk or have taken a university degree in theology—fifty-five novices, and forty-five boys from seven to fourteen. These boys wear gray. No new monks are allowed to come from Russia, but many of the boys will take orders. There are three classes of monks: the novice (both probationer and deacon), the ordinary, and the full monk. We choose our own prior, treasurer, and father-confessor, who are then appointed by the Archbishop.''

We had wandered to the orchard, and here our guide introduced the head gardener, who, in concession to the season, wore a straw farmer's hat. He was the jolliest of all the Valamo monks—an idealized ''Saint Nick.'' In lieu of sugar-plums he offered gooseberries, and from his bulging pack he drew forth apples. Above the wide-spread branches of the fruit-trees soared a dome of the church, as might have soared the dome of a veritable mosque. All was still...then the whirr of wild ducks rising from a fish-pool. All was sunlight and tranquillity. Did equal peace reside, we wondered, in the souls of the cloistered votaries?

The gardener-monk would have us see his vegetables, and we were told an episode of Czar Alexander's visit.

''Yonder, near the cemetery,'' said the novice, ''once stood the log cabin of Nicholai the Beggar, a holy man who had taken the vow of silence. Like many of the hermits, Nicholai had planted a few vegetables. When, in the year 1819, the Czar Alexander I visited Valamo, he came to the hut to honor the holy man. Nicholai pulled a turnip from his garden and offered it to his sovereign, whereupon the Czar, not having a knife on his person, bit off the skin and ate the turnip after the way of common soldiers.''

Not having come to Valamo to talk of cabbages and kings nor yet of czars and turnips, we finally retraced our steps to the double rectangle of buildings dominated by the Church of the Transfiguration. Across the quadrangle stand the abbot's dwelling and quarters for monks, to the right of the main doorway the refectory and the Chapel of the Mother of God, to the left the library and Chapel of Saint Peter and Saint Paul built over the Sacred Gate.

The Church of the Transfiguration, with its dome, cupolas, and imposing belfry, is in reality two churches, the lower antedating the upper (which was not completed until 1896) by a century. The restoration of the monastery, which he found in deplorable condition, was undertaken, with the aid of a Russian archbishop, by the enterprising Igumen (or Prior) Damaskin, who came to Valamo at twenty-four to remain sixty-two years, until his death in 1881. These were the years of the monastery's prosperity. Pilgrims innumerable journeyed from Russia. With the coming of wars and revolutions and the cessation of intercourse across the border, and, moreover, with the independence of Finland, less than two per cent of whose people are members of the Eastern Orthodox Church, the ultimate dissolution of

Valamo may come even in our day. Hasten, therefore, to Valamo to behold life as it once flowed in early Christian centuries.

Over the sacred portal of the Church of the Transfiguration gleams the Eye of the Holy Ghost, a symbol portrayed with golden radiations. Those pilgrims who remain unmoved by its startling though impersonal regard are perhaps dulled by constant familiarity. Few, however, can fail to be stirred by the unescapable rapier glances of the hermits. For ourselves, their spears pierced to the very core of our being. Wearing the imprint of the cross upon their somber habits, to signify they are prepared to die, these fanatics strike unholy terror to the hearts of the credulous. Up and down the aisles of the church they wander at will, their thoughts probably in other spheres, glaring as forbiddingly to right and to left as though watch-dogs of the Spirit.

Vespers! Undiluted sunlight glitters on the icons and golden colonnade of the Church of the Transfiguration. As daylight fades, with the gradual withdrawal of the northern sun, candles from hanging lamps gleam to light before the brilliantly colored panels of the saints—a solid reredos shutting off the Holy of Holies. A few benches against the wall are a concession to the feeble or the foreign. Reverently the congregation stands hour on hour, at intervals individuals prostrating themselves with utterly unconscious abandon. The main body of the church is given over to the monks in serried ranks, incredibly sedate in their tall hats, black belted gowns, and Russian boots. All but the novices are bearded, bushy locks rest on shoulders. When hats are removed, we observe that next to none are bald and that only the hermits are unkempt.

To those unaccustomed to the service of the Greek Orthodox Church, its overwhelming manifestation is its music. There is no organ at Valamo, nor other instrumental accompaniment, but the choir has been trained in the sacred tradition, in almost unbroken continuity, for half a millennium. The chants are in Old Russian or Slavonic and consist for the most part of portions of Hebrew Scriptures. After the fashion of Hebrew poetry, there is invariably repetition, which leads scholars to the conclusion that the plainsong still in use was the original accompaniment to the Psalms. Two hundred years ago the monks at Valamo were noted composers, and parts of the liturgy are of their creation.

At vespers a prince-of-Arabian-Nights individual, shaven, golden-haired, hatless, stands in black robe at a portable lectern (his back to the congregation) and intones a supplication. His detachment is absolute. His voice, an instrument of rare beauty, swells and dies away, pianissimo, fortissimo, high, low, diminishing, resounding. There is magic in it, intoxication.

"Gospode, Gospode...Gospode, Gospode, Gospode," pleads the voice, *"Gospode pomelue"* (God, keep us in Your grace). Repeated, repeated, repeated is the name of Deity. The pilgrims sway like cobras, in ecstasy of religious exaltation. A peasant woman, garbed in black, like the monks belted and booted, a black kerchief on her head, advances to the icon of the Christ. She offers a lighted taper, kneels before the crucifix, touching her head three times to the marble floor. The wife of the subprefect of Paris performs the same ceremony. Other pilgrims follow. On the wings of their emotion they are borne to highest heaven.

A brief intermission. The seven-o'clock service commences...it will last almost to midnight. Here and there a lighted candle gleams in the shadowy recesses beneath the arches where pilgrims crowd. Votive tapers flicker before the icons. The nave is packed with members of the Order, who seem to have grown to gigantic stature, their height accentuated by voluminous veiled hats and pleated cloaks. Resplendent, in contrast to the beetle-black mass of monks in the main body of the church, in front of whom they stand facing the Holy of Holies, three priests are clad in glistening cloaks encrusted with gold. The central figure, with coal-black curly beard, upon his vesture wears an immense Greek cross. Two lesser priests, likewise in gold, suggest by the form of their garments ancient Chinese paintings. We are stirred by

memories of Buddhist ceremonies in Japan. Rome
in our day cannot compare. (Did kings and potentates of Western Europe ever equal this in
splendor?) The Magnificent of Magnificents,
swinging a censer, is moved to pace up and down
the aisles. He brushes close to where we stand,
half-smothering us with pungent incense. Nothing
is static. High and low pace and surge at rhythmic
intervals. Intonation alternates with chanting.
From where we stand we see the abbot installed
in his gilded chair. The choir, concealed from the
nave by colonnades, is partly visible to us. The
leader's hand is raised. He opens a worn book.
Chanting alternates with intonation.

Morning found us again in our places. Sunday,
the Feast of the Theotokos. In honor of the Sacra-
ment the doors have opened, disclosing an inner
sanctuary, the Holy of Holies. The monks, erect
in their places, have removed their hats, there is
profound and repeated bowing and crossing, if not
beating of breasts. The bells!...again the deep-
toned bells which had already summoned us to the
Holy Liturgy—the bells which remind us that a
year before, on the same day of the Virgin, we
had responded to the bells of Chartres...but here,
O Henry Adams! here at Valamo faith falters
not; we regain the credulity of the thirteenth
century.

"Time and Space do not exist," my Illustrator
warns me. True. Is faith illusion? Where, then, to

find the real, the true, the ultimate perfection? Self is undeniably lost here at Valamo in something far greater—in the Dæmon of the artist, the God of the mystic.

"Faith," I said, "is the real, all else is illusion...wars and rumours of wars, fear and the dread of fear. In blindness men fail to see that God is Love. But Einstein can see...the leaders of the race can see with the mind's eye. Though Greek Orthodoxy pass, Love endures."

On the morrow, an hour before our departure, my Illustrator and I mounted breathlessly the stair of the belfry. Having attained the height, we were lost in admiration of the largest bell (its weight is sixteen tons), of bronze forged in the days when bells were bells. Two monks are needed to ring it—one to push and one to pull. Once heard (it rings but twenty-five times a year), the sound can never be forgotten. We had heard it thrice... to have heard it is to be, in part, initiated into the mysteries. The carillon of lesser bells was shown. The full chime is played only at Easter.

From the heights we looked over the hills and dales of the central and other islands, the glimmering waters of the lake. Just visible was the chapel known as Jerusalem because it contains a replica of the Holy Sepulcher. We had walked there, a dusty four miles through field and forest. There lay the isle of John the Baptist where no woman may land—it being one of the hermits'

islands. Nearer us were
the fantastic domes and
cupolas, topped by
golden crosses. Imme-
diately below us, we
knew, in the major dome
of the church monks in
oily smocks were rub-
bing and mixing lus-
cious-looking colors to
restore the frescoes. We
had remarked a Sir
Galahad in the choir
and later recognized
him as the leader of the
artists. On nearer view
his sensuous face looked
dissolute. No knight of
the cross was he but
rather a surviving satyr
—driven, perhaps, by
the Forestry Depart-
ment of the Finnish Re-
public now in charge,
from the forests of
Valamo.

Alas, that visits must
end, even visits to Va-
lamo! Our steamer bore
us swiftly from the

On the Road to Jerusalem

monastery, which, as we neared the archipelago of Sortavala, had once more taken on the appearance of a mighty bubble. The miraculous, the illusion more real than reality, pursued us to the last, for the entire island seemed to float skyward like a released balloon. Unbelievable, as all at Valamo, was the apparition of its ascension before distance obliterated this last mirage. As the vision faded from our eyes, the bells of ancient Russia seemed still to be ringing in our ears, of Rimsky-Korsakov's "Russian Easter," of Moussorgsky's "Gate to Kiev," of Tchaikovsky's symphonies, and, moreover, the Great Bell of Valamo giving utterance, no more, no less, than a temple gong of Old Japan, to the aspirations in the heart of man.

Скитъ во имя Всѣхъ Святыхъ ⊹

† A Monk
of Valamo .

Of medieval Strongholds in Finland
Olavinlinna is incomparably first ·

CHAPTER XVIII

MAGIC OF LAKE AND FOREST

Arrived at the Valtion Hotel at Punkaharju, we were at once confronted with a sign:

Tänään Sauna

Seeing our puzzled looks, the hostess, who might well have been the titled lady at an English country-house, explained the meaning: *Bath To-day!*

"Will you take one?" she asked. "Ours are very nice indeed for ladies—not at all like those in the country. But not like those in the towns either...the true Finnish bath with, afterwards, a dip in the lake. The temperature is now 21 degrees. (When do we consider the water cold? Well, 12 degrees is cold—53 Fahrenheit!) We heat the *sauna* on Wednesdays and Saturdays."

Our drive along the ridge was, it so happened, from *sauna* to *sauna,* for an equally enticing sign awaited us at the far end of the trail. The outward

457

cleanliness of the Finn, unequaled by that of any other people, is, we mused, symbolic of "an inward and spiritual grace," an orderliness and pristine freshness of body, mind, and soul. We remembered the story, told us by a Finn, of the individual who hated his brother-men. He was a tired business man. When he left his office in Helsinki, he thought the world was going to the dogs.

"Look at the faces of the people," he thought, as he walked along the street, bumping into his fellow-citizens without begging their pardon. "There's a miser, look at the fatheads, and the women—cats every one!" He decided to take a Finnish bath. Gradually, as the steam did its work, he relaxed. Perhaps things weren't as bad as he had thought. His own wife was all right at any rate. He would call her up after the bath. "How well I look," he thought, as he caught sight of himself in a mirror.

"Hello, Tilma, that you? Let's go to the concert to-night." He sauntered along the street... and the people he met looked like angels!

To a lover of lake and forest, of peace and quiet, combined with not-too-luxurious comfort, there is no more satisfying haven than the cottage annex of the Valtion Hotel. Such a devotee was already installed on the day of our arrival. She was typically Finnish. Although probably not yet twenty, she was so robust in form, so unquestionably competent in household arts, that the

term "young woman" seemed to describe her
more appropriately than "girl." Spread on a
table before her, outside the villa door, were dic-
tionaries and well-thumbed volumes, in her hand
a note-book. When she greeted us in English, we
could not refrain from asking whether she was
learning our language.

"Oh, no," she said, "I am studying law. There
are only about a dozen women lawyers in Finland.
I hope to pass my finals in October."

The first and only act to be performed at Punkaharju is to drive along the ridge. (There is not,
as at the Grand Cañon, the temptation of a Bright
Angel Trail!) Perhaps in this singleness of excursion lies half the charm of the place. No tiring
sights must be seen; there are no distractions.
What a resort for the scholar! The name Punkaharju, we were told, signifies "Hog's Back." The
back of this Gargantuan hog, whose bristles consist of pine-trees, extends a little more than four
miles. It is known as the Ås of Punkaharju and
consists of moraine—reminder of the glacial
epoch.

Dr. Schoenichen in his introduction to *Finland,*
a remarkable collection of photographs published
in Leipzig, says: "A typical feature of the Finnish and Laplandish landscape is to be seen in the
'Åsar' or narrow ridges of morainic deposits ...
comparable to mighty railroad embankments.
They universally follow the direction of the in-

terior glaciers. One of the most considerable Åsar
and also the most frequently visited is the famous
Ås of Punkaharju. . . . They represent the remnants
of the filling of gigantic fissures in the interior
ice-cap.'' The professor describes how ''the granite base of the Finnish landscape, notably in the
Finnish lake region, was transformed by the forces
of the interior ice-cap into a system of trough-
shaped valleys and waves of primitive rock.'' It is
between two of the water basins, in this heart of
the lake country, that the barrier of the ridge
of Punkaharju rises. The fact that there are narrow channels at both ends makes the Ås actually
an island, of which one is scarcely aware.

At times the ridge narrows until it is hardly
more than the road itself with bordering pine-
trees. It is this aspect that suggests the Tokaido
road leading towards Myanoshita. Only Fuji is
lacking. But if Finland possesses no Sacred Mountain, it is equally true that Japan has no rival to
the Ås of Punkaharju. During all the time we
spent in the lake country my thoughts turned towards Japan. If Ladoga had recalled the Inland
Sea, still more do vistas in the region of Punkaharju remind the discerning eye of remote sites
preserved by the Japanese. These pines are comparable to cryptomerias of Nara.

Like the Japanese, the Finns derive inspiration
from the contemplation of Nature. Foreigners can
share this mood in the music of Sibelius. The soul

The Ås of Punkaharju

of Punkaharju is expressed in the composer's Five
Pieces for Piano. "The Solitary Tree," as the
first is sometimes translated, is assuredly a pine,
and the others, "When the Mountain-Ash Is in
Flower," "The Aspen," "The Birch," and "The
Fir," complete a picture as Finnish as Kipling's
"ash, oak, and thorn" is English. When we come
to the Finnish poets, the language erects a barrier
more insurmountable than the ridge of Punkaharju. *Kalevala,* the national epic, rings not with
the lusts of primitive loves and hates, but breathes
the magic of woods and waters and of quiet ways.
Of it we have a fairly adequate English version.
When it comes to Runeberg and other poets, we
are less fortunate. When Topelius (like Runeberg, writing in Swedish) tells of a tryst beneath
the birch-tree, we can imagine the loveliness of
the original. "Suomi's Song" is typically not a
battle-cry but a rhapsody of "whispering firs and
rushing waters." "The Fairest of Countries is
that in the North...where powerful pine-trees...
seem heaven itself defying," sings another Finnish poet; and again, "Thou northern, infinite
moor of pine." The site—a wooded mound with
vista of lake—is preserved at Punkaharju where
Runeberg wrote his famous lyric "The Fifth of
July."

Nature's cathedral at Punkaharju should be entered reverently at the sunset hour. Then the
forest aisles—bathed in ruddy light, between soar-

ing pine-tree columns, glowing and polished as Nikko's temples—lead the eye to the golden revelation in the sky where cloud-born cherubim and seraphim mount to infinity. No need of Gothic fanes in Finland. At Punkaharju, as at Koli, the mysticism inherent in the people finds outlet. It is not in his churches but in these natural shrines, I venture to state, that the contemplative Finn attains his earth-transcending exaltation.

Idyllic were the hours spent aboard the *Punka-harju II,* a gleaming white shuttle which wove its way between green islands. A shuttle? No, it was a swan these boats most resemble, we thought, as another of like proportions bore down upon us, silently, reflected in the mirror of the lake, which ranged in color from pearl to gray, from midnight blue to burnished ebony.

No uniform was worn by the crew—if the single boatman we beheld might be called a crew. A shabby individual at the wheel, clad in drab coat and tan woodsman's breeches, wore leather boots to the knees. The toes turned upwards—like the horn of a rhinoceros. We were soon to become accustomed to the type, worn by Lapps, skiers, and lumberjacks. Our steersman showed uncanny skill in avoiding to port the orange-red spar buoys that marked the channel, while not grazing to starboard poles of black-and-white striped complexion each topped by a bush, without which adornment some would hardly have been discernible.

Canada was often in our thoughts. Not only the far-away look of the sky recalled the vast New World, but also fields newly cleared, the mounds of gathered stones, the fireweed abloom or in blowing seed, the occasional cabin garden gay with clarkia, monkshood, and luxuriant sweet-peas. There was even, at Harjumienu, a double-chair swing, suggesting those that line the route from Quebec to Murray Bay. But the most poignant reminder of Canada was the never-ending, ever-encroaching forest, dark with evergreens. We recollected a haunting picture at Helsinki called "Death Builds the House." The painting represents a lean youth who, having cleared the land, erects his hut. The wife gives suck to a child who should long since have been weaned; while Death, a gruesome specter unseen by the pair, assists in the building. What unsung Maria Chapelaines dwelt on clearings in these depths of forest? One can but wonder.

The midday climax to the boat trip is the arrival at Savonlinna. Of the few medieval strongholds extant in Finland—Viipuri, Turku, Hämeenlinna, Suomenlinna, for example—Olavinlinna (Olaf's Castle), at entrance to the town of Savonlinna, is incomparably first. This Swedish survivor of the border wars is to-day an historic monument. No museum, prison, or barracks within, as in the case of others, detracts from the evocation of its illustrious past.

Like the Château d'If at Marseilles, which it somewhat resembles, the Olavinlinna is built upon a rocky island scarcely larger than itself. Its three strong towers dominate the approach by steamer, and how much more vast do they appear when seen from the ferryman's skiff. Winter and summer the current races between the island and the mainland at such a pace that never is the stronghold ice-bound. A competent guide is provided— competent I say deservedly, for not only does he know his historic facts, but he expresses them by turn in Finnish, Swedish, and English. In this fashion the visitor may acquire a smattering of hitherto unknown tongues.

Olavinlinna has been called the most beautiful castle in the Northern Countries, a title it well merits. It was founded in 1475 by Erik Alexelsson Tott, Swedish commandant at Viipuri, to safeguard the province of Savo from Russian invasion. During its building the very stones had to be conveyed across the channel under Russian fire, for the Russians hotly contested the Finns' (or rather their Swedish masters') rights to the ground on which it was to stand. It is acknowledged to-day that the island was indeed Russian territory. The castle was taken in 1714 during the "Great Wrath," in 1721 it was ceded to Finland but was retaken by Russia in 1742, and by the Turku peace treaty Russian it remained. It was last besieged in 1788, by Swedish-Finnish forces. Returned to Finland and demilitarized in 1836, the stronghold underwent restorations in 1872.

Our party, consisting of ourselves, several Swedish students, and some nondescript Finns, assembled in an ancient hall, once the church. Above this hall we were conducted to the renovated armory, where we were shown, among other coats of arms, the bow-and-arrow emblem of Gimela Bielke, the only woman commander of the fortress.

"The first feminist!" exclaimed our guide.

Later he was to show us the tower chamber of the married women and another for the unmarried. As we mounted the stair, we remarked upon a mountain-ash growing from a crevice in the wall. Its berries were as red as blood.

"The tree is said to have sprung," said our cicerone, "from the heart of a lady who died for love. To judge from others that cling to the walls, this castle must have beheld many a bleeding heart.

"You notice," he went on, as we now descended the spiral stairs, "that you hold on with the left hand on the central column—that leaves the sword hand free."

At one time there were five towers. Eight hundred men formed a war-time garrison. The ancient walls, in which the apertures are small, are twenty feet in thickness. To lighten the darkness

thirteen thousand candles were burned yearly.
Every summer on Saint Olaf's day a fête is held
in honor of the castle's patron. The last time
there had been a play written by a Finn. A few
years ago opera was performed in the central
courtyard, and the artistic success was notable.
The Finns, however, are not yet educated to pay
the necessary prices, and foreigners were few.
Madame Aino Ackté (lovely Finnish Marguerite
of the Paris opera and to-day one of Helsinki's
most revered citizens) lost thousands on the productions—whether thousands of pounds sterling,
dollars, or Finn marks I am unable to say.

The views from the chemin-de-ronde left us still
further breathless. The cool blue-gray foreground
of ancient stone carried the eye inevitably to
gleaming water, wooded isles, and Savonlinna,
nestling in verdure, its only high point the inevitable view-tower. No visitor to Finland should
overlook a visit to Savonlinna's castle.

On our return to the hotel where we had
lunched, we found awaiting us a Finnish gentleman, managing director of a bank, to whom we
had brought a letter. He complained of the short-
ness of our visit. We were about to sail on the
Heinävesi for Kuopio. I shall remember this gentleman's affability. We told him that we thought
the Finn the most welcoming European known to
man—or to these men. Was the reason that even
the non-Finnish-speaking foreigner is received

with open arms, we conjectured, perhaps similar to the reason that Finnish women were given the vote—the first in Europe...after New Zealand the first in the world?

"Every human being counts," we had been told by a feminist. "There are so few people of any kind in Finland."

Nine miniature steamers floated at the dock. Similar one to another as wild swans in a flock, their whiteness was reflected in the still waters. We stepped aboard the *Heinävesi* and were presented to Captain Ervasti, whose aristocratic appearance suggested a British admiral. We were later to tell him that the voyage reminded us of a trip once taken on the West River from Wu Chow to Canton. It transpired that the captain had weathered many a typhoon in the China Sea, had rounded the Horn a dozen times on vessels bearing timber for Australia. Although but nineteen hours, the trip to Kuopio had all the characteristics of a voyage. Friendships were formed at dinner served with ceremony at four—an hour which permitted the captain's presence. There was the Dane and his youthful wife who had been attending a temperance conference at Helsinki— we had thought them German because of his German newspaper; a solitary Finn; and, to complete the company, there were two Danish youths. It was to the English-speaking one of these youths that our hearts warmed. His was an adventurous

spirit. With eight companions, mostly English-
men, he, too, had sailed the seven seas—sailed in
a windjammer through the Panama Canal only
to be wrecked on a coral reef near Australia,
losing the zoölogical specimens collected for his
museum. We led him on to tell of his present em-
ployment, which sounded odd to our ears. With
the fervor of youth this charming citizen of
Copenhagen is throwing heart and soul into the
extermination of the bedbug! He dwelt on the
beauty of the insect, especially the tiny red ones,
but explained what a problem had arisen in Denmark, indeed in all Scandinavia, because of
wooden walls and rafters and long dark winters.

After a dinner worthy of an ocean liner, the
captain led the group to deck-chairs at the stern,
where coffee was served by a curtsying damsel.
Our Dane told how he and his friend had been
attending a meeting of scientists in Helsinki.

"This," said he, "is my first visit to the
Saimaan Lakes, but it will not be my last. It is intangible, the difference between these and equally
wild lakes in Sweden, but to Finland my inclina-
tion will force me to return."

When he ceased speaking, we floated, silently,
past clustered islands where birch leaves were
turned to shining gold, where, in contrast to dark
pines, the mountain-ash was aflame with berries—
the sunset sky, a conflagration of clouds, was no
more vivid. When the ash is laden with berries,

The Finnish Sauna : A Dip in

there will be a hard winter, according to the natives, but the ash provides food for the birds.

As twilight approached, our boat mounted by means of locks to a region of rocky cliffs. Miniature lighthouses shed their rays to guide us to Heinävesi, where from nine to two in the morning we lay at dock, it being impossible in the blackness to sail among the islands. There was a bustle of third-class passengers boarding our boat, one leading a cantankerous heifer. The captain suggested that we visit a *sauna*—a suggestion carried out by the three Danish gentlemen. They had

the Lake follows the Vapor Bath

expected, they told us, a douche following the vapor bath, but not so: an old woman, after switching them with birch whisks, chased them through the darkness into the ice-cold lake.

Kuopio! and with our usual luck we had arrived on the day of the cattle-fair. This event is held every five years, and, moreover, the date coincided with the seventy-fifth anniversary of the founding of the Kuopio Farmers' Association. The market-square was as gay with costume as any in Brittany. Here thronged Karelians with streamered head-dresses. Here were to be seen the red stripes of Savo, and, too, the black-velvet bodices with terra-cotta skirts—in old days worn only at Alavas. A booth with wares from Lapland attracted us—dagger-like knives, moccasins, articles of reindeer hide, a boy's scarlet coat and shaggy leggings.

Breakfast and lunch were to be had at the Atlas Hotel. This modern establishment was one of the surprises that continued to amaze us—even though, we told each other, we should have realized by now the up-to-dateness of Finnish hotels. This one, built but some half-dozen years ago, attracts by its monumental red columns, flanking the entrance like a transplanted *torii*. Of rooms for the night there were none, but this did not dismay us as we had planned to motor to Koli with return to Kuopio on the morrow.

Kay Gilmour, in the excellent little volume called *Finland,* says: "The wanderer going far beyond the confines where English, German, and Swedish are spoken will find the best means of communication—drawings." Going on this principle, the regal velvet curtains that conceal the entrance to washrooms at the hotel are decorated, one with a stencil representation of manly chic, the other with milady.

Finns, who will not bet on a grand scale, were clustered around the four gambling machines at entrance to the dining-room. It amuses them to play a few marks—with a fair chance of winning for those who knowingly tap the mechanism, and with the knowledge that the money lost goes to the Government and to the support of child-welfare organizations. Lunch at the Atlas is worth waiting for, especially when taken in company with the farmers of the region—any one of whom, if faces can tell a story, could be trusted to act with intelligence and uprightness under any and all circumstances. On every table stood pitchers of milk, and these pitchers were constantly and almost miraculously replenished ... ''and who would ask for wine.'' Total abstainers are many. The climate seems to demand, if any stimulant, *snaps*.

Accompanied by a surgeon from the government hospital and his wife, we visited the Exhibition of the Farmers' Association. We inspected the East Finnish cattle—hornless, red with white stripe accentuating the line of the spine. Horses, pigs, sheep, white Leghorns, bulls, still more bulls—in every case the blue-ribbon winners were sought by our hosts. The doctor, too, showed us with pride the exhibit displaying how, since the founding of the Association, soil, once producing only ''reindeer moss,'' had, after years of chemical treatment, yielded first poor growth, and finally blueberries and ferns.

''Every workman in Kuopio has his own motorboat or at least a rowboat,'' said the doctor's wife. We were standing together at the restaurant on the peninsula of Väinölänniemi overlooking

her island home, from which she had come at the
wheel of her own motor-boat. No matter how brief
the stay in Kuopio, she had told us, the stranger
must not fail to visit Puijo Hill, to northwest of
the town. With our vivacious friend we drove to
the knoll and mounted the one hundred and sixty-
two steps of its view-tower. Bobsleds were housed
here, but the newer fashion is for skiing. A forty-
meter jump was pointed out with the remark that
some in Norway are seventy meters! Hardly Koli
itself offers a more rewarding view of lakes and
islands—the typically Finnish scene—than that
from Puijo Hill.

Kuopio, a town of about twenty-five thousand
inhabitants, is not only the economic center of the
province of Savo. It has long been the intellectual
hub of this central and therefore intrinsically Finnish region. Books by Sinclair Lewis, Pearl Buck,
and even Jack London may be had at local book-
shops, as indeed at many Finnish towns. It was
at Kuopio that Minna Canth, a feminist leader of
her day, wrote and dwelt . . . a boulevard bears her
name. Here J. W. Snellman started the first political journal in Finland, in Swedish to reach
those in power, and a weekly in Finnish to arouse
the dormant peasants. He was at the time, 1843
to 1849, principal of the Kuopio Lyceum. Re-
former as well as statesman, Snellman—whose
statue stands before the Lutheran Church at
Kuopio, as well as before the Bank of Finland at

Helsinki—may be considered the founder of Finland the nation. Runeberg, the poet, had planted the seed of the nationalist movement, Lönnrot, collector of the *Kalevala*, had nurtured it, but it was to the toil of Snellman that Finland owed the harvest.

"One nation, one language," was the creed that Snellman preached, in and out of season. His journal, suppressed at the end of two years by the Russian Government, harped on the fact that the Diet had not met in thirty years. When Alexander II, the liberal Czar, succeeded the tyrannical Nicholas I, Snellman applied for a professorship in philosophy (under a less offensive name!) at Helsinki and received the appointment. He became also a senator and lived to see the Language Rescript become law.

"Kuopio or Koli?" we had been asked at the tourist agency when planning a boat trip. Having decided upon the route to Kuopio, we were still unsatisfied. Was it not at Koli that Sibelius sought inspiration? Ukko-Koli, with the modest altitude of eleven hundred feet was, we knew, the highest hill in Finland exclusive of Lapland. Koli! The very name spelt magic.

What matter if we had no common tongue with a Finnish chauffeur? Did he not know the road to Koli? Four hours in his company would seem to us like one hour, so full of rejoicing we were at the thought that we were on our way to Koli. As is to be expected when motoring in Finland, we set out by ferry. How familiar the sign *Kaapeli* becomes. The ferry was a primitive affair drawn by a cable. That a motorbus was installed ahead of us and that the rear wheels of our automobile protruded over the water seemed of no concern to our Finn. His passengers, however, alighted from the car—barely held by chains from diving overboard. Impressions of ponds with blooming water-lilies come to mind, of a bridge and beside it a cordwood "village." The timber was so piled as, when approached, to resemble houses with roofs and openings like windows. How easy to imagine a footsore wanderer at dusk seeking food and shelter! In vain would he call. No man would hear in this phantom-still village. No bell, as at the ferry, would produce a leisurely response. How startling in this quiet remote place to be confronted with familiar lettering: *"Standard," "Firestone," "Ford"!*

Hurdles no horse could leap—not of brushwood but of grain or hay—loomed in fields bordering the roadway...the damper the fields the higher the hurdles. Mists unfurled, disclosing forest backgrounds. We had come to the Finland of pioneers, extolled in song and story. Lumberjacks were handling white-birch ladders. Countrymen, in hip-boots, rakes over shoulders, rode rusty bicycles. As we rolled by, they tumbled off aghast, hauling their mounts to safety. Sorrel horses, shaggy as Clydesdales, shied at sight of us. Now and then we passed men building log cabins on the edge of the wilderness, and once a woman stood beside an immense well-sweep and wistfully followed us with her eyes. During the four hours of our drive we met no other car. On the morrow we were to return by a longer, more frequented route to Kuopio via Joensuu, commercial center of northern Karelia—Joensuu with high-towered town hall of Saarinen design, with flower-bedded park and busy market-square, with Lutheran and Orthodox churches, Joensuu ... beyond which lies Outokumpu. My illustrator was to tug my sleeve as the latter came to sight.

"A hill-town!" he was to breathe in reminiscent ecstasy.

But no, not in Finland. We were to think our eyes deceiving us. In haste we were to open maps and guidebooks and to find the explanation to the towered storied pile: "Outokumpu, state-owned copper-mine."

Koli—for unnumbered centuries buried beneath the snows of winter, basking lonely in summer sunshine—has yielded to the blandishments of man. Since 1930 the government-owned Hotel Ylämaja has topped the granite eminence that overlooks the water. Though deploring its erection, yet, grudgingly, we admit that, with limited time for a holiday, many who now receive inspiration would never have known Koli had it not been for the coming of inn and highway. A haze enhanced the azure of the lake, as first we saw it, welding earth, sky, and water into a harmonious whole. Looking beyond the forest at our feet, we beheld as on an unfurled map Pielisjärvi and its flotilla of distant isles.

Stillness reigned, there was no motion, save the leisurely drift of clouds on high. Koli was, at that silent hour, tranquil with a God-like, all-pervading peace. To breathe the air was benediction. No sensitive nature, and the taciturn Finns are supremely sensitive to the inner voice, could fail to respond to such a stimulus. Koli! No, holy— the Holy of Holies in Nature's temple. Man has produced Valamo, but Koli is the work of man's Creator. At Koli one comprehends the depths and heights of power inherent in the Finn. At Koli, at a thousand natural shrines, the devout Finn withdraws awhile from the turmoil of modern life, to return blessed with the mantle of the prophet. To Sibelius comes inspiration for a symphony; to Kallio the vision of a coöperative world.

At Valamo we could not distinguish between sound and form and color ... to which might be attributed the chief distinction of the place. So it was at Koli. Having seen its beauty, unsurpassed by Japan itself, whose inland sea it so unquestionably suggests; having watched dawn, sunset, and nightfall, in quietness, then and then only were we ready to have unleashed the symphony of winds. Yes, wood-winds, winds of tree-tops, pine and birch and fir, of slightest zephyrs...of tumultuous tempest—transcending earth. Through the voice of her forests Finland speaks. Let those who have ears to hear comprehend the Magic Word!

Tampere :
A stark Figure at Häme Bridge

Valtionrautatiet ·

CHAPTER XIX

AN INDUSTRIAL UTOPIA

TAMPERE is known as the Manchester of Finland —a title that flatters Manchester. A town of some sixty thousand inhabitants, noted for its textile mills, shoe factories, and machine-shops (in which locomotives are manufactured for the Finnish State Railways), the recognized industrial center of Finland, Tampere astounds the visitor by its spotlessness and beauty. (I apologize for my Illustrator's insistence upon a fleeting whim of smoke!) The town owes its supremacy to the hydro-electric power generated where the Tammerkoski rapids fall from Näsijärvi to another lake. The boulevard Hämeenkatu, embellished by gardens, crosses the rapids at Häme bridge— adorned by four stark symbolic figures, work of the sculptor Aaltonen. After a sojourn at Scandinavian towns and beaches one turns an unstartled eye to flaunting nudes in marble or in the flesh.

The Grand Hotel Tammer recalled the Atlas at Kuopio, whence we had come by way of night journeys to and from Helsinki. True, its entrance columns were of singing blue, not lacquer red, and the view at night, from the French windows of my luxuriously furnished room on the seventh floor, suggested Paris. In the foreground lay the duck-pond with its fountain in bosky setting worthy of the Bois. The river with its statue-adorned bridge suggested the Seine, and beyond rose the Public Library, the Municipal Theater ... surely that shaft against the sky was the obelisk of the Place de la Concorde, not a smoke-stack; and the other, looming farther away, might well have been the Washington Monument. Everywhere along the boulevard electric lights glimmered. The river with its tree-shaded banks was flood-lighted.

Parisian leisure pervaded the salle-à-manger. The hors-d'œuvre was superlative, the strains of *Carmen* from the orchestra were in keeping. The waits between courses were, however, true to Finnish custom. My Illustrator, after a hard day, murmured to wake him when food came. Staid business men, solitary or in pairs, sat immersed in newspapers. The tables were laid with fine linen and, as everywhere in Scandinavia, decorated with flowers as fresh as the food was palatable. The waitresses moved immaculate in

glistening frocks, apronless, in accordance with
the democratic spirit of the place, which also ac-
counted for the head-waiter's jaunty business
suit.

Not the least of the attractions at the Grand
Hotel was the notice posted in three tongues on
bedroom doors:

OPAS—CICERONE—GUIDE

*Bathing between 24-7 o'clock should be
avoided.*

Coo-king strictly prohibited.

*Pay attention that guiding in this city and its
wonderful environs rich of forests and silver-
lakes, and explanations of their sigts etc. are
given by ——————. Our office, alone of this
kind in this place, always has educated interpreters and cicerones to your disposition speaking the world's languages. When wished guiding
in groups takes place at an especially reduced
price. For business people and merchants we
dispose of advisors.*

"Assassinate them?" my Illustrator interpo-
lated. "All advisers should be 'disposed of.'"

A very British hand had added, on the margin:

"This is terrible English, take it away."

We remembered (the italics are mine) the
"Guide, speaking different languages appointed
by the town of Borgå on the arrival of the day

steamer. The guide being *even else to meet with by* telephone"! Let the foreigner who has mastered Finnish criticize.

In Finnish there is no article nor is there any gender although there are two numbers. "The fifteen cases," so I read, "are indicated by suffixes added to the root which often undergoes modification." (For compensation the letters never change their sound, and the accent always falls on the first syllable.) It is because of the extreme difficulty of translation that so little Finnish literature has found its way into our language, the notable exceptions being the *Kalevala* and Kivi's masterpiece, *Seven Brothers,* and, in our day, Sillanpää's *Fallen Asleep While Young.*

In his *Seven Brothers* Aleksis Kivi has given us the outstanding characteristics of the Finns— their robust acceptance of physical toil against, to others, probably insurmountable odds; their indefatigable pursuit of knowledge; their uncompromising moral integrity. Startlingly original, gripping as Tolstoy, this book gives us otherwise unobtainable insight into the hearts and lives of these now legendary pioneers. That Kivi should have been excoriated for writing in the national idiom rather than in the more literary Swedish, should have died in extreme poverty, mentally deranged, is an irony of fate.

Change has come upon the land since the date of Kivi's death, 1872. Finland now lavishes honor upon her beloved son. Two of the most appropriate tributes are the preservation of his cottage in the open-air museum at Helsinki and a statue (one of Aaltonen's most interesting works) before the Public Library at Tampere. The muse is represented as touching the brow of the poet, while at the base is a more realistic portrait bas-relief. To me, as an admirer of Kivi, this spot is hallowed ground. Hydrangeas form an interlaced and blossoming hedge, and their beauty becomes full of meaning to the observer when he notices that they have been set in the ground in tubs. What a people! No odds are too great, no winters long enough, to conquer their indomitable spirit. As I stood beneath the immense maples that guard the approach to the Library and watched the eager faces and buoyant figures of the youths and maidens who, books under arm, were constantly mounting or descending the steps, I rejoiced for the future of Finland. What an example Tampere sets for other factory towns ... these young people were workers in the mills! The Finnish Republic, with the courage and pliability of youth, has so adjusted the conditions of modern industrialism as to make them not incompatible with the advance of civilization.

The Swedish church, with its separate bell-tower, grouped beside Library and Theater, is to me vastly more pleasing than the Finnish Cathedral, a production of our century, which has been by some called "romantic style" but by others merely by the name of its architect, "Sonck."

The translation of the Bible into Finnish had a marked influence on the development of the Finns. Readers know of Borrow's adventures with *The Bible in Spain*, of Wilder's notable creation in *Heaven's My Destination* of the heroic distributor of algebras and of texts worthy of the Gideons, but the casual visitor may not know of the part played by the Bible in the industrialization of Finland. It was in 1819 that a Scotchman, John Patterson, a graduate of the University of Glasgow, paid his sixth visit to the site of Tampere. As an agent of the Russian Bible Society he carried out his duty of promoting the distribution of Bibles throughout Northern Europe. Being a practical man, he had, on previous visits, been much impressed by the possibility of utilizing the power of the Tammerkoski rapids. Hence on this memorable visit he brought his friend James Finlayson, at that time an engineer employed by the Russian Government. Permission was granted for the erection of a cotton-mill, which is to-day an immense establishment still known as Finlayson & Co. Many textile workers in the early days of Tampere's development were imported from Lancashire and Yorkshire, and a certain proportion of these married and were assimilated into the Finnish population. After the discovery of a process for reducing timber to pulp, mills for this purpose sprang into being along the Hymmene River and the lakes near Tampere. Yet despite the multiplication of textile, cotton, spinning, and paper mills, of boot and shoe factories, and of machine-shops, Tampere keeps to the even tenor of its way, remaining immaculately clean, avoiding unnecessary noise, providing adequate housing and education for all its thrifty inhabitants—that is to say, for everyman. Bicycles are almost as popular as in Copenhagen, as most of the workers prefer to live in the outskirts or even beyond the limits of the town.

History was made in Tampere. After the Russian revolution of 1917, on December fourth of the same year Finland declared its independence. "A courageous dictator," says Atchley, "might have saved the country from civil war." The Soviet Government was asked to withdraw its troops, but this it refused to do. Instead, arms and officers were supplied to the Finnish Red Guard—those who largely because of Red propaganda endeavored to set up a soviet form of government in Finland. Helsinki was seized by the Reds, who took possession of government buildings and railway station. It was then that four members of the Senate fled to Vaasa in Ostrobothnia, headquarters of the White Army under General Mannerheim, and established constitutional government temporarily in that city. At the end of the three months' war the White Army numbered seventy

Hämeenlinna·

thousand while the Reds mustered perhaps one hundred thousand—Russians and peasants and workers rebelling against the oppression Finland had suffered under Nicholas II. The headquarters of the Reds was at Tampere, and when General Mannerheim and his troops surrounded the city, ten thousand Reds were taken prisoner. In order to prevent a battle-front west of the White Sea the Germans answered the plea of the Finnish Government and sent troops sufficient to end the war. Had it not been for the defeat of Germany, the Kaiser's brother-in-law, Prince Friedrich Karl of Hesse, would have been crowned King of Finland ... by so narrow a margin was the Finnish nation spared to become a leader in world democracy.

Half-way between Tampere and Helsinki is the town of Hämeenlinna, which should be visited en route to or from Tampere. This capital of the province of Häme possesses a *linna* or castle—dating from the time of Birger Jarl—which provides the dominant note. Yet it was quite another interest that brought us and will increasingly as years pass bring others to Hämeenlinna. Kay Gilmour has anticipated me in saying: "It is, however, as the birthplace of Sibelius that Hämeenlinna is most likely to attract the pilgrim of the future."

Our arrival was after dark. An impeccable chauffeur met us at the station, advancing to carry our luggage—a luxury in a land where porters, even at the magnificent railway terminus in Helsinki, are conspicuous in absence. We were whisked to a villa in Aulanko Park. Perhaps not this side of India have we felt so far from home. There was something about the place that smacked of a dark bungalow—perhaps because our rooms were on the ground floor. We could tell that we were surrounded by lawns and by tropically gigantic trees. In the ray from our window a drooping birch-tree had the white form of a Godiva

swathed in rippling golden tresses. Doors stood
open. Was no one in charge? Doubtfully, next
morning, we rang the bell, which, unexpectedly,
produced hot water. Time being ripe, we repaired
to the breakfast-room, and here we found a non-
English-speaking maid assembling eggs, *knacke-
bröd* and toast, marmalade and honey. With some
relief we hailed a mid-Victorian English couple.
They enlightened us, as no one else had been able
to do, just why we found ourselves in such a remote spot. This, it seemed, was an annex of the
Aulanko-Karlberg Hotel. Fishing had brought the
gentleman, as so many of his compatriots, to Finland, and he expatiated on the pleasures of life
at Aulanko Park. His wife, recalling in appearance provincial housewives satirized in *Punch,*
would vastly have preferred her own parish. Finnish tea was not to her liking, and now that she
had exhausted her supply of knitting wool, it
really was rather a bore when it rained, with
every book in the place in Finnish! Yes, we agreed,
with so few English about one feels farther from
"home" than in India. But, when the weather
permitted, one could always walk.

"Have you been to the top of the View Tower?"
she asked, knowing we had arrived after dark.
"And you *must* see the bears, such darlings. Yes,
the bears are artificial, but so is the sand on the
beach!" (We made a mental reservation that we
would draw the line at the bears.)

Although the historic manor on the Karlberg estate was destroyed by fire in 1928, the "bachelors' wing" is still extant and could tell tales of prodigal hospitality. Fifty acres of the estate dominated by Aulanko Hill was purchased in 1926 by the municipality for a tourist center, while one hundred and seventy acres of woodland with entrancing views on Lake Vanajavesi has become National Park.

All the musical world knows that Sibelius was born in Hämeenlinna (Tavastehus in the Swedish version) on December 8, 1865. Yet no mention is made of the fact in the pictorial presentation of "the town of ancient memories and living parks" in the Otava series of books of photographs with captions in Finnish, Swedish, German, and English. It is only the citizens of Hämeenlinna that are not yet aware of it, we decided, on setting out to see the birthplace. The morning was one of those rare autumn days (for in Finland leaves are turning and rowan berries are red at the end of August) that suggest an Indian summer. Our confident orders to the driver of the taxi were, "To the birthplace of Sibelius." En route we whirled by the modern restaurant and hotel office, the "cavaliers' wing," forming, with outlying villas, the tourist center. Vistas of blue lake flickered between forest trees, tremulous aspens, yellowing birches, and, at last, there flashed upon us the vision of the Castle. It loomed across the lake, a mighty pile of brick. To-day it serves as prison, and entrance is forbidden. We passed a factory at the hour of changing shifts. How plainly I remember robust young women clothed in comfortable slacks; but I wish that I might forget the haunted look on the face of a young man. His physiognomy was one not uncommon in Finland—prominent retroussé nose, high cheek-bones, gaunt countenance, hollow eyes, the face of the Finnish Cain in Gallen-Kallela's portrayal of the murderer in the old ballad. It is not the consciousness of blood-guilt that gnaws at the vitals of these marked men, but of incurable tuberculosis. Let us return to the muttons of our quest!

It became evident, as we drove about the town, that every sight was being pointed out to us except the birthplace of Sibelius. We became insistent, only to make the astounding discovery that our chauffeur actually did not know the address. He inquired at the bank, he inquired at the market-place, he inquired of the man in the street ... everywhere he was met with the Finnish equivalent of a shrug—which is a seemingly endless flow of conversation leading nowhere. Although the most taciturn of men—the small talk of other peoples being completely omitted and casual transactions often made in complete silence—the Finn is the most loquacious when once aroused, or perhaps he requires more and longer words to make a simple statement. Mayhap for this very reason

The Birthplace of Sibelius

he refuses to use words at all unless the occasion warrants. Defeated in our quest, we returned to luncheon at Aulanko.

Whenever in doubt at Hämeenlinna, consult the manager of Aulanko-Karlberg. True, his German flows more merrily than his English, but his knowledge of things Finnish is indisputable.

"The birthplace of Sibelius...yes, here is a picture of it"—the first we had seen—"is to be found at Hallituskatu, Number 11, near the Tori Square." Maps were produced. We had been within a stone's throw.

Armed with knowledge our taxi-driver bore us to a low wooden structure characteristic of Finnish architecture a century ago. He drew up at a gate between duplicate houses, exclaiming with triumphant flourish:

"Birthplace of Sibelius."

"Which house?" I asked. "He couldn't have been born in both. Even twins would most likely have been born in the same house."

"No, he was not a twin," from the taxi-driver.

Well, what then? Neither house being occupied, we opened the gate to the court...a few parked bicycles—no other sign of human life. I turned my attention to a painter in overalls who was embellishing with gray a mansion similar in style to that of Runeberg at Porvoo.

"Which," I asked the man, "is the house of Sibelius?"

"Sibelius?" he queried, "this is the house of..." he rattled off a Finnish name.

A window had been elongated, and a glazier was replacing quaint panes with plate-glass. We repeated our question, in louder tones as one is apt to do to foreigners. The man shook his head, but a departing workman overheard, falling off his bicycle in his eagerness to be helpful.

"That is the one," said he, pointing to the house on the right. "They are making it into a restaurant...wonder if they'll call it for him. Come, I'll show you."

We passed through the room with the modern sash and into the modest bedchamber. We remarked to our guide that someday the window would surely be restored to its former size and there would be a plaque with the words *"Jean Sibelius."*

"The Finns are so slow!" he exclaimed—it was evident he had been to America. "They will wait till he is dead. But they have named a park for him. It is near-by. Follow my bicycle."

The park bears the curious name Tahtipuisto ("Time Bâton"), in reference to the Master's bâton, a subtle nomenclature too obscure to be grasped by the casual tourist. At Number 15 Linnankatu the child Sibelius lived during the time when he attended Finnish school, his family having moved to this rather similar house (still a well-kept residence) facing the "park" or square that now contains the German War Memorial.

Sibelius spent much time, in his youth, in meditation upon the shores of Lake Vanajavesi. One of the most rewarding drives in all Finland is that along the fertile lake-shore to Parola. Here stands Hattula, Old Church—there is a New Church, but it was Old Church that we had come to see. On the day of our visit there were haycocks, bluebells in long grass, scudding clouds, against which might be seen a hoary mountainash laden with berries, a conservative estimate of its age perhaps five hundred years. And Hattula, Old Church, how to describe its primitive allure! Only Lohja, on the route from Helsinki to Turku, can in any way compare. Hattula is said to be the oldest village in the province, and the church dates from the fourteenth century. Its bricks, whitened with age, the exaggerated height of its roof, betray its Swedish origin, as do the lich-gates and separate mortuary tower. A toothless woman, mumbling words even a Finn could not have understood, opened the locked portal with a key the traditional Saint Peter might envy. In the vestibule hung a ship with many sails and a birch-bark hull, a ship fashioned by a worthy son of Viking sires. Perhaps because of the bond of Protestantism and similarity of age, we were reminded, as in Sweden we had been so often, of English village churches. Memories of Saint Nonna's, the "Cathedral of the Moor," at Altarnun in Cornwall trooped to mind; and was not this wooden effigy Saint George himself—by whatever name he might masquerade—arrested in the act of transfixing the dragon? A primitive world-weary Atlas balanced the burden of the pulpit upon his head. The crowning glory of Hattula, Old Church, is its naïve murals.

A night's journey from Tampere (a shorter trip from Hämeenlinna or Helsinki) brings the traveler to the city of Turku (in Swedish Åbo) with its population of almost a hundred thousand. Its harbor is open all the year. Indeed, after Helsinki and Viipuri, Turku ranks third in numbers and in importance among the centers of population in Finland. Commerce looms in the minds of many at mention of the name of Finland's former capital—the very word *Turku* signifies "market." Exports nowadays are largely of timber, tar, and skins, comestibles to Stockholm, butter to England; but imports of salt and other commodities are hardly less vital to the prosperity of the country. In the fourteenth century Åbo (as it was then known) and Stockholm were the only Swedish ports permitted to trade with the outside world.

Turku has been called the "cradle of Finnish culture." Here it was that the Swedes, under Charles VII, landed in 1157, bringing their civilization to Finland. Even before their coming there had been a trading-post, known by the Latin name of Aboa, frequented by merchants from Novgorod. A Papal bull of 1229 decreed the transfer of the Cathedral from Räntämäki Hill to "a more suitable place." It was then that the present site was chosen ... the seven-hundredth anniversary of the founding of the Cathedral was duly celebrated in 1929. The region has been known since the Middle Ages by the name of Finland Proper. Turku has always been the center for this most prosperous of the agricultural provinces. Although Swedish influence may be observed throughout all southwestern Finland, it is particularly evident in this region of long-established stone churches and manor-houses. This district forms a striking contrast to Karelia, which was a mere province at a time when Finland Proper was an integral part of the kingdom of Sweden.

That the town coined its own money is known from mention of an Åbo-mark in a fifteenth-century document. The Castle, dating from 1280 and added to by Gustavus Vasa and his son Johan III, has been the scene of the most lavish courts ever held in Finland. Karl Knutsson Bonde's régime in the fifteenth century is legendary, as is that of Duke Johan, from 1556 to 1563 governor of the Grand-Duchy of Finland. Notorious were the feuds between the sons of Gustavus Vasa. Johan and his Polish wife established themselves in the Castle with a feast of a week's duration. His brother Erik XIV sent an army to capture the valuables which he said should never have been taken from Sweden—and to imprison his brother. It was not long, however, before Johan had deposed his mad kinsman and ascended the throne of Sweden as Johan III. Gustavus Adolphus stayed in the Castle during both his visits to Finland. The governor of the town at the time was Per Brahe—perpetuated in top-boots and costume of a cavalier in cathedral square. On the base of the statue are the words (in Swedish and smacking somewhat of Swedish complacency), "I was well content with the country and the country with me." There was in Brahe's day no court and no powerful nobility. Says Young: "Education was the first thought in every man's mind, and so it has remained to this day in a land where the possession of mental power is valued above wealth or birth." Per Brahe's reputation rests upon the fact that he was the founder, in the year 1640, of the Academy of Åbo, first of the Finnish universities.

Learning has always been associated with Åbo —the name by which the town has, until lately, been most often called. The first monastery and the first school in Finland were built here in the thirteenth century by the Dominican later known as Saint Olaf—whose name the castle at Savonlinna bears. For two centuries after its establishment the Academy of Åbo was the only university in the country. Alas for the city's reputation as a seat of learning, the Great Fire of 1827 destroyed seven-eighths of all buildings—constructed after the fashion of those days of wood. The Russians, having wrested Finland from the Swedes in 1808, had transferred the capital to Helsinki in 1819. The devastating fire following so closely upon the removal of the Government swept away the city's chance to become a Finnish Athens. In 1828, by order of the Czar, Åbo Academy was moved to the new capital. Not until 1919 (after Finland's redemption from foreign rule) was another Åbo Academy erected, followed, in 1922, by Turku University for those to whom Finnish is mother-tongue. One-fifth of the population of the city is still Swedish-speaking.

Personal experiences at Turku center around a visit to the Cathedral, gutted by the Great Fire but admirably restored; the Castle; and an excursion to the summer palace of the President. My

Illustrator and I had a distinct first impression as of return to a familiar scene. Never before had we beheld the like of Helsinki, the astounding and original modern capital of the land—so unlike New York and yet, in spirit, so much more akin to an American than to a European city. Viipuri was, to us, unique, remote, medieval—its close proximity to a Russian hinterland unforgettable. Tampere was an unparalleled model to be copied by industrialists of other nations. The new, the unknown, the incredible, had greeted us on every hand at Helsinki, at Viipuri, at Tampere, but here in Turku we were on known ground. Because of its establishment by the Swedes it bears the imprint of their culture. Six hundred years of Swedish culture was bound to leave a mark no fire could efface. The Castle, the Cathedral, might stand on Swedish soil, so imbued are they in every detail with Swedish spirit. But the look of the town is almost more Danish or even Dutch. All the endearing atmosphere of an Old World city is to be found upon the banks of the Aurojoki. Was this the Seine, we queried. One almost would think so—standing near the Cathedral gardens and looking over bridges and kempt quays. Memories of similar vistas at Quimper came to mind ... yet the ample windmill on the far bank from the docks spoke to us of Dordrecht.

"Mr. and Mrs. Oakley! This is a pleasure!" The words greeted us on entering the Cathedral.

The Finnish accent, the oh-so-Finnish physiognomy, where, oh where, had we heard and seen before? Of course, of course ... the reporter from the *Uusi Suomi,* who had interviewed us on the morning of our arrival at Helsinki. But how much he looked like every other Finn, and did we not look like any other tourists?

"How did you know us?" I involuntarily exclaimed, and then, laughingly, admitted that perhaps he would remember that hilarious hour when the interviewed had turned interviewers. He had treated us royally, owing to a shared interest in the music of Sibelius and our ability, impressions lacking, to fall back upon the *Kalevala*—open-sesame to any Finn.

"Do you speak Finnish now?" he inquired, with the flashing smile that had instantly won us. "You might at least speak as well as I speak American. No, not even that well? ... you flatter me. May I present my comrades from Russia? I am showing them my home town."

We had found the youth conservative. Was that merely the policy of his paper, or had the smile broken down even this, to many White Finns, unconquerable barrier? The Bolshevik "comrades" eyed us with distrust ... as though they sensed we had been to Valamo.

Curious how one clings to the human touch, especially in a foreign land. When I think of the somber Cathedral of Turku, reminiscent of Swed-

ish Uppsala, it is brightened not by the wealth
of gorgeous vestments there on display, not by
colorful chancel painting of Agricola presenting
his translation of the Bible to Gustavus Vasa, but
by the illuminating smile of a Finnish comrade.

The edifice is the nation's Westminster. Gloomy
chapels contain sarcophagi of Åke Tott, grandson
of Erik XIV and a hero of the Thirty Years' War,
with his wife who in effigy stands as in life dutifully at his side; of Evert Horn reclining with
his spouse, in marble, upon a bed-like tomb enlivened by blue ribbons of remembrance, *"Till
Evert Horns minne,"* from the Lotta-Svärd; and,
most memorably, the immense sarcophagus of
Queen Karin (Catharina Mansdotter), the peasant bride of Erik XIV, a few months Queen of
Sweden, imprisoned with her deposed husband by
her own request and, finally, banished by his successor. For forty-four years the exile dwelt on an
estate at Kangasala, near Tampere; and there she
died, mourned by the country-folk whose affec-
tion she had won by her generous heart.

Leaving the busy market-square (on a site
where once stood the medieval town) and following the River Aura, fringed with parked motor-
boats, to its mouth, we come to Finland's oldest
fortress. Although the Castle is protected from
the open sea by an archipelago of wooded islands,
it has at times been captured. In 1509, when
Sweden warred with Denmark, the city was plun-

Turku Castle:
Finland's oldest fortress.

dered by the Danes, who put many prominent citizens to death and even held the bishop's staff and miter for ransom. The Russian invasion at the beginning of the eighteenth century brought famine and plague in its wake. Those inhabitants who were able fled to Sweden. Clark, who visited Turku in the same century, tells that Peter the Great, who established headquarters in the city in 1713, took enough bricks with him on his departure to found Saint Petersburg. When in 1917-18 Turku fell into the hands of the Bolsheviks, there was comparatively little damage.

It may be treason to admit it, but the exterior of Turku Castle is far more to my liking than its cluttered interior. The outer or "new" castle dating from the sixteenth century looms like the carcass of a prehistoric monster above the small fry of wooden cabins clustering, as though for protection, at its feet. Its vast maw (there are some seventy-six chambers) contains a somewhat indigested mass of seventeenth- to nineteenth-century period and other rooms with, in all, twelve thousand exhibits. The assemblage can in no way compare in quality with nor does it attain the perfection of arrangement of the collection in the National Museum in Helsinki. The older portion of the Castle is, apart from its associations, architecturally rewarding.

Every Finnish town, be it large or be it small, has its conspicuous bookshop. Other sources fail-

ing, bookshop information is apt to be reliable.
An exception to the rule was advice obtained at
the shop in Turku. We were counseled to motor
to the suburbs to visit the Castle of Kultaranta—
summer palace of the President of Finland.

"The President is not at home," we were told.
"The house and grounds will be open to you."

As we approached the square-towered structure,
imbedded in a woodland setting, we observed that
the State flag was flying. There was not anything
to distinguish the place from a gentleman's coun-
try-seat except a sentry-box.

"Ask the sentry," we said to our chauffeur, "if
as Americans"—popular beyond deserts in Finland—"we may visit the grounds."

The sentry emerged. He was an own brother to
Tom Sawyer and Huck Finn, knee-high to a grass-
hopper, with a heavy cold in his head. Between
snuffles he explained the situation—orders had
gone forth that no one should come in. Sorry, orders are orders! He pointed to a chain barring
entrance. No helmeted Horse Guard at Saint
James's Palace could have blocked the way more
effectively. In Finland the dictates of law and
order go unchallenged. We accepted the lad as a
symbol of democracy, contrasting with the pomp
that, in another era, surrounded the sons of Vasa.

A consolation was offered in the form of a visit
to the notable church at Naantali, reached by
bridge across the sound from Luonnonmaa, the

island site of the summer palace. Turku is the oldest of Finnish towns, but Naantali, with a population of under a thousand, has the distinction of being the smallest town in Finland. There are two reasons why visitors to Turku are apt to include an excursion to Naantali on their itineraries —to bask on the bathing-beach and to see the church, sole surviving relic of the Bridgittine Convent which was established on this site in 1443. At first we feared that our efforts to enter this shrine, as at the palace, would be futile. Keys to churches are not infrequently as hard of access as keys to knowledge. This particular key resided in the pocket of the verger, and the verger, where was he? A gracious gentleman living opposite to the church traced the truant by telephone. By such a modern method were we enabled to see the historic interior of the edifice and to carry away memories of the tapestry altar-piece, handiwork of nuns almost the contemporaries of the Swedish founder of the order—Saint Birgitta, who had first crossed our path at Vadstena, "the most celebrated saint of the Northern Kingdoms." Much water has run under many bridges since these diligent followers of Birgitta sat at looms and embroidery frames. Our thoughts, spanning the chasm of the centuries, beheld the same indefatigable spirit in these industrious forerunners that is manifested to-day by textile workers in the mills of Turku and Tampere.

Pehr Evind Svinhufvud.

On the Island of Åland.

Last of the Grain Ships

CHAPTER XX

ÅLAND, LAND OF DREAMS

Midway between Finland and Sweden in that arm of the Baltic known as the Gulf of Bothnia (the other arm forms the Gulf of Finland) lies Åland, land of dreams. It possesses points in common with other Scandinavian islands—Bornholm, Gotland, Öland—but to the dwellers on the six thousand or more Åland Islands (many minute and uninhabited) it is the "mainland," the motherland.

"Go to Russia," our Red-Russianized friend had passionately urged before our departure from America.

"No, we must not mix impressions," we had replied.

"Stay at the Kamp in Helsinki"...well, the family hotel frequented by Sibelius had been more to our liking.

"Fly from Stockholm to Helsinki"...the words rang in our ears as we boarded the antiquated *Åland I* from Turku.

"How shall we face our friend from West Chester?"

"Friends be hanged," was my Illustrator's response, "much good it would do us to fly over Mariehamn.

"'Mariehamn is the last stronghold of the famous clippers and sailing ships which, before the age of steam, ploughed the seven seas,'" my Illustrator read. "'Ploughed the seven seas' doesn't sound like Cook's *Handbook* but that's what it is. You wouldn't miss a place with power to make Cook wax poetic?"

"Nothing on earth, nor airplanes in the heavens above, shall make me miss Mariehamn," I said, "not even if I do have to sleep in a bunk that resembles a coffin. I shan't get more air than if it were. The berth above is like a lid ready to shut me in. There's not even room to sit up."

A night aboard the *Åland I* is not, however, an unavoidable preliminary to a visit to Mariehamn, Åland's capital.

We had made a friend on the *Scanpenn* of the American Scantic Line—aptly called the Frantic Line by facetious travelers because of the antics of its boats, scurrying fussily in and out of ports on equal terms with larger vessels. This steamer-friend had written to her relative at Mariehamn to meet us on arrival at Åland. After a breathless night entombed in pseudo-coffins we warmed to the sight of "Cousin Dagmar" waiting on the dock.

"My American friends?" she interrogated. We smiled affirmatively.

Cousin Dagmar was unexpectedly beautiful. Coils of dark hair emerged from beneath a lace shade hat. Her jacket, fashioned of black velvet, was of a cut and texture to tempt a portrait painter and, like its owner, could not be pigeon-holed as belonging to any particular age or category. Cousin Dagmar, citizen of Finland, Swedish to the core, fluent in English (like many another Scandinavian living remote from centers of culture), Cousin Dagmar was the anchor by which we moored our ship of expectations.

It was arranged that we should stay at the Hotel Hjorten, giving upon waters where, with folded wings, clipper ships rested till autumn and the habit of years would lure them to Australia.

"One for each of the seven seas!" I exclaimed, when confronted by their oft-imagined presence ... but my Illustrator was already beyond recall, brows furrowed, sketch-book open.

Captain Gustaf Erikson of the cold, all-seeing, fishy eye, citizen of Mariehamn, is the owner of what is reputed to be the last fleet of clippers and barques to sail the waters—the modern clipper's element being air. Grain races from Australia to

England have given these sailing-ships more than passing fame, a fame which made the wreck of a winner, the *Herzogin Cecilia*—off Hope Cove, Devon, a few years ago, in thick but not stormy weather—notorious. All sorts of theories were advanced by correspondents in the London *Times*. Was there a hidden magnetism in rocks? Was it not a greater danger than the sirens that lured Ulysses? What of Scylla and Charybdis?...so the talk ran.

Alan Villiers has added his bit to the popularization of these ships. Anyone who has heard Villiers, an Australian with breezy speech, and seen his motion-pictures of sailing to the antipodes aboard the *Joseph Conrad* (a square-rigged four-master) is half-convinced that he, too, has made the voyage...next best is to possess Villiers' account of his voyages on the *Parma* of Mariehamn —*Last of the Wind Ships*.

Erikson's fleet consists, nowadays, of fewer than a score of sailing-ships, decreasing, alas! in number. The barques summer at Copenhagen and other harbors, but least expensively at the home port of Mariehamn. Majestic they float before my eyes, at mention of their names, as once we saw them on an August day, svelte of form, gleaming white of hull (above blue water) or lusterless black patched with singing orange. *L'Avenir,* a barque on the verge of departure, welcomed us aboard. For ninety days she would sail via Good

Hope to Spencer's Gulf, then, after loading, race, grain-laden, to England by way of the Horn. We stood upon her much-trodden decks, we handled ropes, we gazed upon her compass (was not this a compass hitched to a star?)—all seemed real and tangible. Then, as night fell and mists descended, this ship, strangely distorted and transformed, took on the semblance of a Flying Dutchman, an unearthly phantom. Eerie flappings of sails came to us across the still water, as of some giant bird about to stretch its wings in flight—flight that would carry it forever beyond our ken. *L'Avenir,* the future . . . the past, rather, unless, indeed, to-day both past and future merge.

Luncheon with Cousin Dagmar was an event. Her house stood upon the well-shaded main street of the country town. It was of one story, shingled, with fire-ladder leading from ground to roof, architecturally of Runeberg's period, like Sibelius' dwellings at Hämeenlinna. Because of its garden, abloom with roses and lavish in sweet-smelling herbs, the place had no rival in Mariehamn. Cousin Dagmar's father had been a citizen of importance, and his daughter, unmarried and of modest means, carried on according to tradition. Having retired from a position of trust in Viipuri, Dagmar had returned to Åland. Time, aided by the owner's feminine grace, had enhanced the inheritance. Even the sturdy fire-ladder at Cousin

Dagmar's had come to life, had become a Jack-
and-the-Bean-Stalk affair surging with living
tendrils.

"To think of your coming on the *Åland I!*" she
greeted us. "I remember traveling on it as a child.
I had no idea it still continued. I remember the
cells in which we slept and the red-plush lethal
chamber into which the bachelors crawled—no
headroom for standing.

"It is an experience," she admitted, "and if the
newer boats did not suit your date for sailing...
It is, of course, too late in the season for the daily
service by air, and, as you know, the larger planes
ignore us, going direct from Helsinki to Stockholm. We stand midway. The larger boats connect
us with Stockholm in seven hours, the smaller
take a night to either shore.

"Do you know what a bone of contention Åland
has been between Finland and Sweden? Our problem was the first to be solved by the League of
Nations. Our citizens are of Swedish descent and
Swedish-speaking, naturally our sympathy lies in
that direction. We sent a petition asking the
League to allow us to become a part of Sweden.
Unfortunately our archipelago seems more closely
to connect with Finland. The verdict of the League
was not to our liking, but it assuaged us somewhat.
We were to remain Finnish, but our official language would be Swedish. We were to become a
demilitarized and semi-autonomous province.

Åland ✦
Finströms Kyrka.

Such is our fate. You will notice that we do not, like foreigners, speak of the Åland Islands, but of Åland. You ask a native, 'Are you Finn or Swede?' He will reply, 'I am an Ålander.' ''

''The Canadians give a like answer in the Province of Quebec,'' I said, ''being neither British by descent nor French by government.''

Finland, we were reminded, had been an integral part of Sweden for centuries, not an unrepresented colony but sending voting members, as did other provinces, to the Swedish Diet. Then, by the Peace of Fredrikshamn, in 1809, Finland, including the Åland Islands, was ceded to Russia. Small wonder that the so-Swedish Ålanders wished to return to the Swedish fold.

Åland, strictly speaking, is the name of the archipelago, and, to the native, the island on which their capital stands is ''mainland.'' Twelve thousand Swedes, we were told, had visited Mariehamn during the summer, lured, perhaps, because of a favorable rate of exchange. We thought, however, as we started a day's motor tour of the northern part of the island, that Åland's attractions were sufficient bait. Wooden windmills of fantastically quaint design dot the fields where cattle graze. Many are unpainted, while others have been washed with red. We passed through Godby, where from a permanent midsummer-pole fluttered wreaths, ship-models, and paper fantasies.

Old stone churches are a relic of Catholic days. The one at Jomala dates from the thirteenth century. As at Rättvik there were rows of log stables, each no larger than a box stall. These are still used in winter, cars being only a few hundred and railroads non-existent on the island. Many natives, never having left Åland, have, therefore, never seen a railway! Finström's church was our favorite, having (to the disgust of some Lutherans) retained its wooden saints and antique crucifix. Its steep roof was receiving a treatment of dripping tar. Last time, we were told, during the tarring, a man had grasped the wrong rope from the pulley and fallen from roof to ground. Unaccountably he was merely stunned. Our chauffeur pointed out a cottage where a Finn has lived for years and still cannot speak Swedish. He seemed to be a unique specimen in this territory flying the Finnish flag.

On another day we were to drive to Geta, passing many fox-farms. Mills were whirring, woodpeckers rapping, dairymaids singing in the fields as milk flowed foaming into buckets. Ant-hills resembled burial-mounds covered with pine-needles and aquiver with busy inmates. It was necessary to leave our car twenty minutes before our destination, Getaberg, and to climb through a forest of spruce and pine and mountain-ash flaunting berries, across a chaos of moss-grown stones, beside glacial boulders, until we came into the open. A rustic rest-house topped the mount, up which the path had led, overlooking lakes, islands, and sea— a view which told us, without need of argument, that we were still in Finland.

Attention has turned of late to Åland because of the phenomenal success of *Katrina,* the Helsingfors Prize Novel of 1936, published that year in Sweden and, put into English, taking the American reading public by storm. Of the heroine Selma Lagerlöf says, to the reader of the book, "You have found something strong, true, patient and loving, untiring—a being that is a credit to humanity." Sally Salminen, the creator of Katrina, was born in the Åland Islands of a Swedish mother and a Finnish father. Her book was written in America, where its author was employed as a domestic. Following her rise to fame, and untainted by it, she has returned to the Åland Islands.

Mills of Don Quixote, of Daudet, of Holland, Sweden, Denmark, your laurels must be looked to! Åland is in league with the winds of heaven— on shore and upon the seven seas. And when the days of windmill and clipper pass, Åland, indefatigable in spirit, will, doubtless, train her sons to flights in air.

Flights in air! Vikings of the modern world, sons and daughters of Scandinavia, no peoples are more firmly rooted in the soil, none less fettered by earthly bonds. Finland! European pioneer in woman's enfranchisement, land where a man by labor may reach highest goal, land presided over by an elected president, land of literacy and moral integrity, land excelling in the arts, home of Sibelius. . . . Suomi! in concert with your Scandinavian brothers, blaze new trails for men!

Kalevala

Index

521

(1)

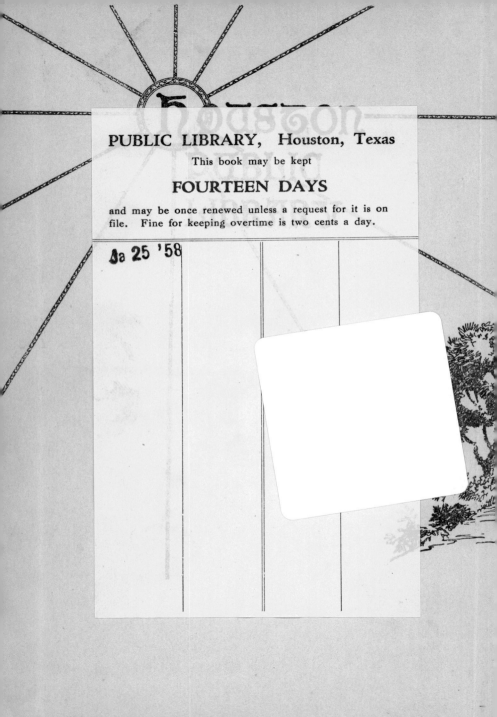